THE FIRST HEBREW READER

THE FIRST HEBREW READER

Jessica W. Goldstein

GUIDED SELECTIONS
FROM THE HEBREW BIBLE

EKS Publishing Co., Albany, California

For B.B.S., my teacher, mentor, and friend

Editor
Timothy J. LaVallée

Proofreader
Robyn Brode

Book Design
Irene Imfeld

EKS Publishing Co.

P.O. Box 9750
Berkeley, CA 94709-0750
e-mail: EKS@wenet.net
Phone (510) 558-9200 Fax (510) 558-9255

First Printing, January 2000

ISBN 0-939144-30-1

INTRODUCTION

The First Hebrew Reader is a practical guide to Hebrew Bible translation. Many students complete a beginning grammar, only to discover that they lack the necessary skills and experience to translate the Bible. This book reviews and enhances the student's knowledge of grammar through direct contact with biblical texts. We have included passages from all biblical genres and arranged them in approximate order of difficulty so that students will achieve competency in a broad range of biblical styles as their skills increase.

We specifically designed *The First Hebrew Reader* for individual or small group study. It is appropriate for any student who has completed an introductory Biblical Hebrew grammar. Students of *The First Hebrew Primer* will find this book particularly helpful, as we reference that text and use terms specific to it. Readers who have studied with another grammar should consult the guide to EKS terminology on page 177.

The First Hebrew Reader can help readers working at different skill levels. For those who require the most guidance, each section includes an interlinear translation, a list of new vocabulary words, a verb analysis chart, and grammatical notes. More advanced students can translate sections independently and use the text as an answer key. The glossary in the back of the book contains all words used in this text, but as students progress, we suggest that they begin using a standard dictionary. All students will find sections much easier to work through if they have a good working vocabulary of Biblical Hebrew. We urge everyone to review basic vocabulary before beginning this book.

Because this book is not intended to be a comprehensive commentary, we have not provided a complete bibliography for each chapter. Instead, we include a general bibliography of translation aids that students may consult as they build their Hebrew language libraries.

Finally, a note about our translations: It is said that poetry is what is lost in the translation, and this maxim is certainly true for Biblical Hebrew. We have attempted a compromise between overly literal and very poetic translations. Word-for-word translations can sound stiff or awkward in English, and lyrical translations, which often capture the essence of the original, are less instructional for language study. A good translation should sound natural in English; however, to be useful to the intermediate student a translation must closely follow the original. Because Hebrew and

English have so little in common, some awkward sentences are inevitable. As your skills increase, allow yourself to experiment with freer translations.

Many of you will notice that we do not use gender-inclusive language in our translations: This was not an oversight. We recognize that bias-free writing is the current standard and do not intend for our language to be interpreted as a political or religious statement. However, the Hebrew language marks all words according to grammatical gender, and because *The First Hebrew Reader* is a learning tool, we have preserved gender assignations in our translations. As a reader and interpreter of biblical text, you may choose to make the language more inclusive.

CONTENTS

How to Use This Book ix

Abbreviations xi

תּוֹרָה The Five Books of Moses 1

Reading 1 Genesis 17:1–10 2
God establishes a covenant with Abraham.

Reading 2 Genesis 22:1–19 10
God asks Abraham to sacrifice Isaac.

Reading 3 Exodus 32:1–14 24
God is angry when the Israelites make a molten calf and worship it.

Reading 4 Leviticus 19:11–18 36
God instructs the Israelites in cultic and ethical obligations.

Reading 5 Numbers 20:1–13 42
Moses makes water flow from a rock.

Reading 6 Deuteronomy 5:1–21 52
Moses recites the ten commandments to the Israelites.

Reading 7 Deuteronomy 6:4–9 66
Moses details the meaning of the first commandment.

נְבִיאִים The Prophets 71

Reading 8 II Samuel 7:1–17 72
Nathan tells King David that he will secure a dynasty.

Reading 9 I Kings 3:3–28 84
Solomon demonstrates his wisdom in a custody case.

Reading 10 Jonah 1:1–2:2 104
Jonah flees from God by taking a boat to Tarshish.

Reading 11 Micah 4:1–5 118
Micah tells Israel about his vision of an ideal future.

כְּתוּבִים The Writings 125

Reading 12 Psalm 23:1–6 126
The psalmist praises God using shepherd imagery.

Reading 13 Psalm 29:1–11 130
God manifests his power in a thunderstorm.

Reading 14 Psalm 67:1–8 136
The psalmist asks for help and thanks God for the harvest.

Reading 15 Psalm 136:1–26 140
God's work in creation and history is described in a song of thanks.

Reading 16 Song of Songs 3:1–5 150
A maiden dreams of searching for her lover.

Reading 17 Ecclesiastes 1:1–9 154
Kohelet, the preacher, proclaims that all of life is futile.

Reading 18 Ecclesiastes 3:1–22 160
Kohelet explains that there is a fixed time for everything.

Guide to EKS Terminology 177

Suggestions for Further Reading 179

Hebrew-English Glossary 181

Index of Grammatical Notes 195

HOW TO USE THIS BOOK

The First Hebrew Reader can be used by any student who has completed an introductory Biblical Hebrew course or textbook. Beginning students may need to rely heavily on the vocabulary lists and interlinear translations, while more advanced students may use the book to check their work. Following is more information on each section.

Hebrew Bible Passage

The core part of each section is a reading from the Hebrew Bible. Our text is based on a medieval manuscript called the Leningrad Codex. Readers searching for the complete text of the Hebrew Bible can consult the *Biblia Hebraica Stuttgartensia* or the *JPS Hebrew-English Tanakh,* both of which appear in our bibliography. We made two important changes to the medieval Hebrew text. First, we deleted all major and minor accents to improve readability, leaving only punctuation that marks the end of a verse. Students who want to work with a fully accented text should consult one of the two Hebrew editions listed above. Second, we numbered each chapter and verse with Arabic numerals. Many editions use Hebrew letters for chapter and verse numbers, but this style can confuse the beginning translator.

Interlinear Translation

The second half of each even-numbered page is a line-by-line Hebrew-English translation. To help you identify Hebrew verbs, which are often the key to understanding a line, they are printed in gray. We occasionally supply words from context or add words to clarify a translation; these additions are printed in parentheses.

New Vocabulary

We assume that all readers have a working vocabulary of the most common Biblical Hebrew words. The premise of this book is that students have learned all the vocabulary in *The First Hebrew Primer.* That 333-word vocabulary is based on frequency in the Hebrew Bible and is comparable to the vocabulary taught in most other beginning grammars. Every word in *The First Hebrew Reader* that is not included in the *Primer* is listed under the heading **New Vocabulary** each time it appears on a new page.

Words in the vocabulary list are spelled exactly as they appear in the context of the larger passage; sometimes this spelling is not the standard form. For example, when a word begins with a *beged kefet* letter, the standard spelling of that word includes a *dagesh* in the first letter (דָּבָר). In context, if that word follows a word ending with a vowel, the dagesh is lost (דָבָר).

Verb Analysis

Hebrew verbs communicate a wealth of information and you must correctly identify them to produce a precise translation. Our verb chart analyzes every verb in *The First Hebrew Reader.* To use the chart effectively, you need to understand the terms used in this book. **Pattern** is equivalent to **stem**, **binyan**, or **conjugation** in other textbooks, and **tense** is the same as **form** or **inflection** in other grammars. **P/G/N** stands for **person** (I, you, or it), **gender** (male, female, or common), and **number** (singlular or plural). **Suffix** refers to the **objective or pronominal suffix**. The **meaning** column provides a definition of each verbal root. This definition is specific to the pattern of the verb as it appears in the corresponding passage. Some of our terms for patterns and tenses are specific to EKS Publishing. If you studied a grammar other than *The First Hebrew Primer*, please see the guide to EKS terminology in this volume.

Grammatical Notes

The information provided in this section (listed according to verse number) should help you with your translation and enhance your knowledge of grammar. Whenever you see an unfamiliar term in the verb analysis section, look for an explanation in **Grammatical Notes**. These notes provide information on subjects such as Hebrew spelling, special verb types, unusual verb conjugations, and syntax. We have also included notes that are not strictly grammatical, but offer information about a text's history or context.

Glossary

All readers can find every word in the *The First Hebrew Reader* in the glossary at the back of the book. Ideally, students should work to improve their knowledge of grammar and vocabulary at the same time. To help you develop a good working vocabulary, the glossary identifies words from *The First Hebrew Primer* with an asterisk (*); everyone should know or learn these words. A double asterisk indicates new vocabulary that appears often in the Hebrew Bible; these words should be added to your working vocabulary. Notations for verbs apply to the root as a whole and appear with the first entry. In the glossary, all words are spelled in their standard form.

ABBREVIATIONS

Abbreviations appear only when necessary and are generally confined to the verb analysis chart. Below is a comprehensive guide to the abbreviations in this text.

rv imperfect	reversing vav imperfect
rv perfect	reversing vav perfect
emph. inf.	infinitive of emphasis
p. participle	passive participle
1	first person (I, we, me, us)
2	second person (you)
3	third person (he, she, it, they, him, her, them)
m	masculine
f	feminine
c	common (one form for both genders)
s	singular
p	plural
lit.	literally reads (in interlinear translations)

SELECTIONS FROM

תּוֹרָה

THE FIVE BOOKS OF MOSES

בְּרֵאשִׁית	2	Genesis 17:1–10
בְּרֵאשִׁית	10	Genesis 22:1–19
שְׁמוֹת	24	Exodus 32:1–14
וַיִּקְרָא	36	Leviticus 19:11–18
בְּמִדְבַּר	42	Numbers 20:1–13
דְּבָרִים	52	Deuteronomy 5:1–21
דְּבָרִים	66	Deuteronomy 6:4–9

17 1 וַיְהִי אַבְרָם בֶּן־תִּשְׁעִים שָׁנָה וְתֵשַׁע שָׁנִים וַיֵּרָא
יְהוָה אֶל־אַבְרָם וַיֹּאמֶר אֵלָיו אֲנִי־אֵל שַׁדַּי הִתְהַלֵּךְ
לְפָנַי וֶהְיֵה תָמִים׃ 2 וְאֶתְּנָה בְרִיתִי בֵּינִי וּבֵינֶךָ וְאַרְבֶּה
אוֹתְךָ בִּמְאֹד מְאֹד׃

1 וַיְהִי אַבְרָם	Now when Abram
בֶּן־תִּשְׁעִים שָׁנָה וְתֵשַׁע שָׁנִים	was 99 years old
וַיֵּרָא יְהוָה אֶל־אַבְרָם	the LORD appeared to Abram
וַיֹּאמֶר אֵלָיו אֲנִי־אֵל שַׁדַּי	and said to him, “I am El Shaddai.
הִתְהַלֵּךְ לְפָנַי וֶהְיֵה תָמִים׃	Walk before me and be blameless.
2 וְאֶתְּנָה בְרִיתִי	And I will establish my covenant
בֵּינִי וּבֵינֶךָ	between me and you,
וְאַרְבֶּה אוֹתְךָ בִּמְאֹד מְאֹד׃	and I will make you exceedingly numerous.”

NEW VOCABULARY

תָּמִים	blameless	אַבְרָם	Abram
וְאֶתְּנָה	and I will establish	תִּשְׁעִים	ninety
וְאַרְבֶּה	I will make (you) numerous	שַׁדַּי	Almighty

VERB ANALYSIS

VERB	ROOT	PATTERN	MEANING	TENSE	P/G/N	SUFFIX
וַיְהִי	ה.י.ה	פָּעַל	be, become	rv imperfect	3ms	
וַיֵּרָא	ר.א.ה	נִפְעַל	appear	rv imperfect	3ms	
וַיֹּאמֶר	א.מ.ר	פָּעַל	say	rv imperfect	3ms	
הִתְהַלֵּךְ	ה.ל.ך	הִתְפַּעֵל	walk about	command	ms	
וֶהְיֵה	ה.י.ה	פָּעַל	be, become	command	ms	
וְאֶתְּנָה	נ.ת.ן	פָּעַל	give, set	cohortative	1cs	
וְאַרְבֶּה	ר.ב.ה	הִפְעִיל	make numerous	imperfect	1cs	

GRAMMATICAL NOTES

17:1 Remember that age in the Hebrew Bible is expressed by בֵּן or בַּת followed by the number of years someone has been alive. See *The First Hebrew Primer,* page 198.

17:1 אֵל שַׁדַּי is traditionally rendered **God Almighty**. We have left it untranslated in this book.

17:2 When הָ or (more often) הָ is attached to a first-person imperfect, as in וְאַרְבֶּה, it signifies the **cohortative**. The cohortative expresses the speaker's wish or intention to do something. It can be translated as **I/we will** or **Let me/us**. Some imperfects are cohortative in meaning but not form; we will label verbs cohortative only when the distinctive ending is present.

17:2 בִּמְאֹד מְאֹד literally means **with muchness, muchness**. In this passage it qualifies the adjective **numerous** and is best translated as **exceedingly**.

3 וַיִּפֹּל אַבְרָם עַל־פָּנָיו וַיְדַבֵּר אִתּוֹ אֱלֹהִים לֵאמֹר׃
4 אֲנִי הִנֵּה בְרִיתִי אִתָּךְ וְהָיִיתָ לְאַב הֲמוֹן גּוֹיִם׃
5 וְלֹא־יִקָּרֵא עוֹד אֶת־שִׁמְךָ אַבְרָם וְהָיָה שִׁמְךָ
אַבְרָהָם כִּי אַב־הֲמוֹן גּוֹיִם נְתַתִּיךָ׃ 6 וְהִפְרֵתִי אֹתְךָ
בִּמְאֹד מְאֹד וּנְתַתִּיךָ לְגוֹיִם וּמְלָכִים מִמְּךָ יֵצֵאוּ׃

3 וַיִּפֹּל אַבְרָם עַל־פָּנָיו	Then Abram fell on his face,
וַיְדַבֵּר אִתּוֹ אֱלֹהִים לֵאמֹר׃	and God spoke to him,
4 אֲנִי הִנֵּה בְרִיתִי אִתָּךְ	"(As for) me, behold my covenant is with you,
וְהָיִיתָ לְאַב הֲמוֹן גּוֹיִם׃	and you will be a father of a multitude of nations.
5 וְלֹא־יִקָּרֵא עוֹד אֶת־שִׁמְךָ אַבְרָם	And your name will no longer be Abram,
וְהָיָה שִׁמְךָ אַבְרָהָם	but your name will be Abraham;
כִּי אַב־הֲמוֹן גּוֹיִם	for father of a multitude of nations
נְתַתִּיךָ׃	I have made you (lit. established you).
6 וְהִפְרֵתִי אֹתְךָ בִּמְאֹד מְאֹד	And I will make you exceedingly fruitful
וּנְתַתִּיךָ לְגוֹיִם	and will make nations of you,
וּמְלָכִים מִמְּךָ יֵצֵאוּ׃	and kings will come forth from you.

NEW VOCABULARY

הֲמוֹן multitude
וְהִפְרֵתִי and I will make (you) fruitful

VERB ANALYSIS

VERB	ROOT	PATTERN	MEANING	TENSE	P/G/N	SUFFIX
וַיִּפֹּל	נ.פ.ל	פָּעַל	fall	rv imperfect	3ms	
וַיְדַבֵּר	ד.ב.ר	פִּעֵל	speak	rv imperfect	3ms	
לֵאמֹר	א.מ.ר	פָּעַל	say	infinitive		
וְהָיִיתָ	ה.י.ה	פָּעַל	be, become	rv perfect	2ms	
יִקָּרֵא	ק.ר.א	נִפְעַל	be called	imperfect	3ms	
וְהָיָה	ה.י.ה	פָּעַל	be, become	rv perfect	3ms	
נְתַתִּיךָ	נ.ת.ן	פָּעַל	give, set	perfect	1cs	2ms
וְהִפְרֵתִי	פ.ר.ה	הִפְעִיל	make fruitful	rv perfect	1cs	
וּנְתַתִּיךָ	נ.ת.ן	פָּעַל	give, set	rv perfect	1cs	2ms
יֵצֵאוּ	י.צ.א	פָּעַל	go out	imperfect	3mp	

GRAMMATICAL NOTES

17:3 לֵאמֹר introduces direct speech and does not need to be translated literally.

17:5 The name אַבְרָם means **exalted father** and is made up of the words for father (אָב) and exalted (רָם). Here, the text suggests that the name אַבְרָהָם means **father of multitudes** and consists of the words for father (אָב) and multitude (הֲמוֹן). It is also possible that the name אַבְרָם was expanded by an additional ה, a common practice in the ancient Middle East, and means the same as אַבְרָהָם. Similar wordplays for the names of people and places appear throughout the Hebrew Bible.

17:5 A literal translation of the first half of this verse would read **And your name will no longer be called** (יִקָּרֵא) **Abram**. **Be called** and **your name will be** are redundant in English, so יִקָּרֵא should be left out of the translation.

7 וַהֲקִמֹתִי אֶת־בְּרִיתִי בֵּינִי וּבֵינֶךָ וּבֵין זַרְעֲךָ אַחֲרֶיךָ
לְדֹרֹתָם לִבְרִית עוֹלָם
לִהְיוֹת לְךָ לֵאלֹהִים וּלְזַרְעֲךָ אַחֲרֶיךָ׃
8 וְנָתַתִּי לְךָ וּלְזַרְעֲךָ אַחֲרֶיךָ אֵת אֶרֶץ מְגֻרֶיךָ אֵת
כָּל־אֶרֶץ כְּנַעַן לַאֲחֻזַּת עוֹלָם

7 וַהֲקִמֹתִי אֶת־בְּרִיתִי	I will establish my covenant
בֵּינִי וּבֵינֶךָ	between me and you
וּבֵין זַרְעֲךָ אַחֲרֶיךָ	and your descendants after you
לְדֹרֹתָם	throughout their generations
לִבְרִית עוֹלָם	as an eternal covenant,
לִהְיוֹת לְךָ לֵאלֹהִים	to be God to you
וּלְזַרְעֲךָ אַחֲרֶיךָ׃	and to your descendants after you.
8 וְנָתַתִּי לְךָ	And I will give to you
וּלְזַרְעֲךָ אַחֲרֶיךָ	and to your descendants after you
אֵת אֶרֶץ מְגֻרֶיךָ	the land of your sojournings,
אֵת כָּל־אֶרֶץ כְּנַעַן	all of the land of Canaan,
לַאֲחֻזַּת עוֹלָם	as an everlasting holding.

NEW VOCABULARY

וַהֲקִמֹתִי	and I will establish
מְגֻרֶיךָ	your sojournings
כְּנַעַן	Canaan
לַאֲחֻזַּת	as a holding

VERB ANALYSIS

VERB	ROOT	PATTERN	MEANING	TENSE	P/G/N	SUFFIX
וַהֲקִמֹתִי	ק.ו.ם	הִפְעִיל	raise up	rv perfect	1cs	
לִהְיוֹת	ה.י.ה	פָּעַל	be, become	infinitive		
וְנָתַתִּי	נ.ת.ן	פָּעַל	give, set	rv perfect	1cs	

GRAMMATICAL NOTE

The ו in reversing ו constructions can be treated several ways. Most often, the ו is translated **and**, as it is with וְנָתַתִּי in verse 8. Other times, ו is translated as **as**, **when**, **so**, or **then**. See וַיִּפֹּל in verse 3 or וַיֹּאמֶר in verse 9 for examples of ו as **then**. Sometimes the ו simply marks the tense of a verb and can be left out of a translation. We did not translate the ו in וַהֲקִמֹתִי in verse 7. Decide whether or how to translate the ו in reversing ו constructions based on narrative context and euphony.

וְהָיִיתִי לָהֶם לֵאלֹהִים׃ 9 וַיֹּאמֶר אֱלֹהִים אֶל־אַבְרָהָם
וְאַתָּה אֶת־בְּרִיתִי תִשְׁמֹר אַתָּה וְזַרְעֲךָ אַחֲרֶיךָ
לְדֹרֹתָם׃ 10 זֹאת בְּרִיתִי אֲשֶׁר תִּשְׁמְרוּ בֵּינִי וּבֵינֵיכֶם
וּבֵין זַרְעֲךָ אַחֲרֶיךָ הִמּוֹל לָכֶם כָּל־זָכָר׃

וְהָיִיתִי לָהֶם לֵאלֹהִים׃	And I will be their God."
9 וַיֹּאמֶר אֱלֹהִים אֶל־אַבְרָהָם	Then God said to Abraham,
וְאַתָּה אֶת־בְּרִיתִי תִשְׁמֹר	"And (as for) you, you shall keep my covenant,
אַתָּה וְזַרְעֲךָ אַחֲרֶיךָ	you and your descendants after you
לְדֹרֹתָם׃	throughout their generations.
10 זֹאת בְּרִיתִי אֲשֶׁר תִּשְׁמְרוּ	This is my covenant, which you shall keep
בֵּינִי וּבֵינֵיכֶם	between me and you
וּבֵין זַרְעֲךָ אַחֲרֶיךָ	and your descendants after you:
הִמּוֹל לָכֶם כָּל־זָכָר׃	Every male among you shall be circumcised."

NEW VOCABULARY

הִמּוֹל shall be circumcised
זָכָר male

VERB ANALYSIS

VERB	ROOT	PATTERN	MEANING	TENSE	P/G/N	SUFFIX
וְהָיִיתִי	ה.י.ה	פָּעַל	be, become	rv perfect	1cs	
וַיֹּאמֶר	א.מ.ר	פָּעַל	say	rv imperfect	3ms	
תִשְׁמֹר	ש.מ.ר	פָּעַל	keep, watch	imperfect	2ms	
תִשְׁמְרוּ	ש.מ.ר	פָּעַל	keep, watch	imperfect	2mp	
הִמּוֹל	מ.ו.ל	נִפְעַל	be circumcised	emph. inf.		

GRAMMATICAL NOTE

17:10 זָכָר (male) derives from the root ז.כ.ר (**to remember**). The relation of זָכָר to ז.כ.ר is obscure.

בְּרֵאשִׁית GENESIS 22:1-19

22 [1] וַיְהִי אַחַר הַדְּבָרִים הָאֵלֶּה וְהָאֱלֹהִים נִסָּה
אֶת־אַבְרָהָם וַיֹּאמֶר אֵלָיו אַבְרָהָם וַיֹּאמֶר הִנֵּנִי׃
[2] וַיֹּאמֶר קַח־נָא אֶת־בִּנְךָ אֶת־יְחִידְךָ אֲשֶׁר־אָהַבְתָּ
אֶת־יִצְחָק וְלֶךְ־לְךָ אֶל־אֶרֶץ הַמֹּרִיָּה וְהַעֲלֵהוּ שָׁם
לְעֹלָה עַל אַחַד הֶהָרִים אֲשֶׁר אֹמַר אֵלֶיךָ׃ [3] וַיַּשְׁכֵּם
אַבְרָהָם בַּבֹּקֶר וַיַּחֲבֹשׁ אֶת־חֲמֹרוֹ

[1] וַיְהִי אַחַר הַדְּבָרִים הָאֵלֶּה	And after these things
וְהָאֱלֹהִים נִסָּה אֶת־אַבְרָהָם	God tested Abraham
וַיֹּאמֶר אֵלָיו אַבְרָהָם	and said to him, "Abraham!"
וַיֹּאמֶר הִנֵּנִי׃	And he (Abraham) said, "Here I am."
[2] וַיֹּאמֶר קַח־נָא אֶת־בִּנְךָ	Then he (God) said, "Take your son,
אֶת־יְחִידְךָ אֲשֶׁר־אָהַבְתָּ אֶת־יִצְחָק	your only son, whom you love, Isaac,
וְלֶךְ־לְךָ אֶל־אֶרֶץ הַמֹּרִיָּה	and go to the land of Moriah.
וְהַעֲלֵהוּ שָׁם	Offer him (lit. make him go up) there
לְעֹלָה עַל אַחַד הֶהָרִים	as a burnt offering upon one of the hills
אֲשֶׁר אֹמַר אֵלֶיךָ׃	of which I will tell you."
[3] וַיַּשְׁכֵּם אַבְרָהָם בַּבֹּקֶר	So Abraham rose early in the morning,
וַיַּחֲבֹשׁ אֶת־חֲמֹרוֹ	saddled (lit. bound) his donkey,

NEW VOCABULARY

נִסָּה	tested
הִנֵּנִי	here I am
יְחִידְךָ	your only son
מֹרִיָּה	Moriah
לְעֹלָה	as a burnt offering
וַיַּשְׁכֵּם	and (he) rose early
וַיַּחֲבֹשׁ	and (he) saddled
חֲמֹרוֹ	his donkey

VERB ANALYSIS

VERB	ROOT	PATTERN	MEANING	TENSE	P/G/N	SUFFIX
וַיְהִי	ה.י.ה	פָּעַל	be, become	rv imperfect	3ms	
נִסָּה	נ.ס.ה	פִּעֵל	test, try	perfect	3ms	
וַיֹּאמֶר	א.מ.ר	פָּעַל	say	rv imperfect	3ms	
קַח	ל.ק.ח	פָּעַל	take	command	ms	
אָהַבְתָּ	א.ה.ב	פָּעַל	love	perfect	2ms	
וְלֶךְ	ה.ל.ך	פָּעַל	walk, go	command	ms	
וְהַעֲלֵהוּ	ע.ל.ה	הִפְעִיל	bring up, offer	command	ms	3ms
אֹמַר	א.מ.ר	פָּעַל	say	imperfect	1cs	
וַיַּשְׁכֵּם	ש.כ.ם	הִפְעִיל	rise early	rv imperfect	3ms	
וַיַּחֲבֹשׁ	ח.ב.ש	פָּעַל	bind	rv imperfect	3ms	

GRAMMATICAL NOTE

22:1 The word הִנֵּה (**here is, behold!**) can take a suffix. When it appears with the first-person ending, translate the word as **here I am**. See page 242 of *The First Hebrew Primer* for other examples of הִנֵּה with suffixes.

וַיִּקַּח אֶת־שְׁנֵי נְעָרָיו אִתּוֹ וְאֵת יִצְחָק בְּנוֹ וַיְבַקַּע
עֲצֵי עֹלָה וַיָּקָם וַיֵּלֶךְ אֶל־הַמָּקוֹם אֲשֶׁר־אָמַר־לוֹ
הָאֱלֹהִים׃ 4 בַּיּוֹם הַשְּׁלִישִׁי וַיִּשָּׂא אַבְרָהָם אֶת־עֵינָיו
וַיַּרְא אֶת־הַמָּקוֹם מֵרָחֹק׃ 5 וַיֹּאמֶר אַבְרָהָם אֶל־נְעָרָיו
שְׁבוּ־לָכֶם פֹּה עִם־הַחֲמוֹר וַאֲנִי וְהַנַּעַר נֵלְכָה
עַד־כֹּה וְנִשְׁתַּחֲוֶה וְנָשׁוּבָה אֲלֵיכֶם׃

וַיִּקַּח אֶת־שְׁנֵי נְעָרָיו אִתּוֹ	and took two of his boys with him
וְאֵת יִצְחָק בְּנוֹ	and his son Isaac.
וַיְבַקַּע עֲצֵי עֹלָה	Then he split wood for (lit. of) the burnt offering
וַיָּקָם וַיֵּלֶךְ אֶל־הַמָּקוֹם	and arose and went to the place
אֲשֶׁר־אָמַר־לוֹ הָאֱלֹהִים׃	of which God had told him.
4 בַּיּוֹם הַשְּׁלִישִׁי	On the third day
וַיִּשָּׂא אַבְרָהָם אֶת־עֵינָיו	Abraham lifted his eyes
וַיַּרְא אֶת־הַמָּקוֹם מֵרָחֹק׃	and saw the place from a distance.
5 וַיֹּאמֶר אַבְרָהָם אֶל־נְעָרָיו	Then Abraham said to his boys,
שְׁבוּ־לָכֶם פֹּה עִם־הַחֲמוֹר	"Stay here with the donkey,
וַאֲנִי וְהַנַּעַר נֵלְכָה עַד־כֹּה	and the boy and I will go as far as here.
וְנִשְׁתַּחֲוֶה וְנָשׁוּבָה אֲלֵיכֶם׃	Then we will worship and return to you."

NEW VOCABULARY

וַיְבַקַּע	then he split
עֹלָה	burnt offering
מֵרָחֹק	from a distance
פֹּה	here
הַחֲמוֹר	the donkey
וְנִשְׁתַּחֲוֶה	then we will worship

VERB ANALYSIS

VERB	ROOT	PATTERN	MEANING	TENSE	P/G/N	SUFFIX
וַיִּקַּח	ל.ק.ח	פָּעַל	take	rv imperfect	3ms	
וַיְבַקַּע	ב.ק.ע	פִּעֵל	cut to pieces	rv imperfect	3ms	
וַיָּקָם	ק.ו.ם	פָּעַל	arise	rv imperfect	3ms	
וַיֵּלֶךְ	ה.ל.ך	פָּעַל	walk, go	rv imperfect	3ms	
אָמַר	א.מ.ר	פָּעַל	say	perfect	3ms	
וַיִּשָּׂא	נ.שׂ.א	פָּעַל	lift, carry	rv imperfect	3ms	
וַיַּרְא	ר.א.ה	פָּעַל	see	rv imperfect	3ms	
וַיֹּאמֶר	א.מ.ר	פָּעַל	say	rv imperfect	3ms	
שְׁבוּ	י.שׁ.ב	פָּעַל	sit, dwell	command	mp	
נֵלְכָה	ה.ל.ך	פָּעַל	walk, go	cohortative	1cp	
וְנִשְׁתַּחֲוֶה	ח.ו.ה	הִשְׁתַּפֵּל	worship	imperfect	1cp	
וְנָשׁוּבָה	שׁ.ו.ב	פָּעַל	turn, return	cohortative	1cp	

GRAMMATICAL NOTE

22:5 The verb נִשְׁתַּחֲוֶה is in a pattern called הִשְׁתַּפֵּל (**Hishtafel**). The Hishtafel pattern is found only for the root ח.ו.ה, and the root ח.ו.ה occurs only in the הִשְׁתַּפֵּל. The form may have been borrowed from a language related to Hebrew; its origin is uncertain and controversial. The basic meaning of ח.ו.ה in the הִשְׁתַּפֵּל is **bow down** or **worship**.

6 וַיִּקַּח אַבְרָהָם אֶת־עֲצֵי הָעֹלָה וַיָּשֶׂם עַל־יִצְחָק בְּנוֹ
וַיִּקַּח בְּיָדוֹ אֶת־הָאֵשׁ וְאֶת־הַמַּאֲכֶלֶת וַיֵּלְכוּ שְׁנֵיהֶם
יַחְדָּו׃ 7 וַיֹּאמֶר יִצְחָק אֶל־אַבְרָהָם אָבִיו וַיֹּאמֶר אָבִי
וַיֹּאמֶר הִנֶּנִּי בְנִי וַיֹּאמֶר הִנֵּה הָאֵשׁ וְהָעֵצִים וְאַיֵּה
הַשֶּׂה לְעֹלָה׃ 8 וַיֹּאמֶר אַבְרָהָם אֱלֹהִים יִרְאֶה־לּוֹ
הַשֶּׂה לְעֹלָה בְּנִי וַיֵּלְכוּ שְׁנֵיהֶם יַחְדָּו׃

6 וַיִּקַּח אַבְרָהָם אֶת־עֲצֵי הָעֹלָה	Abraham took the wood for the burnt offering
וַיָּשֶׂם עַל־יִצְחָק בְּנוֹ	and placed it on his son Isaac.
וַיִּקַּח בְּיָדוֹ אֶת־הָאֵשׁ	He took in his hand the fire
וְאֶת־הַמַּאֲכֶלֶת	and the knife,
וַיֵּלְכוּ שְׁנֵיהֶם יַחְדָּו׃	and the two of them went off together.
7 וַיֹּאמֶר יִצְחָק אֶל־אַבְרָהָם אָבִיו	Then Isaac spoke to his father Abraham,
וַיֹּאמֶר אָבִי וַיֹּאמֶר הִנֶּנִּי בְנִי	and he said, "My father." And he said, "Here I am, my son."
וַיֹּאמֶר הִנֵּה הָאֵשׁ וְהָעֵצִים	And he (Isaac) said, "Here is the fire and the wood,
וְאַיֵּה הַשֶּׂה לְעֹלָה׃	but where is the sheep for the burnt offering?"
8 וַיֹּאמֶר אַבְרָהָם אֱלֹהִים יִרְאֶה־	And Abraham said, "God will see
לּוֹ הַשֶּׂה לְעֹלָה בְּנִי	to it, the sheep for the burnt offering, my son."
וַיֵּלְכוּ שְׁנֵיהֶם יַחְדָּו׃	So the two of them went off together.

NEW VOCABULARY

הָעֹלָה	the burnt offering
הָאֵשׁ	the fire
הַמַּאֲכֶלֶת	the knife
יַחְדָּו	together
וְאַיֵּה	but where (is)
הַשֶּׂה	sheep

VERB ANALYSIS

VERB	ROOT	PATTERN	MEANING	TENSE	P/G/N	SUFFIX
וַיִּקַּח	ל.ק.ח	פָּעַל	take	rv imperfect	3ms	
וַיָּשֶׂם	שׂ.י.ם	פָּעַל	put, place	rv imperfect	3ms	
וַיֵּלְכוּ	ה.ל.ך	פָּעַל	walk, go	rv imperfect	3mp	
וַיֹּאמֶר	א.מ.ר	פָּעַל	say	rv imperfect	3ms	
יִרְאֶה	ר.א.ה	פָּעַל	see	imperfect	3ms	

GRAMMATICAL NOTE

22:6 The word עֹלָה is related to a word that you already know. In פָּעַל, the verb עָלָה means to **go up** or **ascend** and, in הִפְעִיל, to **send up** or **offer**. An עֹלָה is an offered or sent-up object, a burnt offering in which the sacrifice is consumed and sent up in flames.

9 וַיָּבֹאוּ אֶל־הַמָּקוֹם אֲשֶׁר אָמַר־לוֹ הָאֱלֹהִים וַיִּבֶן שָׁם
אַבְרָהָם אֶת־הַמִּזְבֵּחַ וַיַּעֲרֹךְ אֶת־הָעֵצִים וַיַּעֲקֹד
אֶת־יִצְחָק בְּנוֹ וַיָּשֶׂם אֹתוֹ עַל־הַמִּזְבֵּחַ מִמַּעַל
לָעֵצִים׃ 10 וַיִּשְׁלַח אַבְרָהָם אֶת־יָדוֹ וַיִּקַּח
אֶת־הַמַּאֲכֶלֶת לִשְׁחֹט אֶת־בְּנוֹ׃ 11 וַיִּקְרָא אֵלָיו מַלְאַךְ
יְהוָה מִן־הַשָּׁמַיִם

9 וַיָּבֹאוּ אֶל־הַמָּקוֹם	They came to the place
אֲשֶׁר אָמַר־לוֹ הָאֱלֹהִים	of which God had spoken.
וַיִּבֶן שָׁם אַבְרָהָם אֶת־הַמִּזְבֵּחַ	Abraham built an altar there;
וַיַּעֲרֹךְ אֶת־הָעֵצִים	he arranged the wood,
וַיַּעֲקֹד אֶת־יִצְחָק בְּנוֹ	and he bound his son Isaac
וַיָּשֶׂם אֹתוֹ עַל־הַמִּזְבֵּחַ	and placed him upon the altar,
מִמַּעַל לָעֵצִים׃	upon the wood.
10 וַיִּשְׁלַח אַבְרָהָם אֶת־יָדוֹ	Then Abraham stretched out (lit. sent) his hand
וַיִּקַּח אֶת־הַמַּאֲכֶלֶת	and took the knife
לִשְׁחֹט אֶת־בְּנוֹ׃	to slay his son.
11 וַיִּקְרָא אֵלָיו מַלְאַךְ יְהוָה	Then the LORD's messenger called out to him
מִן־הַשָּׁמַיִם	from heaven,

NEW VOCABULARY

וַיַּעֲרֹךְ	he arranged
וַיַּעֲקֹד	and he bound
מִמַּעַל	upon
הַמַּאֲכֶלֶת	the knife
לִשְׁחֹט	to slay

VERB ANALYSIS

VERB	ROOT	PATTERN	MEANING	TENSE	P/G/N	SUFFIX
וַיָּבֹאוּ	ב.ו.א	פָּעַל	come	rv imperfect	3mp	
אָמַר	א.מ.ר	פָּעַל	say	perfect	3ms	
וַיִּבֶן	ב.נ.ה	פָּעַל	build	rv imperfect	3ms	
וַיַּעֲרֹךְ	ע.ר.ך	פָּעַל	arrange	rv imperfect	3ms	
וַיַּעֲקֹד	ע.ק.ד	פָּעַל	bind	rv imperfect	3ms	
וַיָּשֶׂם	שׂ.י.ם	פָּעַל	put, place	rv imperfect	3ms	
וַיִּשְׁלַח	שׁ.ל.ח	פָּעַל	send	rv imperfect	3ms	
וַיִּקַּח	ל.ק.ח	פָּעַל	take	rv imperfect	3ms	
לִשְׁחֹט	שׁ.ח.ט	פָּעַל	slaughter	infinitive		
וַיִּקְרָא	ק.ר.א	פָּעַל	call, proclaim	rv imperfect	3ms	

GRAMMATICAL NOTES

22:9 מִמַּעַל **(above, upon)** is formed from two words that you know: מִן + מַעַל. מַעַל derives from the common preposition עַל, and the ן from מִן disappears when directly attached to another word.

22:10 מַאֲכֶלֶת **(knife)** also derives from a word that you know: אָכַל **(to eat)**. The Hebrew nouns for meal, food, fuel, and foodstuff all come from א.כ.ל. Many of the new nouns introduced in this text derive from roots that you know. As an additional exercise you may wish to identify these roots, look them up in a good dictionary, and see what other words relate to them.

וַיֹּאמֶר אַבְרָהָם אַבְרָהָם וַיֹּאמֶר הִנֵּנִי׃ 12 וַיֹּאמֶר
אַל־תִּשְׁלַח יָדְךָ אֶל־הַנַּעַר וְאַל־תַּעַשׂ לוֹ מְאוּמָה
כִּי עַתָּה יָדַעְתִּי כִּי־יְרֵא אֱלֹהִים אַתָּה וְלֹא חָשַׂכְתָּ
אֶת־בִּנְךָ אֶת־יְחִידְךָ מִמֶּנִּי׃ 13 וַיִּשָּׂא אַבְרָהָם
אֶת־עֵינָיו וַיַּרְא וְהִנֵּה־אַיִל אַחַר נֶאֱחַז בַּסְּבַךְ בְּקַרְנָיו
וַיֵּלֶךְ אַבְרָהָם וַיִּקַּח אֶת־הָאַיִל

וַיֹּאמֶר אַבְרָהָם אַבְרָהָם	and he (the messenger) said, "Abraham! Abraham!"
וַיֹּאמֶר הִנֵּנִי׃	And he (Abraham) said, "Here I am."
12 וַיֹּאמֶר אַל־תִּשְׁלַח יָדְךָ	And he said, "Do not stretch out your hand
אֶל־הַנַּעַר וְאַל־תַּעַשׂ לוֹ מְאוּמָה	against the boy, and do not do anything to him,
כִּי עַתָּה יָדַעְתִּי	for now I know
כִּי־יְרֵא אֱלֹהִים אַתָּה	that you fear God
וְלֹא חָשַׂכְתָּ אֶת־בִּנְךָ	and did not withhold your son,
אֶת־יְחִידְךָ מִמֶּנִּי׃	your only son, from me."
13 וַיִּשָּׂא אַבְרָהָם אֶת־עֵינָיו	Then Abraham lifted his eyes
וַיַּרְא וְהִנֵּה־אַיִל	and looked—and behold!—a ram
אַחַר נֶאֱחַז בַּסְּבַךְ בְּקַרְנָיו	caught behind (him) in the thicket by its horns.
וַיֵּלֶךְ אַבְרָהָם וַיִּקַּח אֶת־הָאַיִל	So Abraham went and took the ram

NEW VOCABULARY

מְאוּמָה	anything
חָשַׂכְתָּ	withhold
יְחִידְךָ	your only son
נֶאֱחַז	caught
בַּסְּבַךְ	in the thicket
בְּקַרְנָיו	by its horns

VERB ANALYSIS

VERB	ROOT	PATTERN	MEANING	TENSE	P/G/N	SUFFIX
וַיֹּאמֶר	א.מ.ר	פָּעַל	say	rv imperfect	3ms	
תִּשְׁלַח	ש.ל.ח	פָּעַל	send	imperfect	2ms	
תַּעַשׂ	ע.שׂ.ה	פָּעַל	make, do	jussive	2ms	
יָדַעְתִּי	י.ד.ע	פָּעַל	know	perfect	1cs	
יְרֵא	י.ר.א	פָּעַל	fear	participle	ms	
חָשַׂכְתָּ	ח.שׂ.ך	פָּעַל	withhold	perfect	2ms	
וַיִּשָּׂא	נ.שׂ.א	פָּעַל	lift, carry	rv imperfect	3ms	
וַיַּרְא	ר.א.ה	פָּעַל	see	rv imperfect	3ms	
נֶאֱחַז	א.ח.ז	נִפְעַל	be caught	perfect	3ms	
וַיֵּלֶךְ	ה.ל.ך	פָּעַל	walk, go	rv imperfect	3ms	
וַיִּקַּח	ל.ק.ח	פָּעַל	take	rv imperfect	3ms	

GRAMMATICAL NOTE

22:12 The verb תַּעַשׂ appears in a tense called **jussive**. Jussives are imperfect verbs in the second or third person that indicate wished for or desired action. When you can translate a verb as **may he/she/you** or **let him/her/you**, it is jussive in meaning; the jussive also can function as a mild command. Jussives often will be identical to imperfects in form. When the two differ, jussives correspond to **clipped forms**. We label verbs jussive only when they show the distinct form. In this verse, the jussive תַּעַשׂ is used with אַל to express a negative command. See page 94 in *The First Hebrew Primer* for other meanings of the imperfect; pages 169, 229, and 304 for clipped forms; and page 197 for negative commands.

וַיַּעֲלֵהוּ לְעֹלָה תַּחַת בְּנוֹ׃ 14 וַיִּקְרָא אַבְרָהָם
שֵׁם־הַמָּקוֹם הַהוּא יְהוָה יִרְאֶה אֲשֶׁר יֵאָמֵר הַיּוֹם
בְּהַר יְהוָה יֵרָאֶה׃ 15 וַיִּקְרָא מַלְאַךְ יְהוָה אֶל־אַבְרָהָם
שֵׁנִית מִן־הַשָּׁמָיִם׃ 16 וַיֹּאמֶר בִּי נִשְׁבַּעְתִּי נְאֻם־יְהוָה
כִּי יַעַן אֲשֶׁר עָשִׂיתָ אֶת־הַדָּבָר הַזֶּה וְלֹא חָשַׂכְתָּ
אֶת־בִּנְךָ אֶת־יְחִידֶךָ׃

וַיַּעֲלֵהוּ לְעֹלָה תַּחַת בְּנוֹ׃	and offered it as a burnt offering in place of his son.
14 וַיִּקְרָא אַבְרָהָם	Abraham called
שֵׁם־הַמָּקוֹם הַהוּא	the name of that place
יְהוָה יִרְאֶה אֲשֶׁר יֵאָמֵר הַיּוֹם	"The LORD will see," whence it is said today,
בְּהַר יְהוָה יֵרָאֶה׃	"On the mountain the LORD will see."
15 וַיִּקְרָא מַלְאַךְ יְהוָה	Then the messenger of the LORD called out
אֶל־אַבְרָהָם שֵׁנִית מִן־הַשָּׁמָיִם׃	to Abraham a second time from the heavens.
16 וַיֹּאמֶר בִּי נִשְׁבַּעְתִּי	He said, "By myself I have sworn,"
נְאֻם־יְהוָה כִּי יַעַן אֲשֶׁר עָשִׂיתָ	says the LORD, "on account of what you did,
אֶת־הַדָּבָר הַזֶּה	this thing,
וְלֹא חָשַׂכְתָּ אֶת־בִּנְךָ	and (your) not withholding your son,
אֶת־יְחִידֶךָ׃	your only son.

NEW VOCABULARY

לְעֹלָה	as a burnt offering
נִשְׁבַּעְתִּי	I have sworn
נְאֻם	says
יַ֫עַן אֲשֶׁר	on account of
חָשַׂכְתָּ	(your) withholding
יְחִידְךָ	your only son

VERB ANALYSIS

VERB	ROOT	PATTERN	MEANING	TENSE	P/G/N	SUFFIX
וַיַּעֲלֵהוּ	ע.ל.ה	הִפְעִיל	bring up, offer	rv imperfect	3ms	3ms
וַיִּקְרָא	ק.ר.א	פָּעַל	call, proclaim	rv imperfect	3ms	
יִרְאֶה	ר.א.ה	פָּעַל	see	imperfect	3ms	
יֵאָמֵר	א.מ.ר	נִפְעַל	be said	imperfect	3ms	
יֵרָאֶה	ר.א.ה	נִפְעַל	appear	imperfect	3ms	
וַיֹּאמֶר	א.מ.ר	פָּעַל	say	rv imperfect	3ms	
נִשְׁבַּעְתִּי	שׁ.ב.ע	נִפְעַל	swear	perfect	1cs	
עָשִׂיתָ	ע.שׂ.ה	פָּעַל	make, do	perfect	2ms	
חָשַׂכְתָּ	ח.שׂ.ך	פָּעַל	withhold	perfect	2ms	

GRAMMATICAL NOTES

22:14 You may choose to leave **the name of** for שֵׁם־ out of your translation. See Genesis 17:5 on pages 4–5 for a similar construction.

22:16 Note that אֲשֶׁר can be used with prepositions. Here, יַ֫עַן אֲשֶׁר means **because of** or **on account of**. Look for עֵקֶב אֲשֶׁר (**because of**) in Genesis 22:18. כַּאֲשֶׁר (**as, even as, when**), אַחֲרֵי אֲשֶׁר (**after**), and עַד אֲשֶׁר (**until**) are common uses of אֲשֶׁר with prepositions.

22:16 נְאֻם is a noun meaning **oracle** and apears most often in the formula נְאֻם־יְהוָה (**oracle of the LORD**). That formula is used throughout prophecy and is not always literally translated.

17 כִּי־בָרֵךְ אֲבָרֶכְךָ וְהַרְבָּה אַרְבֶּה אֶת־זַרְעֲךָ כְּכוֹכְבֵי
הַשָּׁמַיִם וְכַחוֹל אֲשֶׁר עַל־שְׂפַת הַיָּם וְיִרַשׁ זַרְעֲךָ אֵת שַׁעַר
אֹיְבָיו׃ 18 וְהִתְבָּרְכוּ בְזַרְעֲךָ כֹּל גּוֹיֵי הָאָרֶץ עֵקֶב אֲשֶׁר
שָׁמַעְתָּ בְּקֹלִי׃ 19 וַיָּשָׁב אַבְרָהָם אֶל־נְעָרָיו וַיָּקֻמוּ וַיֵּלְכוּ
יַחְדָּו אֶל־בְּאֵר שָׁבַע וַיֵּשֶׁב אַבְרָהָם בִּבְאֵר שָׁבַע׃

17 כִּי־בָרֵךְ אֲבָרֶכְךָ	For I indeed bless you
וְהַרְבָּה אַרְבֶּה אֶת־זַרְעֲךָ	and surely make your descendants as numerous
כְּכוֹכְבֵי הַשָּׁמַיִם	as the stars of heaven
וְכַחוֹל אֲשֶׁר עַל־שְׂפַת הַיָּם	and as the sand which is on the seashore;
וְיִרַשׁ זַרְעֲךָ	and your descendants will possess
אֵת שַׁעַר אֹיְבָיו׃	the gate of their enemies.
18 וְהִתְבָּרְכוּ בְזַרְעֲךָ	And they will bless themselves by your descendants,
כֹּל גּוֹיֵי הָאָרֶץ	all the nations of the earth,
עֵקֶב אֲשֶׁר שָׁמַעְתָּ בְּקֹלִי׃	because you obeyed (lit. heard) my voice.”
19 וַיָּשָׁב אַבְרָהָם אֶל־נְעָרָיו	Abraham returned to his boys.
וַיָּקֻמוּ וַיֵּלְכוּ יַחְדָּו אֶל־בְּאֵר שָׁבַע	They arose and went together to Be’er Sheva;
וַיֵּשֶׁב אַבְרָהָם בִּבְאֵר שָׁבַע׃	and Abraham stayed in Be’er Sheva.

NEW VOCABULARY

וְהַרְבָּה אַרְבֶּה	and surely make numerous
כְּכוֹכְבֵי	stars
וְכַחוֹל	and the sand
אֹיְבָיו	their enemies
עֵקֶב אֲשֶׁר	because
יַחְדָּו	together
בְּאֵר שָׁבַע	Be'er Sheva

VERB ANALYSIS

VERB	ROOT	PATTERN	MEANING	TENSE	P/G/N	SUFFIX
בָּרֵךְ	ב.ר.ך	פִּעֵל	bless	emph. inf.		
אֲבָרֶכְךָ	ב.ר.ך	פִּעֵל	bless	imperfect	1cs	2ms
וְהַרְבָּה	ר.ב.ה	הִפְעִיל	make numerous	emph. inf		
אַרְבֶּה	ר.ב.ה	הִפְעִיל	make numerous	imperfect	1cs	
וְיִרַשׁ	י.ר.ש	פָּעַל	possess	imperfect	3ms	
אֹיְבָיו	א.י.ב	פָּעַל	be hostile to	participle	mp	3ms
וְהִתְבָּרְכוּ	ב.ר.ך	הִתְפַּעֵל	bless oneself	rv perfect	3cp	
שָׁמַעְתָּ	ש.מ.ע	פָּעַל	hear	perfect	2ms	
וַיָּשָׁב	ש.ו.ב	פָּעַל	turn, return	rv imperfect	3ms	
וַיָּקֻמוּ	ק.ו.ם	פָּעַל	arise	rv imperfect	3mp	
וַיֵּלְכוּ	ה.ל.ך	פָּעַל	walk, go	rv imperfect	3mp	
וַיֵּשֶׁב	י.ש.ב	פָּעַל	sit, dwell	rv imperfect	3ms	

GRAMMATICAL NOTE

22:17 חוֹל **(sand)** is a symbol for something that is innumerable.

32 ¹ וַיַּרְא הָעָם כִּי־בֹשֵׁשׁ מֹשֶׁה לָרֶדֶת מִן־הָהָר וַיִּקָּהֵל
הָעָם עַל־אַהֲרֹן וַיֹּאמְרוּ אֵלָיו קוּם עֲשֵׂה־לָנוּ
אֱלֹהִים אֲשֶׁר יֵלְכוּ לְפָנֵינוּ כִּי־זֶה מֹשֶׁה הָאִישׁ אֲשֶׁר
הֶעֱלָנוּ מֵאֶרֶץ מִצְרַיִם לֹא יָדַעְנוּ מֶה־הָיָה לוֹ׃ ²וַיֹּאמֶר
אֲלֵהֶם אַהֲרֹן פָּרְקוּ נִזְמֵי הַזָּהָב אֲשֶׁר בְּאָזְנֵי נְשֵׁיכֶם
בְּנֵיכֶם

¹וַיַּרְא הָעָם כִּי־בֹשֵׁשׁ מֹשֶׁה	When the people saw that Moses was delayed
לָרֶדֶת מִן־הָהָר	in coming down from the mountain,
וַיִּקָּהֵל הָעָם עַל־אַהֲרֹן	the people gathered around Aaron
וַיֹּאמְרוּ אֵלָיו	and said to him,
קוּם עֲשֵׂה־לָנוּ אֱלֹהִים	"Arise, make gods for us
אֲשֶׁר יֵלְכוּ לְפָנֵינוּ	who will go before us;
כִּי־זֶה מֹשֶׁה הָאִישׁ	as for this Moses, the man
אֲשֶׁר הֶעֱלָנוּ מֵאֶרֶץ מִצְרַיִם	who brought us out from the land of Egypt—
לֹא יָדַעְנוּ מֶה־הָיָה לוֹ׃	we do not know what has happened to him."
²וַיֹּאמֶר אֲלֵהֶם אַהֲרֹן	And Aaron said to them,
פָּרְקוּ נִזְמֵי הַזָּהָב	"Remove the gold rings
אֲשֶׁר בְּאָזְנֵי נְשֵׁיכֶם בְּנֵיכֶם	that are in the ears of your wives, your sons,

NEW VOCABULARY

בֹּשֵׁשׁ	was delayed
לָרֶדֶת	in coming down
וַיִּקָּהֵל	(they) gathered
פָּרְקוּ	remove
נִזְמֵי	rings of

VERB ANALYSIS

VERB	ROOT	PATTERN	MEANING	TENSE	P/G/N	SUFFIX
וַיַּרְא	ר.א.ה	פָּעַל	see	rv imperfect	3ms	
בֹּשֵׁשׁ	ב.ו.ש	פּוֹלֵל	delay	perfect	3ms	
לָרֶדֶת	י.ר.ד	פָּעַל	come down	infinitive		
וַיִּקָּהֵל	ק.ה.ל	נִפְעַל	assemble	rv imperfect	3ms	
וַיֹּאמְרוּ	א.מ.ר	פָּעַל	say	rv imperfect	3mp	
קוּם	ק.ו.ם	פָּעַל	arise	command	ms	
עֲשֵׂה	ע.ש.ה	פָּעַל	make, do	command	ms	
יֵלְכוּ	ה.ל.ך	פָּעַל	walk, go	imperfect	3mp	
הֶעֱלָנוּ	ע.ל.ה	הִפְעִיל	bring up, offer	perfect	3ms	1cp
יָדַעְנוּ	י.ד.ע	פָּעַל	know	perfect	1cp	
הָיָה	ה.י.ה	פָּעַל	be, become	perfect	3ms	
וַיֹּאמֶר	א.מ.ר	פָּעַל	say	rv imperfect	3ms	
פָּרְקוּ	פ.ר.ק	פִּעֵל	remove	command	mp	

GRAMMATICAL NOTE

32:1 The verb בֹּשֵׁשׁ is unusual in meaning and form. Most words derived from the root ב.ו.ש relate to being ashamed or causing shame; here the verb means to delay, and its relation to the root is unclear. בֹּשֵׁשׁ appears in a pattern called פּוֹלֵל (**Po'lel**), which frequently functions as a substitute for the פָּעַל in hollow verbs. It is not important for you to learn the פּוֹלֵל pattern at this time.

וּבְנֹתֵיכֶם וְהָבִיאוּ אֵלָי׃ 3 וַיִּתְפָּרְקוּ כָּל־הָעָם אֶת־נִזְמֵי
הַזָּהָב אֲשֶׁר בְּאָזְנֵיהֶם וַיָּבִיאוּ אֶל־אַהֲרֹן׃ 4 וַיִּקַּח מִיָּדָם
וַיָּצַר אֹתוֹ בַּחֶרֶט וַיַּעֲשֵׂהוּ עֵגֶל מַסֵּכָה וַיֹּאמְרוּ אֵלֶּה
אֱלֹהֶיךָ יִשְׂרָאֵל אֲשֶׁר הֶעֱלוּךָ מֵאֶרֶץ מִצְרָיִם׃ 5 וַיַּרְא
אַהֲרֹן וַיִּבֶן מִזְבֵּחַ לְפָנָיו וַיִּקְרָא אַהֲרֹן וַיֹּאמַר חַג
לַיהוָה מָחָר׃

וּבְנֹתֵיכֶם וְהָבִיאוּ אֵלָי׃	and your daughters, and bring them to me."
3 וַיִּתְפָּרְקוּ כָּל־הָעָם	So all the people took off
אֶת־נִזְמֵי הַזָּהָב אֲשֶׁר בְּאָזְנֵיהֶם	the gold rings that were in their ears
וַיָּבִיאוּ אֶל־אַהֲרֹן׃	and brought (them) to Aaron.
4 וַיִּקַּח מִיָּדָם	He took from their hands,
וַיָּצַר אֹתוֹ בַּחֶרֶט	and formed it with the engraving tool,
וַיַּעֲשֵׂהוּ עֵגֶל מַסֵּכָה	and made it—a molten calf;
וַיֹּאמְרוּ אֵלֶּה אֱלֹהֶיךָ יִשְׂרָאֵל	and they said, "These are your gods, Israel,
אֲשֶׁר הֶעֱלוּךָ מֵאֶרֶץ מִצְרָיִם׃	who brought you up from the land of Egypt."
5 וַיַּרְא אַהֲרֹן וַיִּבֶן מִזְבֵּחַ לְפָנָיו	Aaron saw (this) and built an altar before it;
וַיִּקְרָא אַהֲרֹן וַיֹּאמַר	and Aaron called and said,
חַג לַיהוָה מָחָר׃	"(There will be) a feast for the LORD tomorrow."

NEW VOCABULARY

וַיִּתְפָּרְקוּ	so (they) took off
נִזְמֵי	rings of
וַיָּצַר	and (he) formed
בַּחֶרֶט	with the engraving tool
עֵגֶל	calf
מַסֵּכָה	molten
חַג	feast
מָחָר	tomorrow

VERB ANALYSIS

VERB	ROOT	PATTERN	MEANING	TENSE	P/G/N	SUFFIX
וְהָבִיאוּ	ב.ו.א	הִפְעִיל	bring	command	mp	
וַיִּתְפָּרְקוּ	פ.ר.ק	הִתְפַּעֵל	remove	rv imperfect	3mp	
וַיָּבִיאוּ	ב.ו.א	הִפְעִיל	bring	rv imperfect	3mp	
וַיִּקַּח	ל.ק.ח	פָּעַל	take	rv imperfect	3ms	
וַיָּצַר	צ.ו.ר	פָּעַל	form, fashion	rv imperfect	3ms	
וַיַּעֲשֵׂהוּ	ע.שׂ.ה	פָּעַל	make, do	rv imperfect	3ms	3ms
וַיֹּאמְרוּ	א.מ.ר	פָּעַל	say	rv imperfect	3mp	
הֶעֱלוּךָ	ע.ל.ה	הִפְעִיל	bring up, offer	perfect	3cp	2ms
וַיַּרְא	ר.א.ה	פָּעַל	see	rv imperfect	3ms	
וַיִּבֶן	ב.נ.ה	פָּעַל	build	rv imperfect	3ms	
וַיִּקְרָא	ק.ר.א	פָּעַל	call, proclaim	rv imperfect	3ms	
וַיֹּאמַר	א.מ.ר	פָּעַל	say	rv imperfect	3ms	

GRAMMATICAL NOTE

32:5 וַיֹּאמַר is a regular alternative to the expected rv imperfect 3ms form וַיֹּאמֶר.

6 וַיַּשְׁכִּימוּ מִמָּחֳרָת וַיַּעֲלוּ עֹלֹת וַיַּגִּשׁוּ שְׁלָמִים וַיֵּשֶׁב
הָעָם לֶאֱכֹל וְשָׁתוֹ וַיָּקֻמוּ לְצַחֵק׃ 7 וַיְדַבֵּר יְהוָה
אֶל־מֹשֶׁה לֶךְ־רֵד כִּי שִׁחֵת עַמְּךָ אֲשֶׁר הֶעֱלֵיתָ
מֵאֶרֶץ מִצְרָיִם׃ 8 סָרוּ מַהֵר מִן־הַדֶּרֶךְ אֲשֶׁר צִוִּיתִם
עָשׂוּ לָהֶם עֵגֶל מַסֵּכָה וַיִּשְׁתַּחֲווּ־לוֹ וַיִּזְבְּחוּ־לוֹ

6 וַיַּשְׁכִּימוּ מִמָּחֳרָת	So they rose early the next day
וַיַּעֲלוּ עֹלֹת	and offered burnt offerings,
וַיַּגִּשׁוּ שְׁלָמִים	and brought peace offerings;
וַיֵּשֶׁב הָעָם לֶאֱכֹל וְשָׁתוֹ	and the people sat down to eat and drink,
וַיָּקֻמוּ לְצַחֵק׃	and got up to celebrate.
7 וַיְדַבֵּר יְהוָה אֶל־מֹשֶׁה	Then the LORD said to Moses,
לֶךְ־רֵד כִּי שִׁחֵת עַמְּךָ	"Go down; for your people have acted perversely,
אֲשֶׁר הֶעֱלֵיתָ מֵאֶרֶץ מִצְרָיִם׃	the ones you brought up from the land of Egypt.
8 סָרוּ מַהֵר	They have turned away quickly
מִן־הַדֶּרֶךְ אֲשֶׁר צִוִּיתִם	from the path that I commanded them.
עָשׂוּ לָהֶם עֵגֶל מַסֵּכָה	They have made themselves a molten calf,
וַיִּשְׁתַּחֲווּ־לוֹ וַיִּזְבְּחוּ־לוֹ	and have worshipped it and sacrificed to it,

NEW VOCABULARY

שִׁחֵת	have acted perversely	וַיַּשְׁכִּימוּ	so they rose early
מַהֵר	quickly	מִמָּחֳרָת	the next day
עֵגֶל	calf	עֹלֹת	burnt offerings
מַסֵּכָה	molten	וַיַּגִּשׁוּ	(they) brought
וַיִּשְׁתַּחֲווּ	and they have worshipped	שְׁלָמִים	peace offerings
וַיִּזְבְּחוּ	and (they) sacrificed	לְצַחֵק	to celebrate

VERB ANALYSIS

VERB	ROOT	PATTERN	MEANING	TENSE	P/G/N	SUFFIX
וַיַּשְׁכִּימוּ	ש.כ.ם	הִפְעִיל	rise early	rv imperfect	3mp	
וַיַּעֲלוּ	ע.ל.ה	הִפְעִיל	bring up, offer	rv imperfect	3mp	
וַיַּגִּשׁוּ	נ.ג.ש	הִפְעִיל	bring	rv imperfect	3mp	
וַיֵּשֶׁב	י.ש.ב	פָּעַל	sit, dwell	rv imperfect	3ms	
לֶאֱכֹל	א.כ.ל	פָּעַל	eat, consume	infinitive		
וְשָׁתוֹ	ש.ת.ה	פָּעַל	drink	infinitive		
וַיָּקֻמוּ	ק.ו.ם	פָּעַל	arise	rv imperfect	3mp	
לְצַחֵק	צ.ח.ק	פִּעֵל	laugh	infinitive		
וַיְדַבֵּר	ד.ב.ר	פִּעֵל	speak	rv imperfect	3ms	
לֵךְ	ה.ל.ך	פָּעַל	walk, go	command	ms	
רֵד	י.ר.ד	פָּעַל	go down	command	ms	
שִׁחֵת	ש.ח.ת	פִּעֵל	go to ruin	perfect	3ms	
הֶעֱלִיתָ	ע.ל.ה	הִפְעִיל	bring up, offer	perfect	2ms	
סָרוּ	ס.ו.ר	פָּעַל	turn aside	perfect	3cp	
צִוִּיתִם	צ.ו.ה	פִּעֵל	command	perfect	1cs	3mp
עָשׂוּ	ע.ש.ה	פָּעַל	make, do	perfect	3cp	
וַיִּשְׁתַּחֲווּ	ח.ו.ה	הִשְׁתַּפֵּל	worship	rv imperfect	3mp	
וַיִּזְבְּחוּ	ז.ב.ח	פָּעַל	sacrifice	rv imperfect	3mp	

וַיֹּאמְרוּ אֵלֶּה אֱלֹהֶיךָ יִשְׂרָאֵל אֲשֶׁר הֶעֱלוּךָ מֵאֶרֶץ
מִצְרָיִם׃ 9 וַיֹּאמֶר יְהוָה אֶל־מֹשֶׁה רָאִיתִי אֶת־הָעָם
הַזֶּה וְהִנֵּה עַם־קְשֵׁה־עֹרֶף הוּא׃ 10 וְעַתָּה הַנִּיחָה לִּי
וְיִחַר־אַפִּי בָהֶם וַאֲכַלֵּם וְאֶעֱשֶׂה אוֹתְךָ לְגוֹי גָּדוֹל׃
11 וַיְחַל מֹשֶׁה אֶת־פְּנֵי יְהוָה אֱלֹהָיו וַיֹּאמֶר לָמָה יְהוָה
יֶחֱרֶה אַפְּךָ בְּעַמֶּךָ

וַיֹּאמְרוּ אֵלֶּה אֱלֹהֶיךָ יִשְׂרָאֵל	and they said, 'These are your gods, Israel,
אֲשֶׁר הֶעֱלוּךָ מֵאֶרֶץ מִצְרָיִם׃	who brought you up from the land of Egypt.'"
9 וַיֹּאמֶר יְהוָה אֶל־מֹשֶׁה	The LORD said to Moses,
רָאִיתִי אֶת־הָעָם הַזֶּה	"I have seen this people,
וְהִנֵּה עַם־קְשֵׁה־עֹרֶף הוּא׃	and look, it is a stiff-necked people.
10 וְעַתָּה הַנִּיחָה לִּי	Now let me be,
וְיִחַר־אַפִּי בָהֶם	so that my anger might burn against them,
וַאֲכַלֵּם	and I might bring them to an end
וְאֶעֱשֶׂה אוֹתְךָ לְגוֹי גָּדוֹל׃	and make you into a mighty nation."
11 וַיְחַל מֹשֶׁה אֶת־פְּנֵי יְהוָה	But Moses implored the face of the LORD
אֱלֹהָיו וַיֹּאמֶר לָמָה יְהוָה	his God and said, "Why, LORD,
יֶחֱרֶה אַפְּךָ בְּעַמֶּךָ	does your anger burn against your people,

NEW VOCABULARY

קָשֵׁה	stiff
עֹרֶף	neck
הַנִּיחָה	let me be
וַיְחַל	but (he) implored

VERB ANALYSIS

VERB	ROOT	PATTERN	MEANING	TENSE	P/G/N	SUFFIX
וַיֹּאמְרוּ	א.מ.ר	פָּעַל	say	rv imperfect	3mp	
הֶעֱלוּךָ	ע.ל.ה	הִפְעִיל	bring up, offer	perfect	3cp	2ms
וַיֹּאמֶר	א.מ.ר	פָּעַל	say	rv imperfect	3ms	
רָאִיתִי	ר.א.ה	פָּעַל	see	perfect	1cs	
הַנִּיחָה	נ.ו.ח	הִפְעִיל	give rest to	command	ms	
וְיִחַר	ח.ר.ה	פָּעַל	burn	jussive	3ms	
וַאֲכַלֵּם	כ.ל.ה	פִּעֵל	complete	imperfect	1cs	3mp
וְאֶעֱשֶׂה	ע.שׂ.ה	פָּעַל	make, do	imperfect	1cs	
וַיְחַל	ח.ל.ה	פִּעֵל	implore	rv imperfect	3ms	
יֶחֱרֶה	ח.ר.ה	פָּעַל	burn	imperfect	3ms	

GRAMMATICAL NOTES

32:8 קְשֵׁה־עֹרֶף **(stiff-necked)** is the biblical idiom for stubborn. In Exodus 32:8, Israel is stubborn because the nation will not listen to the LORD and abandon earlier forms of worship.

32:10 The command הַנִּיחָה has הָא attached to the end; the expected form is הָנֵּחַ. This ending may appear on any 2ms command. Remember that when הָא is attached to a 1cs or 1cp imperfect, the resulting form is the cohortative.

32:10 The word אַף and words derived from the root ח.ר.ה often appear together in the Hebrew Bible to express anger. For other uses of the word אַף, see page 349 in *The First Hebrew Primer.*

32:11 Throughout this book, the vowel Ẋ and the marker for the *shin* (שׁ) are written as one mark. Therefore, **Moses** is spelled מֹשֶׁה in verse 11, and **was delayed** is spelled בֹשֵׁשׁ in verse 1 on page 24.

אֲשֶׁר הוֹצֵאתָ מֵאֶרֶץ מִצְרַיִם בְּכֹחַ גָּדוֹל וּבְיָד חֲזָקָה׃
12 לָמָּה יֹאמְרוּ מִצְרַיִם לֵאמֹר בְּרָעָה הוֹצִיאָם לַהֲרֹג
אֹתָם בֶּהָרִים וּלְכַלֹּתָם מֵעַל פְּנֵי הָאֲדָמָה שׁוּב מֵחֲרוֹן
אַפֶּךָ וְהִנָּחֵם עַל־הָרָעָה לְעַמֶּךָ׃ 13 זְכֹר לְאַבְרָהָם
לְיִצְחָק וּלְיִשְׂרָאֵל עֲבָדֶיךָ אֲשֶׁר נִשְׁבַּעְתָּ לָהֶם בָּךְ

אֲשֶׁר הוֹצֵאתָ מֵאֶרֶץ מִצְרַיִם	whom you brought out from the land of Egypt
בְּכֹחַ גָּדוֹל וּבְיָד חֲזָקָה׃	with great power and with a mighty hand?
12 לָמָּה יֹאמְרוּ מִצְרַיִם לֵאמֹר	Why should the Egyptians say,
בְּרָעָה הוֹצִיאָם	'With evil (intent) he brought them out
לַהֲרֹג אֹתָם בֶּהָרִים וּלְכַלֹּתָם	to kill them in the mountains and finish them off
מֵעַל פְּנֵי הָאֲדָמָה	from upon the face of the earth'?
שׁוּב מֵחֲרוֹן אַפֶּךָ	Repent from your burning anger
וְהִנָּחֵם עַל־הָרָעָה לְעַמֶּךָ׃	and abandon the evil (plan) for your people.
13 זְכֹר לְאַבְרָהָם לְיִצְחָק	Remember Abraham, Isaac,
וּלְיִשְׂרָאֵל עֲבָדֶיךָ	and Israel, your servants,
אֲשֶׁר נִשְׁבַּעְתָּ לָהֶם בָּךְ	how you promised to them by your own self

NEW VOCABULARY

לַהֲרֹג	to kill
וּלְכַלֹּתָם	and finish them off
מֵחֲרוֹן	from (your) burning
וְהִנָּחֵם	and abandon
נִשְׁבַּעְתָּ	you promised

VERB ANALYSIS

VERB	ROOT	PATTERN	MEANING	TENSE	P/G/N	SUFFIX
הוֹצֵאתָ	י.צ.א	הִפְעִיל	bring out	perfect	2ms	
יֹאמְרוּ	א.מ.ר	פָּעַל	say	imperfect	3mp	
לֵאמֹר	א.מ.ר	פָּעַל	say	infinitive		
הוֹצִיאָם	י.צ.א	הִפְעִיל	bring out	perfect	3ms	3mp
לַהֲרֹג	ה.ר.ג	פָּעַל	kill	infinitive		
וּלְכַלֹּתָם	כ.ל.ה	פִּעֵל	complete	infinitive		3mp
שׁוּב	שׁ.ו.ב	פָּעַל	turn, return	command	ms	
וְהִנָּחֵם	נ.ח.ם	נִפְעַל	be sorry	command	ms	
זְכֹר	ז.כ.ר	פָּעַל	remember	command	ms	
נִשְׁבַּעְתָּ	שׁ.ב.ע	נִפְעַל	swear	perfect	2ms	

GRAMMATICAL NOTES

32:12 לָמָּה often precedes an imperfect to form a rhetorical question, specifically why a certain action should or should not be undertaken.

32:12 The basic meaning of שׁוּב in פָּעַל is to turn or return, but it can also be used in figures of speech. שׁוּב can express an idea or plan being **repented** and certain conditions being **restored**.

32:13 נִפְעַל verbs are usually passive and correspond to an active פָּעַל form. However, some verb roots appear in the נִפְעַל and are not passive in meaning; שׁ.ב.ע is one such verb. For more information on the נִפְעַל, see pages 331–335 in *The First Hebrew Primer.*

וַתְּדַבֵּר אֲלֵהֶם אַרְבֶּה אֶת־זַרְעֲכֶם כְּכוֹכְבֵי הַשָּׁמָיִם
וְכָל־הָאָרֶץ הַזֹּאת אֲשֶׁר אָמַרְתִּי אֶתֵּן לְזַרְעֲכֶם וְנָחֲלוּ
לְעֹלָם׃ 14 וַיִּנָּחֶם יְהוָה עַל־הָרָעָה אֲשֶׁר דִּבֶּר לַעֲשׂוֹת
לְעַמּוֹ׃

וַתְּדַבֵּר אֲלֵהֶם	and said to them,
אַרְבֶּה אֶת־זַרְעֲכֶם	'I will make your descendants as numerous
כְּכוֹכְבֵי הַשָּׁמָיִם	as the stars of heaven.
וְכָל־הָאָרֶץ הַזֹּאת אֲשֶׁר אָמַרְתִּי	And all of this land, about which I spoke,
אֶתֵּן לְזַרְעֲכֶם	I will give to your descendants,
וְנָחֲלוּ לְעֹלָם׃	and they shall inherit it forever.'"
14 וַיִּנָּחֶם יְהוָה עַל־הָרָעָה	So the LORD abandoned the evil (plan)
אֲשֶׁר דִּבֶּר לַעֲשׂוֹת לְעַמּוֹ׃	that he said he would do to his people.

NEW VOCABULARY

אַרְבֶּה	I will make numerous
כְּכוֹכְבֵי	as the stars of
וְנָחֲלוּ	they shall inherit
וַיִּנָּחֶם	so (he) abandoned

VERB ANALYSIS

VERB	ROOT	PATTERN	MEANING	TENSE	P/G/N	SUFFIX
וַתְּדַבֵּר	ד.ב.ר	פִּעֵל	speak	rv imperfect	2ms	
אַרְבֶּה	ר.ב.ה	הִפְעִיל	make numerous	imperfect	1cs	
אָמַרְתִּי	א.מ.ר	פָּעַל	say	perfect	1cs	
אֶתֵּן	נ.ת.ן	פָּעַל	give, set	imperfect	1cs	
וְנָחֲלוּ	נ.ח.ל	פָּעַל	inherit	rv perfect	3cp	
וַיִּנָּחֶם	נ.ח.ם	נִפְעַל	be sorry	rv imperfect	3ms	
דִּבֶּר	ד.ב.ר	פִּעֵל	speak	perfect	3ms	
לַעֲשׂוֹת	ע.שׂ.ה	פָּעַל	make, do	infinitive		

GRAMMATICAL NOTES

32:14 נ.ח.ם literally means to be sorry or have compassion for someone or something. Here the word is used as a synonym for שׁ.ו.ב (32:12) and indicates repentance for a thought or course of action. We translated וַיִּנָּחֶם as **and (he) abandoned** to make the English idiomatic.

Exodus 32:12–14 refers to the covenant established between Israel and its God. The LORD promises to make Israel's future generations numerous, to give the Hebrews the land of Canaan as their own, and to preserve Israel's inheritance through future generations. Genesis 17:1-11 outlines the terms and conditions of Israel's covenant with the LORD.

19 11 לֹא תִּגְנֹבוּ וְלֹא־תְכַחֲשׁוּ וְלֹא־תְשַׁקְּרוּ אִישׁ
בַּעֲמִיתוֹ׃ 12 וְלֹא־תִשָּׁבְעוּ בִשְׁמִי לַשָּׁקֶר וְחִלַּלְתָּ
אֶת־שֵׁם אֱלֹהֶיךָ אֲנִי יְהוָה׃ 13 לֹא־תַעֲשֹׁק אֶת־רֵעֲךָ
וְלֹא תִגְזֹל לֹא־תָלִין פְּעֻלַּת שָׂכִיר אִתְּךָ עַד־בֹּקֶר׃
14 לֹא־תְקַלֵּל חֵרֵשׁ וְלִפְנֵי עִוֵּר לֹא תִתֵּן מִכְשֹׁל

11 לֹא תִּגְנֹבוּ וְלֹא־תְכַחֲשׁוּ	"You are not to steal, and you are not to lie,
וְלֹא־תְשַׁקְּרוּ אִישׁ בַּעֲמִיתוֹ׃	and you are not to cheat one another.
12 וְלֹא־תִשָּׁבְעוּ בִשְׁמִי לַשָּׁקֶר	You are not to swear falsely by my name
וְחִלַּלְתָּ אֶת־שֵׁם אֱלֹהֶיךָ	and profane the name of your God:
אֲנִי יְהוָה׃	I am the LORD.
13 לֹא־תַעֲשֹׁק אֶת־רֵעֲךָ	You are not to oppress your neighbor,
וְלֹא תִגְזֹל	and you are not to rob (him);
לֹא־תָלִין פְּעֻלַּת שָׂכִיר	the wages of a worker are not to remain overnight
אִתְּךָ עַד־בֹּקֶר׃	with you until morning.
14 לֹא־תְקַלֵּל חֵרֵשׁ	You are not to insult the deaf,
וְלִפְנֵי עִוֵּר	and before the blind
לֹא תִתֵּן מִכְשֹׁל	you are not to place a stumbling block;

NEW VOCABULARY

תִגְזֹל	you rob	תִּגְנֹבוּ	you steal
תָלִין	(it) remains overnight	תְכַחֲשׁוּ	you lie
פְּעֻלַּת	the wages	תְשַׁקְּרוּ	you cheat
שָׂכִיר	worker	בַּעֲמִיתוֹ	one another
תְקַלֵּל	you insult	תִשָּׁבְעוּ	you swear
חֵרֵשׁ	the deaf	לַשָּׁקֶר	falsely
עִוֵּר	the blind	וְחִלַּלְתָּ	you profane
מִכְשֹׁל	a stumbling block	תַעֲשֹׁק	you oppress

VERB ANALYSIS

VERB	ROOT	PATTERN	MEANING	TENSE	P/G/N	SUFFIX
תִּגְנֹבוּ	ג.נ.ב	פָּעַל	steal	imperfect	2mp	
תְכַחֲשׁוּ	כ.ח.ש	פִּעֵל	deceive	imperfect	2mp	
תְשַׁקְּרוּ	ש.ק.ר	פִּעֵל	deal falsely	imperfect	2mp	
תִשָּׁבְעוּ	ש.ב.ע	נִפְעַל	swear	imperfect	2mp	
וְחִלַּלְתָּ	ח.ל.ל	פִּעֵל	defile, profane	rv perfect	2ms	
תַעֲשֹׁק	ע.ש.ק	פָּעַל	oppress	imperfect	2ms	
תִגְזֹל	ג.ז.ל	פָּעַל	seize, rob	imperfect	2ms	
תָלִין	ל.ו.ן	פָּעַל	pass the night	imperfect	3fs	
תְקַלֵּל	ק.ל.ל	פִּעֵל	curse, insult	imperfect	2ms	
תִתֵּן	נ.ת.ן	פָּעַל	give, set	imperfect	2ms	

GRAMMATICAL NOTES

19:2 Hebrew expresses general prohibitions with לֹא + the imperfect. For a full explanation, see Deuteronomy 5:8 on page 57.

19:11 בַּעֲמִיתוֹ literally means **in your association** or **with your associate**.

19:14 Adjectives can work like nouns in Hebrew. In verse 14, **deaf** means **the deaf** or **the deaf one**, and **blind** means **the blind** or **the blind one**.

וְיָרֵאתָ מֵּאֱלֹהֶיךָ אֲנִי יְהוָה׃ 15 לֹא־תַעֲשׂוּ עָוֶל
בַּמִּשְׁפָּט לֹא־תִשָּׂא פְנֵי־דָל וְלֹא תֶהְדַּר פְּנֵי גָדוֹל
בְּצֶדֶק תִּשְׁפֹּט עֲמִיתֶךָ׃ 16 לֹא־תֵלֵךְ רָכִיל בְּעַמֶּיךָ לֹא
תַעֲמֹד עַל־דַּם רֵעֶךָ אֲנִי יְהוָה׃ 17 לֹא־תִשְׂנָא
אֶת־אָחִיךָ בִּלְבָבֶךָ הוֹכֵחַ תּוֹכִיחַ אֶת־עֲמִיתֶךָ

but you are to fear your God: I am the LORD.	וְיָרֵאתָ מֵּאֱלֹהֶיךָ אֲנִי יְהוָה׃
You are to do no injustice in (rendering) judgment:	15 לֹא־תַעֲשׂוּ עָוֶל בַּמִּשְׁפָּט
you are not to favor the poor,	לֹא־תִשָּׂא פְנֵי־דָל
and you are not to defer to the great;	וְלֹא תֶהְדַּר פְּנֵי גָדוֹל
you are to judge your fellow with righteousness.	בְּצֶדֶק תִּשְׁפֹּט עֲמִיתֶךָ׃
You are not to go about as a slanderer	16 לֹא־תֵלֵךְ רָכִיל
among your people;	בְּעַמֶּיךָ
you are not to stand by the blood of your neighbor:	לֹא תַעֲמֹד עַל־דַּם רֵעֶךָ
I am the LORD.	אֲנִי יְהוָה׃
You are not to hate your neighbor in your heart;	17 לֹא־תִשְׂנָא אֶת־אָחִיךָ בִּלְבָבֶךָ
you are certainly to rebuke your fellow,	הוֹכֵחַ תּוֹכִיחַ אֶת־עֲמִיתֶךָ

NEW VOCABULARY

בְּצֶדֶק	with righteousness	עָוֶל	injustice
שׁרָכִיל	slanderer	דָל	poor
תִשְׂנָא	you hate	תֶהְדַּר	defer
הוֹכֵחַ תוֹכִיחַ	you certainly rebuke	עֲמִיתֶךָ	your fellow

VERB ANALYSIS

VERB	ROOT	PATTERN	MEANING	TENSE	P/G/N	SUFFIX
וְיָרֵאתָ	י.ר.א	פָּעַל	fear	rv perfect	2ms	
תַעֲשׂוּ	ע.שׂ.ה	פָּעַל	make, do	imperfect	2mp	
תִשָּׂא	נ.שׂ.א	פָּעַל	lift, carry	imperfect	2ms	
תֶהְדַּר	ה.ד.ר	פָּעַל	swell, honor	imperfect	2ms	
תִשְׁפֹּט	שׁ.פ.ט	פָּעַל	judge	imperfect	2ms	
תֵלֵךְ	ה.ל.ך	פָּעַל	walk, go	imperfect	2ms	
תַעֲמֹד	ע.מ.ד	פָּעַל	stand	imperfect	2ms	
תִשְׂנָא	שׂ.נ.א	פָּעַל	hate	imperfect	2ms	
הוֹכֵחַ	י.כ.ח	הִפְעִיל	judge, reprove	emph. inf.		
תוֹכִיחַ	י.כ.ח	הִפְעִיל	judge, reprove	imperfect	2ms	

GRAMMATICAL NOTES

19:15 **נ.שׂ.א** (**lift**, **carry**) and **ה.ד.ר** (**swell, honor**) can convey negative associations. To carry someone in a bad sense is to show partiality; to honor someone excessively is to defer to that person.

19:16 The meaning of **stand by the blood of your neighbor** is unclear. It might mean benefit from someone's death or call for the death of a person.

19:17 Recall that the infinitive of emphasis frequently is used with other forms of the same verb. See page 213 in *The First Hebrew Primer* and note the use of the infinitive of emphasis in Genesis 22:17 on page 22.

וְלֹא־תִשָּׂא עָלָיו חֵטְא׃ 18 לֹא־תִקֹּם וְלֹא־תִטֹּר
אֶת־בְּנֵי עַמֶּךָ וְאָהַבְתָּ לְרֵעֲךָ כָּמוֹךָ אֲנִי יְהוָה׃

וְלֹא־תִשָּׂא עָלָיו חֵטְא׃	but you are not to bear sin because of him.
18 לֹא־תִקֹּם	You are not to take vengeance
וְלֹא־תִטֹּר	and you are not to maintain (anger)
אֶת־בְּנֵי עַמֶּךָ	against the children of your people,
וְאָהַבְתָּ לְרֵעֲךָ כָּמוֹךָ	but love your neighbor as yourself:
אֲנִי יְהוָה׃	I am the LORD."

NEW VOCABULARY

חֵטְא sin
תִּקֹּם you take vengeance
תִּטֹּר you maintain

VERB ANALYSIS

VERB	ROOT	PATTERN	MEANING	TENSE	P/G/N	SUFFIX
תִשָּׂא	נ.שׂ.א	פָּעַל	lift, carry	imperfect	2ms	
תִקֹּם	נ.ק.ם	פָּעַל	avenge	imperfect	2ms	
תִטֹּר	נ.ט.ר	פָּעַל	keep, maintain	imperfect	2ms	
וְאָהַבְתָּ	א.ה.ב	פָּעַל	love	imperfect	2ms	

GRAMMATICAL NOTES

19:18 נ.ט.ר is used several times in the Hebrew Bible with the direct object אַף to mean **maintain anger**. We supplied אַף from context for this verse.

Leviticus 19:11–18 is part of a passage called the Holiness Code, which combines cultic and ethical obligations. These instructions reach a climax with the command to **love your neighbor as yourself**. The New Testament quotes this passage in Mark 12:31.

The Hebrew title of Leviticus is וַיִּקְרָא, **and he called**; it is the first word in the book and is not a descriptive title. Many ancient texts bear this type of title, called an *incipit* (Latin for **it begins**), including several books in the Hebrew Bible.

20 1 וַיָּבֹאוּ בְנֵי־יִשְׂרָאֵל כָּל־הָעֵדָה מִדְבַּר־צִן בַּחֹדֶשׁ
הָרִאשׁוֹן וַיֵּשֶׁב הָעָם בְּקָדֵשׁ וַתָּמָת שָׁם מִרְיָם וַתִּקָּבֵר
שָׁם׃ 2 וְלֹא־הָיָה מַיִם לָעֵדָה וַיִּקָּהֲלוּ עַל־מֹשֶׁה
וְעַל־אַהֲרֹן׃ 3 וַיָּרֶב הָעָם עִם־מֹשֶׁה וַיֹּאמְרוּ לֵאמֹר וְלוּ
גָוַעְנוּ בִּגְוַע אַחֵינוּ לִפְנֵי יְהוָה׃ 4 וְלָמָה הֲבֵאתֶם
אֶת־קְהַל יְהוָה

1 וַיָּבֹאוּ בְנֵי־יִשְׂרָאֵל כָּל־הָעֵדָה	And the Israelites came, the whole congregation,
מִדְבַּר־צִן בַּחֹדֶשׁ הָרִאשׁוֹן	to the wilderness of Zin in the first month,
וַיֵּשֶׁב הָעָם בְּקָדֵשׁ	and the people stayed at Kadesh.
וַתָּמָת שָׁם מִרְיָם וַתִּקָּבֵר שָׁם׃	Miriam died there, and she was buried there.
2 וְלֹא־הָיָה מַיִם לָעֵדָה	But there was no water for the congregation,
וַיִּקָּהֲלוּ עַל־מֹשֶׁה	so they assembled against Moses
וְעַל־אַהֲרֹן׃	and against Aaron.
3 וַיָּרֶב הָעָם עִם־מֹשֶׁה	The people quarrelled with Moses
וַיֹּאמְרוּ לֵאמֹר	and they said,
וְלוּ גָוַעְנוּ	"If only we had died
בִּגְוַע אַחֵינוּ לִפְנֵי יְהוָה׃	when our brothers died before the LORD!
4 וְלָמָה הֲבֵאתֶם אֶת־קְהַל יְהוָה	And why did you bring the assembly of the LORD

NEW VOCABULARY

לָעֵדָה	for the congregation	הָעֵדָה	the congregation
וַיִּקָּהֲלוּ	so they assembled	צִן	Zin
וַיָּרֶב	and quarrelled	הָרִאשׁוֹן	the first
וְלוּ	if only	בְּקָדֵשׁ	at Kadesh
גָוַעְנוּ	we had died	מִרְיָם	Miriam
בִּגְוַע	when died	וַתִּקָּבֵר	and she was buried
קָהָל	assembly		

VERB ANALYSIS

VERB	ROOT	PATTERN	MEANING	TENSE	P/G/N	SUFFIX
וַיָּבֹאוּ	ב.ו.א	פָּעַל	come	rv imperfect	3mp	
וַיֵּשֶׁב	י.שׁ.ב	פָּעַל	sit, dwell	rv imperfect	3ms	
וַתָּמָת	מ.ו.ת	פָּעַל	die	rv imperfect	3fs	
וַתִּקָּבֵר	ק.ב.ר	נִפְעַל	be buried	rv imperfect	3fs	
הָיָה	ה.י.ה	פָּעַל	be, become	perfect	3ms	
וַיִּקָּהֲלוּ	ק.ה.ל	נִפְעַל	assemble	rv imperfect	3mp	
וַיָּרֶב	ר.י.ב	פָּעַל	quarrel	rv imperfect	3ms	
וַיֹּאמְרוּ	א.מ.ר	פָּעַל	say	rv imperfect	3mp	
לֵאמֹר	א.מ.ר	פָּעַל	say	infinitive		
גָוַעְנוּ	ג.ו.ע	פָּעַל	perish, die	perfect	1cp	
בִּגְוַע	ג.ו.ע	פָּעַל	perish, die	infinitive		
הֲבֵאתֶם	ב.ו.א	הִפְעִיל	bring	perfect	2mp	

GRAMMATICAL NOTES

A shorter version of this story appears in Exodus 17:1–7. The two accounts differ, so you may want to compare them.

20:1 This Kadesh is a wilderness in southern Israel, unlike the Kadesh of Psalm 29:8 on page 132. In Exodus 17, the wilderness of Zin is spelled סִין.

אֶל־הַמִּדְבָּר הַזֶּה לָמוּת שָׁם אֲנַחְנוּ וּבְעִירֵנוּ׃ 5 וְלָמָה
הֶעֱלִיתֻנוּ מִמִּצְרַיִם לְהָבִיא אֹתָנוּ אֶל־הַמָּקוֹם הָרָע
הַזֶּה לֹא מְקוֹם זֶרַע וּתְאֵנָה וְגֶפֶן וְרִמּוֹן וּמַיִם אַיִן
לִשְׁתּוֹת׃ 6 וַיָּבֹא מֹשֶׁה וְאַהֲרֹן מִפְּנֵי הַקָּהָל אֶל־פֶּתַח
אֹהֶל מוֹעֵד וַיִּפְּלוּ עַל־פְּנֵיהֶם וַיֵּרָא כְבוֹד־יְהוָה
אֲלֵיהֶם׃

אֶל־הַמִּדְבָּר הַזֶּה	into this wilderness,
לָמוּת שָׁם אֲנַחְנוּ וּבְעִירֵנוּ׃	to die there, we and our cattle?
5 וְלָמָה הֶעֱלִיתֻנוּ מִמִּצְרַיִם	And why did you bring us up from Egypt
לְהָבִיא אֹתָנוּ	to bring us
אֶל־הַמָּקוֹם הָרָע הַזֶּה	to this evil place?
לֹא מְקוֹם זֶרַע וּתְאֵנָה	It is not a place of grain, and fig-tree(s),
וְגֶפֶן וְרִמּוֹן	and vine(s), and pomegranate(s),
וּמַיִם אַיִן לִשְׁתּוֹת׃	and there is no water to drink!"
6 וַיָּבֹא מֹשֶׁה וְאַהֲרֹן מִפְּנֵי הַקָּהָל	So Moses and Aaron came from the assembly,
אֶל־פֶּתַח אֹהֶל מוֹעֵד	to the entrance of the meeting tent,
וַיִּפְּלוּ עַל־פְּנֵיהֶם	and they fell on their faces.
וַיֵּרָא כְבוֹד־יְהוָה אֲלֵיהֶם׃	And the glory of the LORD appeared to them.

NEW VOCABULARY

וּבְעִירֵנוּ	and our cattle
וּתְאֵנָה	and fig-tree(s)
וְגֶפֶן	and vine(s)
וְרִמּוֹן	and pomegranate(s)
מִפְּנֵי	from
הַקָּהָל	the assembly

VERB ANALYSIS

VERB	ROOT	PATTERN	MEANING	TENSE	P/G/N	SUFFIX
לָמוּת	מ.ו.ת	פָּעַל	die	infinitive		
הֶעֱלִיתֻנוּ	ע.ל.ה	הִפְעִיל	bring up, offer	perfect	2mp	1cp
לְהָבִיא	ב.ו.א	הִפְעִיל	bring	infinitive		
לִשְׁתּוֹת	ש.ת.ה	פָּעַל	drink	infinitive		
וַיָּבֹא	ב.ו.א	פָּעַל	come	rv imperfect	3ms	
וַיִּפְּלוּ	נ.פ.ל	פָּעַל	fall	rv imperfect	3mp	
וַיֵּרָא	ר.א.ה	נִפְעַל	appear	rv imperfect	3ms	

GRAMMATICAL NOTES

20:4 בְּעִיר is a term for cattle or the general category **beasts of burden**.

20:5 זֶרַע literally means **seed**, but in this verse is a collective plural for grain that is sown. **Fig-tree**, **vine**, and **pomegranate** are also collective plurals, and the series is part of an idealized memory of Egypt.

20:6 The expression **to fall on one's face** (נ.פ.ל + פָּנִים) is a common phrase in ancient Middle Eastern writing, especially as part of a letter's greeting.

7 וַיְדַבֵּר יְהוָה אֶל־מֹשֶׁה לֵּאמֹר׃ 8 קַח אֶת־הַמַּטֶּה
וְהַקְהֵל אֶת־הָעֵדָה אַתָּה וְאַהֲרֹן אָחִיךָ וְדִבַּרְתֶּם
אֶל־הַסֶּלַע לְעֵינֵיהֶם וְנָתַן מֵימָיו וְהוֹצֵאתָ לָהֶם מַיִם
מִן־הַסֶּלַע וְהִשְׁקִיתָ אֶת־הָעֵדָה וְאֶת־בְּעִירָם׃ 9 וַיִּקַּח
מֹשֶׁה אֶת־הַמַּטֶּה מִלִּפְנֵי יְהוָה כַּאֲשֶׁר צִוָּהוּ׃

7 וַיְדַבֵּר יְהוָה אֶל־מֹשֶׁה לֵּאמֹר׃	And the LORD spoke to Moses,
8 קַח אֶת־הַמַּטֶּה	"Take the staff
וְהַקְהֵל אֶת־הָעֵדָה	and assemble the congregation,
אַתָּה וְאַהֲרֹן אָחִיךָ	you and your brother Aaron,
וְדִבַּרְתֶּם אֶל־הַסֶּלַע לְעֵינֵיהֶם	and speak to the rock before their eyes,
וְנָתַן מֵימָיו	so that it will give its water.
וְהוֹצֵאתָ לָהֶם מַיִם מִן־הַסֶּלַע	You will bring up water for them from the rock,
וְהִשְׁקִיתָ אֶת־הָעֵדָה	and you will give drink to the congregation
וְאֶת־בְּעִירָם׃	and their cattle."
9 וַיִּקַּח מֹשֶׁה אֶת־הַמַּטֶּה	So Moses took the staff
מִלִּפְנֵי יְהוָה	from before the LORD,
כַּאֲשֶׁר צִוָּהוּ׃	as he (the LORD) had commanded him.

NEW VOCABULARY

הַמַּטֶּה	the staff
וְהַקְהֵל	and assemble
הָעֵדָה	the congregation
הַסֶּלַע	the rock
וְהִשְׁקִיתָ	and you will give drink
בְּעִירָם	their cattle

VERB ANALYSIS

VERB	ROOT	PATTERN	MEANING	TENSE	P/G/N	SUFFIX
וַיְדַבֵּר	ד.ב.ר	פִּעֵל	speak	rv imperfect	3ms	
לֵאמֹר	א.מ.ר	פָּעַל	say	infinitive		
קַח	ל.ק.ח	פָּעַל	take	command	ms	
וְהַקְהֵל	ק.ה.ל	הִפְעִיל	call assembly	command	ms	
וְדִבַּרְתֶּם	ד.ב.ר	פִּעֵל	speak	rv perfect	2mp	
וְנָתַן	נ.ת.ן	פָּעַל	give, set	rv perfect	3ms	
וְהוֹצֵאתָ	י.צ.א	הִפְעִיל	bring out	rv perfect	2ms	
וְהִשְׁקִיתָ	ש.ק.ה	הִפְעִיל	give drink	rv perfect	2ms	
וַיִּקַּח	ל.ק.ח	פָּעַל	take	rv imperfect	3ms	
צִוָּהוּ	צ.ו.ה	פִּעֵל	command	perfect	3ms	3ms

GRAMMATICAL NOTES

20:8 מַטֶּה can signifiy a **staff** or **tribe** (as in **the tribes of Israel**) and derives from the root נ.ט.ה (**stretch out**). A **staff** is something you stretch out, and a **tribe** is ruled by a chief who carries a staff.

20:8 סֶלַע is a **rock** or a **crag**. According to Exodus 17, the water comes from a **צוּר** (**rock**).

20:9 Some translations read **as he was commanded** for כַּאֲשֶׁר צִוָּהוּ. This is called an impersonal construction and is explained on page 101 for I Kings 3:24.

10 וַיַּקְהִלוּ מֹשֶׁה וְאַהֲרֹן אֶת־הַקָּהָל אֶל־פְּנֵי הַסָּלַע
וַיֹּאמֶר לָהֶם שִׁמְעוּ־נָא הַמֹּרִים הֲמִן־הַסֶּלַע הַזֶּה
נוֹצִיא לָכֶם מָיִם׃ 11 וַיָּרֶם מֹשֶׁה אֶת־יָדוֹ וַיַּךְ
אֶת־הַסֶּלַע בְּמַטֵּהוּ פַּעֲמָיִם וַיֵּצְאוּ מַיִם רַבִּים וַתֵּשְׁתְּ
הָעֵדָה וּבְעִירָם׃ 12 וַיֹּאמֶר יְהוָה אֶל־מֹשֶׁה
וְאֶל־אַהֲרֹן יַעַן לֹא־הֶאֱמַנְתֶּם בִּי

10 וַיַּקְהִלוּ מֹשֶׁה וְאַהֲרֹן אֶת־הַקָּהָל	Moses and Aaron summoned the assembly
אֶל־פְּנֵי הַסָּלַע וַיֹּאמֶר לָהֶם	before the rock and said to them,
שִׁמְעוּ־נָא הַמֹּרִים	"Listen, (you) rebels,
הֲמִן־הַסֶּלַע הַזֶּה נוֹצִיא לָכֶם מָיִם׃	shall we bring water out of this rock for you?"
11 וַיָּרֶם מֹשֶׁה אֶת־יָדוֹ	Then Moses raised his hand
וַיַּךְ אֶת־הַסֶּלַע בְּמַטֵּהוּ פַּעֲמָיִם	and struck the rock with his staff two times;
וַיֵּצְאוּ מַיִם רַבִּים	much water came out,
וַתֵּשְׁתְּ הָעֵדָה וּבְעִירָם׃	and the congregation drank, and (then) their cattle.
12 וַיֹּאמֶר יְהוָה	Then the LORD said
אֶל־מֹשֶׁה וְאֶל־אַהֲרֹן	to Moses and to Aaron,
יַעַן לֹא־הֶאֱמַנְתֶּם בִּי	"Because you did not believe in me,

NEW VOCABULARY

הָעֵדָה	the congregation	הַסָּלַע	the rock
וּבְעִירָם	and their cattle	הַמֹּרִים	(you) rebels
יַעַן	because	וַיָּרֶם	then (he) raised
הֶאֱמַנְתֶּם	you believe	בְּמַטֵּהוּ	with his staff

VERB ANALYSIS

VERB	ROOT	PATTERN	MEANING	TENSE	P/G/N	SUFFIX
וַיַּקְהִלוּ	ק.ה.ל	הִפְעִיל	call assembly	rv imperfect	3mp	
וַיֹּאמֶר	א.מ.ר	פָּעַל	say	rv imperfect	3ms	
שִׁמְעוּ	שׁ.מ.ע	פָּעַל	hear	command	mp	
הַמֹּרִים	מ.ר.ה	פָּעַל	be rebellious	participle	mp	
נוֹצִיא	י.צ.א	הִפְעִיל	bring out	imperfect	1cp	
וַיָּרֶם	ר.ו.ם	הִפְעִיל	raise, lift	rv imperfect	3ms	
וַיַּךְ	נ.כ.ה	הִפְעִיל	strike, smite	rv imperfect	3ms	
וַיֵּצְאוּ	י.צ.א	פָּעַל	go out	rv imperfect	3mp	
וַתֵּשְׁתְּ	שׁ.ת.ה	פָּעַל	drink	rv perfect	3fs	
וַיֹּאמֶר	א.מ.ר	פָּעַל	say	rv imperfect	3ms	
הֶאֱמַנְתֶּם	א.מ.ן	הִפְעִיל	believe	perfect	2mp	

GRAMMATICAL NOTES

20:11 The dual ending often appears in words like מַיִם where you cannot translate it. For פַּעַם (**time, occurrence**), the ending should be translated literally.

20:11 Notice that וַתֵּשְׁתְּ is a feminine singular verb. The subject of the verb is עֵדָה (**congregation**). **Their cattle** is an addition and does not affect the verb.

20:12 See Genesis 22:16 on page 21 for the use of יַעַן + אֲשֶׁר.

לְהַקְדִּישֵׁנִי לְעֵינֵי בְּנֵי יִשְׂרָאֵל לָכֵן לֹא תָבִיאוּ
אֶת־הַקָּהָל הַזֶּה אֶל־הָאָרֶץ אֲשֶׁר־נָתַתִּי לָהֶם׃ 13 הֵמָּה
מֵי מְרִיבָה אֲשֶׁר־רָבוּ בְנֵי־יִשְׂרָאֵל אֶת־יְהוָה וַיִּקָּדֵשׁ
בָּם׃

לְהַקְדִּישֵׁנִי לְעֵינֵי בְּנֵי יִשְׂרָאֵל	to venerate me in the eyes of the Israelites,
לָכֵן לֹא תָבִיאוּ אֶת־הַקָּהָל הַזֶּה	therefore you will not bring this assembly
אֶל־הָאָרֶץ אֲשֶׁר־נָתַתִּי לָהֶם׃	to the land that I have given them."
13 הֵמָּה מֵי מְרִיבָה	These are the waters of Meribah,
אֲשֶׁר־רָבוּ בְנֵי־יִשְׂרָאֵל אֶת־יְהוָה	where the Israelites quarrelled with the LORD,
וַיִּקָּדֵשׁ בָּם׃	and he was sanctified by them.

NEW VOCABULARY

לָכֵן	therefore
הַקָּהָל	the assembly
מְרִיבָה	Meribah
רָבוּ	(they) quarrelled

VERB ANALYSIS

VERB	ROOT	PATTERN	MEANING	TENSE	P/G/N	SUFFIX
לְהַקְדִּישֵׁנִי	ק.ד.ש	הִפְעִיל	treat as sacred	infinitive		1cs
תָּבִיאוּ	ב.ו.א	הִפְעִיל	bring	imperfect	2mp	
נָתַתִּי	נ.ת.ן	פָּעַל	give, set	perfect	1cs	
רָבוּ	ר.י.ב	פָּעַל	quarrel	perfect	3cp	
וַיִּקָּדֵשׁ	ק.ד.ש	נִפְעַל	be sanctified	rv imperfect	3ms	

GRAMMATICAL NOTES

20:13 This story explains the origin of the place name Meribah. מְרִיבָה (**Meribah**) derives from the root ר.י.ב and means **strife** or **contention**. Thus, the spring is named after the Israelites' bad behavior. In Exodus 17:7, the spring bears two names: Meribah and Massah. מַסָּה (**Massah**) means **test** and refers to the Israelites' testing God in the account. This type of story, one which explains the origin of a personal or place name, is called an **etiology** and is common in the Hebrew Bible.

The English title **Numbers** comes from the census desribed in the first 10 chapters of the book. The Hebrew title בְּמִדְבַּר originates from the first sentence of the book and describes the location of the subsequent action.

5 1 וַיִּקְרָא מֹשֶׁה אֶל־כָּל־יִשְׂרָאֵל וַיֹּאמֶר אֲלֵהֶם שְׁמַע
יִשְׂרָאֵל אֶת־הַחֻקִּים וְאֶת־הַמִּשְׁפָּטִים אֲשֶׁר אָנֹכִי
דֹּבֵר בְּאָזְנֵיכֶם הַיּוֹם וּלְמַדְתֶּם אֹתָם וּשְׁמַרְתֶּם
לַעֲשֹׂתָם׃ 2 יְהוָה אֱלֹהֵינוּ כָּרַת עִמָּנוּ בְּרִית בְּחֹרֵב׃
3 לֹא אֶת־אֲבֹתֵינוּ כָּרַת יְהוָה אֶת־הַבְּרִית הַזֹּאת כִּי
אִתָּנוּ אֲנַחְנוּ אֵלֶּה פֹה הַיּוֹם כֻּלָּנוּ חַיִּים׃

1 וַיִּקְרָא מֹשֶׁה אֶל־כָּל־יִשְׂרָאֵל	Moses called to all of Israel
וַיֹּאמֶר אֲלֵהֶם שְׁמַע יִשְׂרָאֵל	and said to them, “Hear, Israel,
אֶת־הַחֻקִּים וְאֶת־הַמִּשְׁפָּטִים	the statutes and the laws
אֲשֶׁר אָנֹכִי דֹּבֵר בְּאָזְנֵיכֶם הַיּוֹם	that I speak in your hearing (lit. ears) today.
וּלְמַדְתֶּם אֹתָם וּשְׁמַרְתֶּם לַעֲשֹׂתָם׃	Learn them and take care to observe them.
2 יְהוָה אֱלֹהֵינוּ כָּרַת	The LORD our God made (lit. cut)
עִמָּנוּ בְּרִית בְּחֹרֵב׃	a covenant with us at Horeb.
3 לֹא אֶת־אֲבֹתֵינוּ	Not with our fathers
כָּרַת יְהוָה אֶת־הַבְּרִית הַזֹּאת	did the LORD make this covenant,
כִּי אִתָּנוּ אֲנַחְנוּ	but with us, we,
אֵלֶּה פֹה הַיּוֹם כֻּלָּנוּ חַיִּים׃	these here today, all of us (who) are living.

NEW VOCABULARY

הַחֻקִּים	the statutes
וּלְמַדְתֶּם	learn them
בְּחֹרֵב	at Horeb
פֹּה	here

VERB ANALYSIS

VERB	ROOT	PATTERN	MEANING	TENSE	P/G/N	SUFFIX
וַיִּקְרָא	ק.ר.א	פָּעַל	call, proclaim	rv imperfect	3ms	
וַיֹּאמֶר	א.מ.ר	פָּעַל	say	rv imperfect	3ms	
שְׁמַע	שׁ.מ.ע	פָּעַל	hear	command	ms	
דֹּבֵר	ד.ב.ר	פָּעַל	speak	participle	ms	
וּלְמַדְתֶּם	ל.מ.ד	פָּעַל	learn	rv perfect	2mp	
וּשְׁמַרְתֶּם	שׁ.מ.ר	פָּעַל	keep, watch	rv perfect	2mp	
לַעֲשֹׂתָם	ע.שׂ.ה	פָּעַל	make, do	infinitive		3mp
כָּרַת	כ.ר.ת	פָּעַל	cut, make	perfect	3ms	

GRAMMATICAL NOTES

5:1 Notice that דֹּבֵר is a פָּעַל verb. ד.ב.ר usually occurs in the פִּעֵל, but appears a few times in the Hebrew Bible as a פָּעַל infinitive or participle.

5:1 The word **ears** is used when **hearing** is clearly meant. This is a figure of speech called **metonymy**: use of a literal name of one thing for that of another associated with it.

5:2 The idiom **cut a covenant** (**make a covenant**) may derive from cutting a sacrificial animal during a covenant ratification ceremony.

4 פָּנִים בְּפָנִים דִּבֶּר יְהוָה עִמָּכֶם בָּהָר מִתּוֹךְ הָאֵשׁ׃
5 אָנֹכִי עֹמֵד בֵּין־יְהוָה וּבֵינֵיכֶם בָּעֵת הַהִוא לְהַגִּיד
לָכֶם אֶת־דְּבַר יְהוָה כִּי יְרֵאתֶם מִפְּנֵי הָאֵשׁ
וְלֹא־עֲלִיתֶם בָּהָר לֵאמֹר׃ 6 אָנֹכִי יְהוָה אֱלֹהֶיךָ אֲשֶׁר
הוֹצֵאתִיךָ מֵאֶרֶץ מִצְרַיִם מִבֵּית עֲבָדִים׃

4 פָּנִים בְּפָנִים דִּבֶּר יְהוָה עִמָּכֶם	The LORD spoke with you face to face
בָּהָר מִתּוֹךְ הָאֵשׁ׃	at the mountain from the middle of the fire—
5 אָנֹכִי עֹמֵד בֵּין־יְהוָה וּבֵינֵיכֶם	I was standing between the LORD and you
בָּעֵת הַהִוא	at that time
לְהַגִּיד לָכֶם אֶת־דְּבַר יְהוָה	to report to you the word of the LORD,
כִּי יְרֵאתֶם	because you were afraid
מִפְּנֵי הָאֵשׁ	in the presence of the fire
וְלֹא־עֲלִיתֶם בָּהָר לֵאמֹר׃	and did not go up to the mountain—
6 אָנֹכִי יְהוָה אֱלֹהֶיךָ	'I am the LORD your God,
אֲשֶׁר הוֹצֵאתִיךָ מֵאֶרֶץ מִצְרַיִם	who brought you out from the land of Egypt,
מִבֵּית עֲבָדִים׃	from a house of slaves.

NEW VOCABULARY

הָאֵשׁ the fire

מִפְּנֵי in the presence of

VERB ANALYSIS

VERB	ROOT	PATTERN	MEANING	TENSE	P/G/N	SUFFIX
דִּבֶּר	ד.ב.ר	פִּעֵל	speak	perfect	3ms	
עֹמֵד	ע.מ.ד	פָּעַל	stand	participle	ms	
לְהַגִּיד	נ.ג.ד	הִפְעִיל	declare, tell	infinitive		
יְרֵאתֶם	י.ר.א	פָּעַל	fear	perfect	2mp	
עֲלִיתֶם	ע.ל.ה	פָּעַל	go up	perfect	2mp	
לֵאמֹר	א.מ.ר	פָּעַל	say	infinitive		
הוֹצֵאתִיךָ	י.צ.א	הִפְעִיל	bring out	perfect	1cs	2ms

GRAMMATICAL NOTES

5:4 פָּנִים בְּפָנִים translates literally as **face with face**; we changed the preposition to **to** so that the English idiom would be preserved.

5:4 דִּבֶּר is a regular alternative to the expected 3ms form דִּבֵּר.

5:5 Look at the word הַהִוא. The consonants coordinate with those for the word הַהוּא, but the vowels match those for the word הַהִיא. This phenomenon is the work of scribes who wanted to alter the text of the Hebrew Bible, but revered it too much to change the consonants. (During the Middle Ages, scribes added vowels to the Hebrew Bible; before the Middle Ages, the Hebrew Bible was essentially a consonantal text.) The scribes' solution was to superimpose on the consonantal text what ought to be read. This combination of mismatched consonants and vowels is called כְּתִיב קְרֵי (Aramaic for **what is written, to be read**). In the first five books of the Hebrew Bible, הִיא is almost always written הִוא. The most famous כְּתִיב קְרֵי of all is יְהוָה for the name of Israel's God.

5:6 Many translations give **from a house of bondage** for מִבֵּית עֲבָדִים, assuming that the language is figurative.

7לֹא־יִהְיֶה לְךָ אֱלֹהִים אֲחֵרִים עַל־פָּנָי׃ 8לֹא־תַעֲשֶׂה
לְךָ פֶּסֶל כָּל־תְּמוּנָה אֲשֶׁר בַּשָּׁמַיִם מִמַּעַל וַאֲשֶׁר
בָּאָרֶץ מִתָּחַת וַאֲשֶׁר בַּמַּיִם מִתַּחַת לָאָרֶץ׃
9לֹא־תִשְׁתַּחֲוֶה לָהֶם וְלֹא תָעָבְדֵם כִּי אָנֹכִי יְהוָה
אֱלֹהֶיךָ אֵל קַנָּא פֹּקֵד עֲוֹן אָבוֹת

7לֹא־יִהְיֶה לְךָ אֱלֹהִים אֲחֵרִים	You are not to have other gods
עַל־פָּנָי׃	besides me (lit. my face).
8לֹא־תַעֲשֶׂה לְךָ	You are not to make for yourself
פֶּסֶל כָּל־תְּמוּנָה	a sculpted image of any form
אֲשֶׁר בַּשָּׁמַיִם מִמַּעַל	that is in the heavens above,
וַאֲשֶׁר בָּאָרֶץ מִתָּחַת	or that is on the earth below,
וַאֲשֶׁר בַּמַּיִם מִתַּחַת לָאָרֶץ׃	or that is in the water below the earth.
9לֹא־תִשְׁתַּחֲוֶה לָהֶם	You are not to bow down to them,
וְלֹא תָעָבְדֵם	and you are not to serve them,
כִּי אָנֹכִי יְהוָה אֱלֹהֶיךָ	for I, the LORD your God,
אֵל קַנָּא	am a jealous God,
פֹּקֵד עֲוֹן אָבוֹת	visiting the iniquity of the fathers

NEW VOCABULARY

מִתָּחַת	below	פֶּסֶל	sculpted image
תִשְׁתַּחֲוֶה	you bow down	תְּמוּנָה	form
קַנָּא	jealous	מִמַּעַל	above
פֹּקֵד	visiting		

VERB ANALYSIS

VERB	ROOT	PATTERN	MEANING	TENSE	P/G/N	SUFFIX
יִהְיֶה	ה.י.ה	פָּעַל	be, become	imperfect	3ms	
תַעֲשֶׂה	ע.שׂ.ה	פָּעַל	make, do	imperfect	2ms	
תִשְׁתַּחֲוֶה	ח.ו.ה	הִשְׁתַּפֵּל	worship	imperfect	2ms	
תָעָבְדֵם	ע.ב.ד	הָפְעַל	work, serve	imperfect	2ms	3mp
פֹּקֵד	פ.ק.ד	פָּעַל	attend to, visit	participle	ms	

GRAMMATICAL NOTES

5:7 **You are not to have other gods besides me.** The text literally reads: **You are not to have other gods besides my face.** By substituting **my face** for **me**, the text employs a figure of speech called **synecdoche**, the use of a part of something to signify the whole.

5:8 Though Hebrew commands have their own form, negative commands are expressed by לֹא or אַל + the imperfect. אַל is used to forbid specific actions and לֹא is used for general prohibitions. Since the Ten Commandments are general prohibitions, look for לֹא + the 2ms imperfect in this passage. See page 197 in *The First Hebrew Primer.*

5:8 The regular spelling for מִתָּחַת is מִתַּחַת. See I Kings 3:22 on page 99 for an explanation of similar spelling changes.

5:9 For a discussion of the הִשְׁתַּפֵּל, please see Genesis 22:5 on page 13.

5:9 תָעָבְדֵם appears in a pattern called הָפְעַל (**Hofal**). The הָפְעַל pattern is a passive counterpart of the הִפְעִיל, although תָעָבְדֵם is not passive in this verse. You do not need to learn the הָפְעַל at this time.

עַל־בָּנִים וְעַל־שִׁלֵּשִׁים וְעַל־רִבֵּעִים לְשֹׂנְאָי׃ 10 וְעֹשֶׂה
חֶסֶד לַאֲלָפִים לְאֹהֲבַי וּלְשֹׁמְרֵי מִצְוֹתָו׃ 11 לֹא תִשָּׂא
אֶת־שֵׁם־יְהוָה אֱלֹהֶיךָ לַשָּׁוְא כִּי לֹא יְנַקֶּה יְהוָה אֵת
אֲשֶׁר־יִשָּׂא אֶת־שְׁמוֹ לַשָּׁוְא׃ 12 שָׁמוֹר אֶת־יוֹם הַשַּׁבָּת
לְקַדְּשׁוֹ כַּאֲשֶׁר צִוְּךָ יְהוָה אֱלֹהֶיךָ׃ 13 שֵׁשֶׁת יָמִים
תַּעֲבֹד וְעָשִׂיתָ כָּל־מְלַאכְתֶּךָ׃

עַל־בָּנִים וְעַל־שִׁלֵּשִׁים	upon the sons, and upon (the) third (generation)
וְעַל־רִבֵּעִים לְשֹׂנְאָי׃	and upon (the) fourth (generation) of those who hate me,
10 וְעֹשֶׂה חֶסֶד לַאֲלָפִים	but showing lovingkindness to thousands
לְאֹהֲבַי וּלְשֹׁמְרֵי מִצְוֹתָו׃	who love me and keep my commandments.
11 לֹא תִשָּׂא אֶת־שֵׁם־יְהוָה	You are not to take up the name of the LORD
אֱלֹהֶיךָ לַשָּׁוְא	your God for no purpose,
כִּי לֹא יְנַקֶּה יְהוָה	for the LORD will not exonerate
אֵת אֲשֶׁר־יִשָּׂא אֶת־שְׁמוֹ לַשָּׁוְא׃	those who take up his name for no purpose.
12 שָׁמוֹר אֶת־יוֹם הַשַּׁבָּת לְקַדְּשׁוֹ	Observe the Sabbath day to make it holy
כַּאֲשֶׁר צִוְּךָ יְהוָה אֱלֹהֶיךָ׃	as the LORD your God commanded you.
13 שֵׁשֶׁת יָמִים תַּעֲבֹד	Six days you may work
וְעָשִׂיתָ כָּל־מְלַאכְתֶּךָ׃	and do all your labor,

NEW VOCABULARY

חֶסֶד	lovingkindness	שִׁלֵּשִׁים	third (generation)
לַשָּׁוְא	for no purpose	רִבֵּעִים	fourth (generation)
יְנַקֶּה	(he) will exonerate	לְשֹׂנְאָי	of those who hate me
מְלַאכְתֶּךָ	your labor		

VERB ANALYSIS

VERB	ROOT	PATTERN	MEANING	TENSE	P/G/N	SUFFIX
לְשֹׂנְאָי	שׂ.נ.א	פָּעַל	hate	participle	mp	1cs
וְעֹשֶׂה	ע.שׂ.ה	פָּעַל	make, do	participle	ms	
לְאֹהֲבַי	א.ה.ב	פָּעַל	love	participle	mp	1cs
וּלְשֹׁמְרֵי	שׁ.מ.ר	פָּעַל	keep, watch	participle	mp	
תִשָּׂא	נ.שׂ.א	פָּעַל	lift, carry	imperfect	2ms	
יְנַקֶּה	נ.ק.ה	פִּעֵל	exonerate	imperfect	3ms	
יִשָּׂא	נ.שׂ.א	פָּעַל	lift, carry	imperfect	3ms	
שָׁמוֹר	שׁ.מ.ר	פָּעַל	keep, watch	emph. inf.		
לְקַדְּשׁוֹ	ק.ד.שׁ	פִּעֵל	sanctify	infinitive		3ms
צִוְּךָ	צ.ו.ה	פִּעֵל	command	perfect	3ms	2ms
תַּעֲבֹד	ע.ב.ד	פָּעַל	work, serve	imperfect	2ms	
וְעָשִׂיתָ	ע.שׂ.ה	פָּעַל	make, do	rv perfect	2ms	

GRAMMATICAL NOTES

5:9 שִׁלֵּשִׁים and רִבֵּעִים mean **those of (the) third and those of (the) fourth**. In this context **generation** should be supplied; the text refers to sons, grandsons, and great-grandsons.

5:9 לַאֲלָפִים could signify **thousands** or **the thousandth generation**.

5:10 מִצְוֹתָו (**his commandments**) probably should read מִצְוֹתָי (**my commandments**), as it does in Exodus 20:6, a parallel verse.

14 וְיוֹם הַשְּׁבִיעִי שַׁבָּת לַיהוָה אֱלֹהֶיךָ לֹא־תַעֲשֶׂה
כָל־מְלָאכָה אַתָּה וּבִנְךָ־וּבִתֶּךָ וְעַבְדְּךָ־וַאֲמָתֶךָ
וְשׁוֹרְךָ וַחֲמֹרְךָ וְכָל־בְּהֶמְתֶּךָ וְגֵרְךָ אֲשֶׁר בִּשְׁעָרֶיךָ
לְמַעַן יָנוּחַ עַבְדְּךָ וַאֲמָתְךָ כָּמוֹךָ׃ 15 וְזָכַרְתָּ כִּי עֶבֶד
הָיִיתָ בְּאֶרֶץ מִצְרַיִם וַיֹּצִאֲךָ יְהוָה אֱלֹהֶיךָ

14 וְיוֹם הַשְּׁבִיעִי שַׁבָּת	but the seventh day is a Sabbath
לַיהוָה אֱלֹהֶיךָ	for the LORD your God;
לֹא־תַעֲשֶׂה כָל־מְלָאכָה	you are not to do any work,
אַתָּה וּבִנְךָ־וּבִתֶּךָ	you, or your son, or your daughter,
וְעַבְדְּךָ־וַאֲמָתֶךָ	or your manservant, or your maidservant,
וְשׁוֹרְךָ וַחֲמֹרְךָ וְכָל־בְּהֶמְתֶּךָ	or your ox, or your donkey, or any of your cattle,
וְגֵרְךָ אֲשֶׁר בִּשְׁעָרֶיךָ	or your visitor who is within your gates,
לְמַעַן יָנוּחַ	so that they may rest,
עַבְדְּךָ וַאֲמָתְךָ כָּמוֹךָ׃	your manservant and your maidservant, like you.
15 וְזָכַרְתָּ כִּי עֶבֶד הָיִיתָ	You are to remember that you were a slave
בְּאֶרֶץ מִצְרַיִם	in the land of Egypt,
וַיֹּצִאֲךָ יְהוָה אֱלֹהֶיךָ	and the LORD your God brought you out

NEW VOCABULARY

הַשְּׁבִיעִי	the seventh	וַחֲמֹרְךָ	or your donkey
מְלָאכָה	work	וְגֵרְךָ	or your visitor
וַאֲמָתֶךָ	or your maidservant	יָנוּחַ	so that they may rest
וְשׁוֹרְךָ	or your ox	וַאֲמָתְךָ	and your maidservant

VERB ANALYSIS

VERB	ROOT	PATTERN	MEANING	TENSE	P/G/N	SUFFIX
תַעֲשֶׂה	ע.שׂ.ה	פָּעַל	make, do	imperfect	2ms	
יָנוּחַ	נ.ו.ח	פָּעַל	rest	imperfect	3ms	
וְזָכַרְתָּ	ז.כ.ר	פָּעַל	remember	rv perfect	2ms	
הָיִיתָ	ה.י.ה	פָּעַל	be, become	perfect	2ms	
וַיֹּצִאֲךָ	י.צ.א	הִפְעִיל	bring out	rv imperfect	3ms	2ms

GRAMMATICAL NOTES

5:14 We translated לְמַעַן יָנוּחַ as **so that they may rest**, even though יָנוּחַ is a 3ms verb. The singular refers to any person or animal in the preceding list. We used the plural to make the English sound natural.

5:15 The story of the Ten Commandments is also told in Exodus 20:1-17. There are some interesting differences between the two accounts, of which one is the fourth commandment to remember the Sabbath day. In Exodus 20:8-11, the speech exhorts the reader to remember the Sabbath and describes the creation of the world in six days. The commandment is the same in Deuteronomy 5:12-15, but no reference to the creation story is made. Instead, the speaker reiterates that the reader should remember Israel's captivity in Egypt and God's role in the exodus from Egypt.

מִשָּׁם בְּיָד חֲזָקָה וּבִזְרֹעַ נְטוּיָה עַל־כֵּן צִוְּךָ יְהוָה
אֱלֹהֶיךָ לַעֲשׂוֹת אֶת־יוֹם הַשַּׁבָּת׃ 16 כַּבֵּד אֶת־אָבִיךָ
וְאֶת־אִמֶּךָ כַּאֲשֶׁר צִוְּךָ יְהוָה אֱלֹהֶיךָ לְמַעַן יַאֲרִיכֻן
יָמֶיךָ וּלְמַעַן יִיטַב לָךְ עַל הָאֲדָמָה אֲשֶׁר־יְהוָה
אֱלֹהֶיךָ נֹתֵן לָךְ׃ 17 לֹא תִּרְצָח 18 וְלֹא תִּנְאָף 19 וְלֹא
תִּגְנֹב

מִשָּׁם בְּיָד חֲזָקָה	from there with a strong hand
וּבִזְרֹעַ נְטוּיָה	and with an arm outstretched;
עַל־כֵּן צִוְּךָ יְהוָה אֱלֹהֶיךָ	therefore the LORD your God commanded you
לַעֲשׂוֹת אֶת־יוֹם הַשַּׁבָּת׃	to observe the Sabbath day.
16 כַּבֵּד אֶת־אָבִיךָ וְאֶת־אִמֶּךָ	Honor your father and your mother
כַּאֲשֶׁר צִוְּךָ יְהוָה אֱלֹהֶיךָ	as the LORD your God commanded you,
לְמַעַן יַאֲרִיכֻן יָמֶיךָ	so that your days may be prolonged
וּלְמַעַן יִיטַב לָךְ עַל הָאֲדָמָה	and so that the land will be good for you,
אֲשֶׁר־יְהוָה אֱלֹהֶיךָ נֹתֵן לָךְ׃	which (land) the LORD your God is giving to you.
17 לֹא תִּרְצָח	You are not to murder.
18 וְלֹא תִּנְאָף	You are not to commit adultery.
19 וְלֹא תִּגְנֹב	You are not to steal.

NEW VOCABULARY

יַאֲרִיכֻן	(they) may be prolonged	חֲזָקָה	strong
יִיטַב	(it) will be good	וּבִזְרֹעַ	and an arm
תִּרְצָח	you murder	נְטוּיָה	outstretched
תִּנְאָף	you commit adultery	כַּבֵּד	honor
תִּגְנֹב	you steal		

VERB ANALYSIS

VERB	ROOT	PATTERN	MEANING	TENSE	P/G/N	SUFFIX
נְטוּיָה	נ.ט.ה	פָּעַל	stretch out	p. participle	fs	
צִוְּךָ	צ.ו.ה	פִּעֵל	command	perfect	3ms	2ms
לַעֲשׂוֹת	ע.שׂ.ה	פָּעַל	make, do	infinitive		
כַּבֵּד	כ.ב.ד	פִּעֵל	honor	command	ms	
יַאֲרִיכֻן	א.ר.ך	הִפְעִיל	prolong	imperfect	3mp	
יִיטַב	י.ט.ב	פָּעַל	be pleasing	imperfect	3ms	
נֹתֵן	נ.ת.ן	פָּעַל	give, set	participle	ms	
תִּרְצָח	ר.צ.ח	פָּעַל	murder	imperfect	2ms	
תִּנְאָף	נ.א.ף	פָּעַל	commit adultery	imperfect	2ms	
תִּגְנֹב	ג.נ.ב	פָּעַל	steal	imperfect	2ms	

GRAMMATICAL NOTE

5:16 יַאֲרִיכֻן has an extra **nun** at the end. The expected 3mp form is יַאֲרִיכוּ. This additional letter is called the **paragogic nun**. It can appear at the end of several types of verbs, but occurs most often at the end of 3mp imperfects. The paragogic nun should not affect your translation.

20 וְלֹא־תַעֲנֶה בְרֵעֲךָ עֵד שָׁוְא׃ 21 וְלֹא תַחְמֹד אֵשֶׁת
רֵעֶךָ וְלֹא תִתְאַוֶּה בֵּית רֵעֶךָ שָׂדֵהוּ וְעַבְדּוֹ וַאֲמָתוֹ
שׁוֹרוֹ וַחֲמֹרוֹ וְכֹל אֲשֶׁר לְרֵעֶךָ׃

20 וְלֹא־תַעֲנֶה בְרֵעֲךָ	You are not to answer against your neighbor
עֵד שָׁוְא׃	as a lying witness.
21 וְלֹא תַחְמֹד אֵשֶׁת רֵעֶךָ	You are not to desire your neighbor's wife,
וְלֹא תִתְאַוֶּה בֵּית רֵעֶךָ	and you are not to crave your neighbor's house,
שָׂדֵהוּ וְעַבְדּוֹ וַאֲמָתוֹ	his field, or his manservant, or his maidservant,
שׁוֹרוֹ וַחֲמֹרוֹ	his ox, or his donkey,
וְכֹל אֲשֶׁר לְרֵעֶךָ׃	or anything that is your neighbor's.'

NEW VOCABULARY

עֵד	witness
שָׁוְא	lying
תַחְמֹד	desire
תִתְאַוֶּה	crave
וַאֲמָתוֹ	or his maidservant
שׁוֹרוֹ	his ox
וַחֲמֹרוֹ	or his donkey

VERB ANALYSIS

VERB	ROOT	PATTERN	MEANING	TENSE	P/G/N	SUFFIX
תַעֲנֶה	ע.נ.ה	פָּעַל	answer	imperfect	2ms	
תַחְמֹד	ח.מ.ד	פָּעַל	desire	imperfect	2ms	
תִתְאַוֶּה	א.ו.ה	הִתְפַּעֵל	crave	imperfect	2ms	

GRAMMATICAL NOTES

5:20 **שָׁוְא** is a difficult word to render in English. It can be translated as **vanity**, **futility**, **emptiness**, and **nothingness**, among other possibilities. In Deuteronomy 5:11 the sense of the word is vanity or emptiness; you are not to take up God's name to no good purpose. Here the sense is a little different. An **עֵד שָׁוְא** is a witness whose speech is empty or false. You will see **שָׁוְא** again in selections from Ecclesiastes.

5:17–5:21 There are different traditions for numbering these verses. In some manuscripts every commandment from the prohibition against murder (verse 17) to the law against coveting (verse 21) is included in verses 17 and 18. The Hebrew text is the same in both systems; only the numbers are different.

6 4 שְׁמַע יִשְׂרָאֵל יְהוָה אֱלֹהֵינוּ יְהוָה אֶחָד׃ 5 וְאָהַבְתָּ
אֵת יְהוָה אֱלֹהֶיךָ בְּכָל־לְבָבְךָ וּבְכָל־נַפְשְׁךָ
וּבְכָל־מְאֹדֶךָ׃ 6 וְהָיוּ הַדְּבָרִים הָאֵלֶּה אֲשֶׁר אָנֹכִי מְצַוְּךָ
הַיּוֹם עַל־לְבָבֶךָ׃

4 שְׁמַע יִשְׂרָאֵל	Listen, Israel,
יְהוָה אֱלֹהֵינוּ	the LORD (is) our God;
יְהוָה אֶחָד׃	the LORD (is) one.
5 וְאָהַבְתָּ אֵת יְהוָה אֱלֹהֶיךָ	You are to love the LORD your God
בְּכָל־לְבָבְךָ	with all your heart,
וּבְכָל־נַפְשְׁךָ	and with all your being,
וּבְכָל־מְאֹדֶךָ׃	and with all your might.
6 וְהָיוּ הַדְּבָרִים הָאֵלֶּה	And these words are to be,
אֲשֶׁר אָנֹכִי מְצַוְּךָ הַיּוֹם	which I am commanding you today,
עַל־לְבָבֶךָ׃	upon your heart.

NEW VOCABULARY

מְאֹדֶךָ your might

VERB ANALYSIS

VERB	ROOT	PATTERN	MEANING	TENSE	P/G/N	SUFFIX
שְׁמַע	שׁ.מ.ע	פָּעַל	hear	command	ms	
וְאָהַבְתָּ	א.ה.ב	פָּעַל	love	rv perfect	2ms	
וְהָיוּ	ה.י.ה	פָּעַל	be, become	rv perfect	3cp	
מְצַוְּךָ	צ.ו.ה	פִּעֵל	command	participle	ms	2ms

GRAMMATICAL NOTES

In Jewish tradition Deuteronomy 6:4–9 is called the *Shema* (שְׁמַע), after the first word in verse 4.

6:4 This verse is a restatement of the first commandment. (See Exodus 20:2–3 or Deuteronomy 5:6–7 on pages 54–57. Like Leviticus 19:18, on pages 40–41, this line is quoted in Mark 12:29–31.) Despite the importance of this verse, its precise meaning is unclear. Some suggest that the commandment means Israel should worship only the LORD. Others interpret the line as a monotheistic creed, specifying that Israel's God, unlike the gods of Israel's neighbors, is alone and has no consort.

6:5 This verse states that Israel should love God with its collective לֵב (**heart**), נֶפֶשׁ (**soul, self**), and מְאֹד (**might, power**). These words merit a brief discussion. לֵב (**heart**) in Hebrew can signify the mind or will. See I Kings 3:9 on page 89 for another example of this usage. נֶפֶשׁ (**soul, self**) is often translated as soul, but this can be misleading. The word does not imply a contrast to the physical body; instead, think of נֶפֶשׁ as **life** or **being**. Finally, מְאֹד (**might, power**) is a word you know as **very**. Some interpret the word as **excess**, others as **might** or **capacity**.

6:6 The injunction to keep these words **upon your heart** probably means always to think about them.

7 וְשִׁנַּנְתָּם לְבָנֶיךָ וְדִבַּרְתָּ בָּם בְּשִׁבְתְּךָ בְּבֵיתֶךָ
וּבְלֶכְתְּךָ בַדֶּרֶךְ וּבְשָׁכְבְּךָ וּבְקוּמֶךָ׃ 8 וּקְשַׁרְתָּם לְאוֹת
עַל־יָדֶךָ וְהָיוּ לְטֹטָפֹת בֵּין עֵינֶיךָ׃ 9 וּכְתַבְתָּם
עַל־מְזֻזוֹת בֵּיתֶךָ וּבִשְׁעָרֶיךָ׃

7 וְשִׁנַּנְתָּם לְבָנֶיךָ	And you are to teach them to your children diligently,
וְדִבַּרְתָּ בָּם	and you are to speak about them
בְּשִׁבְתְּךָ בְּבֵיתֶךָ	when you sit in your house,
וּבְלֶכְתְּךָ בַדֶּרֶךְ	and when you walk in the way,
וּבְשָׁכְבְּךָ וּבְקוּמֶךָ׃	and when you lie down, and when you rise up.
8 וּקְשַׁרְתָּם לְאוֹת	And you are to bind them as a sign
עַל־יָדֶךָ	on your hands,
וְהָיוּ לְטֹטָפֹת	and they are to be like bands
בֵּין עֵינֶיךָ׃	between your eyes.
9 וּכְתַבְתָּם עַל־מְזֻזוֹת	And you are to write them on the doorposts
בֵּיתֶךָ וּבִשְׁעָרֶיךָ׃	of your houses and on your gates.”

NEW VOCABULARY

וְשִׁנַּנְתָּם	and you are to teach them diligently
וּקְשַׁרְתָּם	and you are to bind them
לְאוֹת	as a sign
לְטֹטָפֹת	like bands
מְזֻזוֹת	doorposts

VERB ANALYSIS

VERB	ROOT	PATTERN	MEANING	TENSE	P/G/N	SUFFIX
וְשִׁנַּנְתָּם	שׁ.נ.ן	פִּעֵל	teach diligently	rv perfect	2ms	3mp
וְדִבַּרְתָּ	ד.ב.ר	פִּעֵל	speak	rv perfect	2ms	
בְּשִׁבְתְּךָ	י.שׁ.ב	פָּעַל	sit, dwell	infinitive		2ms
וּבְלֶכְתְּךָ	ה.ל.ך	פָּעַל	walk, go	infinitive		2ms
וּבְשָׁכְבְּךָ	שׁ.כ.ב	פָּעַל	lie, lie down	infinitive		2ms
וּבְקוּמֶךָ	ק.ו.ם	פָּעַל	arise	infinitive		2ms
וּקְשַׁרְתָּם	ק.שׁ.ר	פָּעַל	bind, join	rv perfect	2ms	3mp
וְהָיוּ	ה.י.ה	פָּעַל	be, become	rv perfect	3cp	
וּכְתַבְתָּם	כ.ת.ב	פָּעַל	write	rv perfect	2ms	3mp

GRAMMATICAL NOTES

6:7 Sometimes the preposition בְּ is used with verbs of speaking, thinking, and knowing to denote the object of the action. In this verse בְּ appears beside ד.ב.ר and means **about**.

6:7 In the second half of verse 7, בְּ means **when** and is used with infinitives. The regular infinitive is used frequently in temporal clauses such as these, often accompanied by בְּ. See page 210 in *The First Hebrew Primer* and I Kings 3:18 on page 95 for more information.

6:8 The language in this verse is unusual. ק.שׁ.ר usually means **to confine** or **to bind** something and is used with concrete nouns. טֹטָפוֹת or **bands** is an uncommon word in any context. This verse may be a figurative restating of verse 5. In later Jewish tradition this injunction was interpreted literally and observed by wearing phylacteries.

SELECTIONS FROM

THE PROPHETS

שְׁמוּאֵל ב	72	**II Samuel 7:1–17**
מְלָכִים א	84	**I Kings 3:3–28**
יוֹנָה	104	**Jonah 1:1–2:2**
מִיכָה	118	**Micah 4:1–5**

7 1 וַיְהִי כִּי־יָשַׁב הַמֶּלֶךְ בְּבֵיתוֹ וַיהוָה הֵנִיחַ־לוֹ מִסָּבִיב
מִכָּל־אֹיְבָיו׃ 2 וַיֹּאמֶר הַמֶּלֶךְ אֶל־נָתָן הַנָּבִיא רְאֵה נָא
אָנֹכִי יוֹשֵׁב בְּבֵית אֲרָזִים וַאֲרוֹן הָאֱלֹהִים יֹשֵׁב בְּתוֹךְ
הַיְרִיעָה׃ 3 וַיֹּאמֶר נָתָן אֶל־הַמֶּלֶךְ כֹּל אֲשֶׁר בִּלְבָבְךָ
לֵךְ עֲשֵׂה כִּי יְהוָה עִמָּךְ׃ 4 וַיְהִי בַּלַּיְלָה הַהוּא וַיְהִי
דְּבַר־יְהוָה אֶל־נָתָן לֵאמֹר׃

1 וַיְהִי כִּי־יָשַׁב הַמֶּלֶךְ בְּבֵיתוֹ	When the king dwelled in his house,
וַיהוָה הֵנִיחַ־לוֹ	and the LORD had given him rest
מִסָּבִיב מִכָּל־אֹיְבָיו׃	from all his enemies round about,
2 וַיֹּאמֶר הַמֶּלֶךְ אֶל־נָתָן הַנָּבִיא	the king said to Nathan the prophet,
רְאֵה נָא אָנֹכִי יוֹשֵׁב בְּבֵית אֲרָזִים	"Look, I dwell in a cedar house,
וַאֲרוֹן הָאֱלֹהִים	but the ark of God
יֹשֵׁב בְּתוֹךְ הַיְרִיעָה׃	sits in the middle of the tent curtains!"
3 וַיֹּאמֶר נָתָן אֶל־הַמֶּלֶךְ	And Nathan said to the king,
כֹּל אֲשֶׁר בִּלְבָבְךָ	"All that is in your heart,
לֵךְ עֲשֵׂה כִּי יְהוָה עִמָּךְ׃	go (and) do (it), for the LORD is with you."
4 וַיְהִי בַּלַּיְלָה הַהוּא	That same night,
וַיְהִי דְּבַר־יְהוָה אֶל־נָתָן לֵאמֹר׃	the word of the LORD came to Nathan,

NEW VOCABULARY

הֵנִיחַ	had given (him) rest
אֹיְבָיו	his enemies
נָתָן	Nathan
אֲרָזִים	cedar
הַיְרִיעָה	the tent curtains

VERB ANALYSIS

VERB	ROOT	PATTERN	MEANING	TENSE	P/G/N	SUFFIX
וַיְהִי	ה.י.ה	פָּעַל	be, become	rv imperfect	3ms	
יָשַׁב	י.שׁ.ב	פָּעַל	sit, dwell	perfect	3ms	
הֵנִיחַ	נ.ו.ח	הִפְעִיל	give rest to	perfect	3ms	
אֹיְבָיו	א.י.ב	פָּעַל	be hostile to	participle	mp	3ms
וַיֹּאמֶר	א.מ.ר	פָּעַל	say	rv imperfect	3ms	
רְאֵה	ר.א.ה	פָּעַל	see	command	ms	
יוֹשֵׁב	י.שׁ.ב	פָּעַל	sit, dwell	participle	ms	
יֹשֵׁב	י.שׁ.ב	פָּעַל	sit, dwell	participle	ms	
לֵךְ	ה.ל.ך	פָּעַל	walk, go	command	ms	
עֲשֵׂה	ע.שׂ.ה	פָּעַל	make, do	command	ms	
לֵאמֹר	א.מ.ר	פָּעַל	say	infinitive		

GRAMMATICAL NOTES

7:2 Many people translate הַיְרִיעָה as **a tent**. The word literally means **the curtains**, and here almost certainly refers to **tent curtains**. We translated the passage as **but the ark of God sits in the middle of the tent curtains** to preserve the grammatical structure of the Hebrew and the sense of the English.

7:2 As you learned in *The First Hebrew Primer*, participles may be spelled with an **אוֹ** or a **אֹ** vowel. When a letter is used to mark a vowel—such as ו, י, or ה in וּ, אִי, or אָה—that letter is called a *mater lectionis* or **mother of reading**. In verse 2 the participle of **שׁ.ו.ב** is spelled with and without the *mater*.

5 לֵךְ וְאָמַרְתָּ אֶל־עַבְדִּי אֶל־דָּוִד כֹּה אָמַר יְהוָה
הַאַתָּה תִּבְנֶה־לִּי בַיִת לְשִׁבְתִּי׃ 6 כִּי לֹא יָשַׁבְתִּי
בְּבַיִת לְמִיּוֹם הַעֲלֹתִי אֶת־בְּנֵי יִשְׂרָאֵל מִמִּצְרַיִם וְעַד
הַיּוֹם הַזֶּה וָאֶהְיֶה מִתְהַלֵּךְ בְּאֹהֶל וּבְמִשְׁכָּן׃
7 בְּכֹל אֲשֶׁר־הִתְהַלַּכְתִּי בְּכָל־בְּנֵי יִשְׂרָאֵל
הֲדָבָר דִּבַּרְתִּי אֶת־אַחַד שִׁבְטֵי יִשְׂרָאֵל

5 לֵךְ וְאָמַרְתָּ אֶל־עַבְדִּי אֶל־דָּוִד	"Go and say to my servant, to David,
כֹּה אָמַר יְהוָה	'Thus says the LORD,
הַאַתָּה תִּבְנֶה־לִּי בַיִת לְשִׁבְתִּי׃	Will you build a house for me to dwell in?
6 כִּי לֹא יָשַׁבְתִּי בְּבַיִת	For I haven't dwelled in a house
לְמִיּוֹם הַעֲלֹתִי	from the day (that) I brought
אֶת־בְּנֵי יִשְׂרָאֵל מִמִּצְרַיִם	the Israelites out of Egypt
וְעַד הַיּוֹם הַזֶּה	until today.
וָאֶהְיֶה מִתְהַלֵּךְ בְּאֹהֶל וּבְמִשְׁכָּן׃	But I have traveled in a tent and in a tabernacle.
7 בְּכֹל אֲשֶׁר־הִתְהַלַּכְתִּי	In all (of the places) where I walked about
בְּכָל־בְּנֵי יִשְׂרָאֵל	with all the Israelites,
הֲדָבָר דִּבַּרְתִּי אֶת־אַחַד	did I speak one word
שִׁבְטֵי יִשְׂרָאֵל	(to) the tribes of Israel,

NEW VOCABULARY

וּבְמִשְׁכָּן	and in a tabernacle
שִׁבְטֵי	tribes of

VERB ANALYSIS

VERB	ROOT	PATTERN	MEANING	TENSE	P/G/N	SUFFIX
לֵךְ	ה.ל.ך	פָּעַל	walk, go	command	ms	
וְאָמַרְתָּ	א.מ.ר	פָּעַל	say	rv perfect	2ms	
אָמַר	א.מ.ר	פָּעַל	say	perfect	3ms	
תִּבְנֶה	ב.נ.ה	פָּעַל	build	imperfect	2ms	
לְשִׁבְתִּי	י.שׁ.ב	פָּעַל	sit, dwell	infinitive	1cs	
יָשַׁבְתִּי	י.שׁ.ב	פָּעַל	sit, dwell	perfect	1cs	
הַעֲלֹתִי	ע.ל.ה	הִפְעִיל	bring up, offer	infinitive		1cs
וָאֶהְיֶה	ה.י.ה	פָּעַל	be, become	rv imperfect	1cs	
מִתְהַלֵּךְ	ה.ל.ך	הִתְפַּעֵל	walk about	participle	ms	
הִתְהַלַּכְתִּי	ה.ל.ך	הִתְפַּעֵל	walk about	perfect		1cs
דִּבַּרְתִּי	ד.ב.ר	פִּעֵל	speak	perfect	1cs	

GRAMMATICAL NOTES

7:5 A house (בַּיִת) for God is a temple, and a house for a king or queen is a palace. II Samuel 7 engages in much wordplay with the word בַּיִת; see further notes for 7:11.

7:6 You are likely to see many translations of בְּנֵי יִשְׂרָאֵל, including **sons of Israel**, **children of Israel**, and **people of Israel**. According to biblical tradition, the people of Israel descended from and were named after Isaac's son Jacob/Israel, so all of these translations are correct. We simply translate the term **Israelites**.

7:7 Most translations give **chiefs of Israel** for שִׁבְטֵי יִשְׂרָאֵל (**tribes of Israel**), following a parallel section in I Chronicles 17:6 and assuming that God was more likely to talk to tribal leaders than the entire membership.

אֲשֶׁר צִוִּיתִי לִרְעוֹת אֶת־עַמִּי אֶת־יִשְׂרָאֵל לֵאמֹר
לָמָּה לֹא־בְנִיתֶם לִי בֵּית אֲרָזִים׃ 8 וְעַתָּה כֹּה־תֹאמַר
לְעַבְדִּי לְדָוִד כֹּה אָמַר יְהוָה צְבָאוֹת אֲנִי לְקַחְתִּיךָ
מִן־הַנָּוֶה מֵאַחַר הַצֹּאן לִהְיוֹת נָגִיד עַל־עַמִּי
עַל־יִשְׂרָאֵל׃ 9 וָאֶהְיֶה עִמְּךָ בְּכֹל אֲשֶׁר הָלַכְתָּ
וָאַכְרִתָה אֶת־כָּל־אֹיְבֶיךָ מִפָּנֶיךָ

אֲשֶׁר צִוִּיתִי לִרְעוֹת	whom I commanded to shepherd
אֶת־עַמִּי אֶת־יִשְׂרָאֵל לֵאמֹר	my people Israel, saying,
לָמָּה לֹא־בְנִיתֶם לִי בֵּית אֲרָזִים׃	"Why have you not built me a cedar house?"'
8 וְעַתָּה כֹּה־תֹאמַר לְעַבְדִּי לְדָוִד	So now, thus you shall say to my servant David,
כֹּה אָמַר יְהוָה צְבָאוֹת	'Thus says the LORD of hosts,
אֲנִי לְקַחְתִּיךָ מִן־הַנָּוֶה	I took you from the pasture,
מֵאַחַר הַצֹּאן	from behind the flock,
לִהְיוֹת נָגִיד עַל־עַמִּי עַל־יִשְׂרָאֵל׃	to be prince over my people, over Israel.
9 וָאֶהְיֶה עִמְּךָ	I was with you
בְּכֹל אֲשֶׁר הָלַכְתָּ	in all (the places) where you went,
וָאַכְרִתָה אֶת־כָּל־אֹיְבֶיךָ מִפָּנֶיךָ	and I cut off your enemies before you.

NEW VOCABULARY

מִן־הַנָּוֶה	from the pasture	לִרְעוֹת	to shepherd
נָגִיד	prince	אֲרָזִים	cedar
אֹיְבֶיךָ	your enemies	צְבָאוֹת	of hosts

VERB ANALYSIS

VERB	ROOT	PATTERN	MEANING	TENSE	P/G/N	SUFFIX
צִוִּיתִי	צ.ו.ה	פִּעֵל	command	perfect	1cs	
לִרְעוֹת	ר.ע.ה	פָּעַל	shepherd	infinitive		
לֵאמֹר	א.מ.ר	פָּעַל	say	infinitive		
בְנִיתֶם	ב.נ.ה	פָּעַל	build	perfect	2mp	
תֹאמַר	א.מ.ר	פָּעַל	say	imperfect	2ms	
אָמַר	א.מ.ר	פָּעַל	say	perfect	3ms	
לְקַחְתִּיךָ	ל.ק.ח	פָּעַל	take	perfect	1cs	2ms
לִהְיוֹת	ה.י.ה	פָּעַל	be, become	infinitive		
וָאֶהְיֶה	ה.י.ה	פָּעַל	be, become	rv imperfect	1cs	
הָלַכְתָּ	ה.ל.ך	פָּעַל	walk, go	perfect	2ms	
וָאַכְרִתָה	כ.ר.ת	הִפְעִיל	cut off	rv imperfect	1cs	
אֹיְבֶיךָ	א.י.ב	פָּעַל	be hostile to	participle	mp	2ms

GRAMMATICAL NOTES

7:8 Parallel construction, the repetition of a sentence or phrase using synonyms, is typical of the Hebrew Bible's style and is found in poetry and prose. Within the context of verse 8, the prepositional phrase **from the pasture** is synonymous with **behind the flock**, and **my people** is equivalent to **Israel**. English literature uses parallel construction much less often than its Hebrew counterpart. The style often strikes the English-speaking reader as dull or repetitive.

7:8 צְבָאוֹת is the unexpected masculine plural form for the noun צָבָא.

וְעָשִׂתִי לְךָ שֵׁם גָּדוֹל כְּשֵׁם הַגְּדֹלִים אֲשֶׁר בָּאָרֶץ׃
10 וְשַׂמְתִּי מָקוֹם לְעַמִּי לְיִשְׂרָאֵל וּנְטַעְתִּיו וְשָׁכַן
תַּחְתָּיו וְלֹא יִרְגַּז עוֹד וְלֹא־יֹסִיפוּ בְנֵי־עַוְלָה לְעַנּוֹתוֹ
כַּאֲשֶׁר בָּרִאשׁוֹנָה׃ 11 וּלְמִן־הַיּוֹם אֲשֶׁר צִוִּיתִי שֹׁפְטִים
עַל־עַמִּי יִשְׂרָאֵל וַהֲנִיחֹתִי לְךָ מִכָּל־אֹיְבֶיךָ וְהִגִּיד
לְךָ יְהוָה

וְעָשִׂתִי לְךָ שֵׁם גָּדוֹל	Now I have made you a great name,
כְּשֵׁם הַגְּדֹלִים אֲשֶׁר בָּאָרֶץ׃	like the great names that are in the land.
10 וְשַׂמְתִּי מָקוֹם לְעַמִּי לְיִשְׂרָאֵל	And I will set a place for my people, for Israel,
וּנְטַעְתִּיו	and I will plant it (Israel),
וְשָׁכַן תַּחְתָּיו	and it will dwell in its own place
וְלֹא יִרְגַּז עוֹד	and not be disturbed again.
וְלֹא־יֹסִיפוּ בְנֵי־עַוְלָה לְעַנּוֹתוֹ	And the unrighteous will afflict them no more,
כַּאֲשֶׁר בָּרִאשׁוֹנָה׃	as (they did) formerly,
11 וּלְמִן־הַיּוֹם אֲשֶׁר צִוִּיתִי שֹׁפְטִים	from the time I appointed judges
עַל־עַמִּי יִשְׂרָאֵל	over my people Israel.
וַהֲנִיחֹתִי לְךָ מִכָּל־אֹיְבֶיךָ	And I will give you rest from all your enemies.
וְהִגִּיד לְךָ יְהוָה	The LORD declares to you

NEW VOCABULARY

עַוְלָה	the unrighteous	וּנְטַעְתִּיו	and I will plant it
לְעַנּוֹתוֹ	will afflict them	וְשָׁכַן	and it will dwell
בָּרִאשׁוֹנָה	formerly	יִרְגַּז	be disturbed
וַהֲנִיחֹתִי	and I will give (you) rest	יֹסִיפוּ	they will do again
אֹיְבֶיךָ	your enemies		

VERB ANALYSIS

VERB	ROOT	PATTERN	MEANING	TENSE	P/G/N	SUFFIX
וְעָשִׂתִי	ע.ש.ה	פָּעַל	make, do	rv perfect	1cs	
וְשַׂמְתִּי	ש.י.ם	פָּעַל	put, place	rv perfect	1cs	
וּנְטַעְתִּיו	נ.ט.ע	פָּעַל	plant	rv perfect	1cs	3ms
וְשָׁכַן	ש.כ.ן	פָּעַל	dwell	rv perfect	3ms	
יִרְגַּז	ר.ג.ז	פָּעַל	be perturbed	imperfect	3ms	
יֹסִיפוּ	י.ס.ף	הִפְעִיל	add to	imperfect	3mp	
לְעַנּוֹתוֹ	ע.נ.ה	פִּעֵל	afflict	infinitive		3ms
צִוִּיתִי	צ.ו.ה	פִּעֵל	command	perfect	1cs	
שֹׁפְטִים	ש.פ.ט	פָּעַל	judge	participle	mp	
וַהֲנִיחֹתִי	נ.ו.ח	הִפְעִיל	give rest to	rv perfect	1cs	
אֹיְבֶיךָ	א.י.ב	פָּעַל	be hostile to	participle	mp	2ms
וְהִגִּיד	נ.ג.ד	הִפְעִיל	declare, tell	perfect	3ms	

GRAMMATICAL NOTES

7:9 שֵׁם means much more than **name** as a designation for a person or thing. It may also convey the notion of **reputation**, **fame**, or **glory**.

7:10 You may have translated תַּחְתָּיו as **behind it**. תַּחַת with the 3ms suffix is an idiom meaning **in its place** or **where one stands**.

7:10 The verb יֹסִיפוּ functions as a helping verb in this sentence. Used with the infinitive, י.ס.ף in הִפְעִיל means to do more of some action or to do something again. In this case the repeated action is **to afflict**.

כִּי־בַיִת יַעֲשֶׂה־לְּךָ יְהוָה׃ 12 כִּי יִמְלְאוּ יָמֶיךָ וְשָׁכַבְתָּ
אֶת־אֲבֹתֶיךָ וַהֲקִימֹתִי אֶת־זַרְעֲךָ אַחֲרֶיךָ אֲשֶׁר יֵצֵא
מִמֵּעֶיךָ וַהֲכִינֹתִי אֶת־מַמְלַכְתּוֹ׃ 13 הוּא יִבְנֶה־בַּיִת
לִשְׁמִי וְכֹנַנְתִּי אֶת־כִּסֵּא מַמְלַכְתּוֹ עַד־עוֹלָם׃ 14 אֲנִי
אֶהְיֶה־לּוֹ לְאָב וְהוּא יִהְיֶה־לִּי לְבֵן אֲשֶׁר בְּהַעֲוֺתוֹ

כִּי־בַיִת יַעֲשֶׂה־לְּךָ יְהוָה׃	that the LORD will make a house for you.
12 כִּי יִמְלְאוּ יָמֶיךָ	When your days are ended
וְשָׁכַבְתָּ אֶת־אֲבֹתֶיךָ	and you lie down with your fathers,
וַהֲקִימֹתִי אֶת־זַרְעֲךָ אַחֲרֶיךָ	I will raise up your offspring after you,
אֲשֶׁר יֵצֵא מִמֵּעֶיךָ	who will come out from you,
וַהֲכִינֹתִי אֶת־מַמְלַכְתּוֹ׃	and I will establish his kingdom.
13 הוּא יִבְנֶה־בַּיִת לִשְׁמִי	He will build a house for my name,
וְכֹנַנְתִּי אֶת־כִּסֵּא מַמְלַכְתּוֹ	and I will set up the throne of his kingdom
עַד־עוֹלָם׃	forever.
14 אֲנִי אֶהְיֶה־לּוֹ לְאָב	I will be like a father for him,
וְהוּא יִהְיֶה־לִּי לְבֵן	and he will be like a son for me.
אֲשֶׁר בְּהַעֲוֺתוֹ	When he sins,

NEW VOCABULARY

יִמְלְאוּ	are ended
מִמֵּעֶיךָ	out from you
מַמְלַכְתּוֹ	his kingdom
וְכֹנַנְתִּי	and I will set up
בְּהַעֲוֺתוֹ	when he sins

VERB ANALYSIS

VERB	ROOT	PATTERN	MEANING	TENSE	P/G/N	SUFFIX
יַעֲשֶׂה	ע.שׂ.ה	פָּעַל	make, do	imperfect	3ms	
יִמְלְאוּ	מ.ל.א	פָּעַל	be full, fill	imperfect	3mp	
וְשָׁכַבְתָּ	שׁ.כ.ב	פָּעַל	lie, lie down	rv perfect	2ms	
וַהֲקִימֹתִי	ק.ו.ם	הִפְעִיל	raise up	rv perfect	1cs	
יֵצֵא	י.צ.א	פָּעַל	go out	imperfect	3ms	
וַהֲכִינֹתִי	כ.ו.ן	הִפְעִיל	establish	rv perfect	1cs	
יִבְנֶה	ב.נ.ה	פָּעַל	build	imperfect	3ms	
וְכֹנַנְתִּי	כ.ו.ן	פּוֹלֵל	set up	rv perfect	1cs	
אֶהְיֶה	ה.י.ה	פָּעַל	be, become	imperfect	1cs	
יִהְיֶה	ה.י.ה	פָּעַל	be, become	imperfect	3ms	
בְּהַעֲוֺתוֹ	ע.ו.ה	הִפְעִיל	sin	infinitive		3ms

GRAMMATICAL NOTES

7:11 בַּיִת is much more than a house or dwelling; it can also be the entire household. Sometimes בַּיִת indicates a division or subgroup within a people. In this verse, בַּיִת refers to a succession of rulers from the same line of descent, or **dynasty**.

7:13 Recall that a suffixed noun is definite, so אֶת־כִּסֵּא מַמְלַכְתּוֹ is **the** throne of his kingdom, not **a** throne.

7:13 וְכֹנַנְתִּי is in the פּוֹלֵל pattern. For further explanation, see the note for בֹּשֵׁשׁ in Exodus 32:1 on page 25.

וְהֹכַחְתִּיו בְּשֵׁבֶט אֲנָשִׁים וּבְנִגְעֵי בְּנֵי אָדָם׃
15 וְחַסְדִּי לֹא־יָסוּר מִמֶּנּוּ כַּאֲשֶׁר הֲסִרֹתִי מֵעִם שָׁאוּל
אֲשֶׁר הֲסִרֹתִי מִלְּפָנֶיךָ׃ 16 וְנֶאְמַן בֵּיתְךָ וּמַמְלַכְתְּךָ
עַד־עוֹלָם לְפָנֶיךָ כִּסְאֲךָ יִהְיֶה נָכוֹן עַד־עוֹלָם׃ 17 כְּכֹל
הַדְּבָרִים הָאֵלֶּה וּכְכֹל הַחִזָּיוֹן הַזֶּה כֵּן דִּבֶּר נָתָן
אֶל־דָּוִד׃

וְהֹכַחְתִּיו בְּשֵׁבֶט אֲנָשִׁים	I will admonish him with the rod of man
וּבְנִגְעֵי בְּנֵי אָדָם׃	and with the straps of the sons of man.
15 וְחַסְדִּי לֹא־יָסוּר מִמֶּנּוּ	But my kindness will not depart (from) him
כַּאֲשֶׁר הֲסִרֹתִי מֵעִם שָׁאוּל	as I took it away from Saul,
אֲשֶׁר הֲסִרֹתִי מִלְּפָנֶיךָ׃	whom I removed before you.
16 וְנֶאְמַן בֵּיתְךָ וּמַמְלַכְתְּךָ	Your house and your kingdom will be secured
עַד־עוֹלָם לְפָנֶיךָ	before you forever;
כִּסְאֲךָ יִהְיֶה נָכוֹן עַד־עוֹלָם׃	your throne will be established forever.'"
17 כְּכֹל הַדְּבָרִים הָאֵלֶּה	In accordance with all these things,
וּכְכֹל הַחִזָּיוֹן הַזֶּה	and in accordance with this entire vision,
כֵּן דִּבֶּר נָתָן אֶל־דָּוִד׃	thus Nathan spoke to David.

NEW VOCABULARY

וְהֹכַחְתִּיו	I will admonish him
בְּשֵׁבֶט	with the rod of
וּבְנִגְעֵי	and with the straps of
וְחַסְדִּי	but my kindness
שָׁאוּל	Saul
וְנֶאְמַן	will be secured
וּמַמְלַכְתְּךָ	and your kingdom
כִּסְאֲךָ	your throne
הַחִזָּיוֹן	the vision

VERB ANALYSIS

VERB	ROOT	PATTERN	MEANING	TENSE	P/G/N	SUFFIX
וְהֹכַחְתִּיו	י.כ.ח	הִפְעִיל	judge, reprove	rv perfect	1cs	3ms
יָסוּר	ס.ו.ר	פָּעַל	turn aside	imperfect	3ms	
הֲסִרֹתִי	ס.ו.ר	הִפְעִיל	remove	perfect	1cs	
וְנֶאְמַן	א.מ.ן	נִפְעַל	made sure	rv perfect	3ms	
יִהְיֶה	ה.י.ה	פָּעַל	be, become	imperfect	3ms	
נָכוֹן	כ.ו.ן	נִפְעַל	be established	participle	ms	
דִּבֶּר	ד.ב.ר	פִּעֵל	speak	perfect	3ms	

GRAMMATICAL NOTE

7:15 Note the shift of person in the last sentence of this verse. In **my kindness will not depart (from) him**, the subject is **my kindness** and there is no object. But in the second half of the sentence, **as I took it away from Saul**, the doer is the speaker (God), and the implied object is **my kindness**. The result is a confusing, disjointed sentence. Some manuscripts of the Hebrew Bible read, **I will not take my kindness from him, as I took it away from Saul**, and many translations follow that reading. We left the passage as is, but you may choose to alter your translation.

3 [3]וַיֶּאֱהַב שְׁלֹמֹה אֶת־יְהוָה לָלֶכֶת בְּחֻקּוֹת דָּוִד אָבִיו
רַק בַּבָּמוֹת הוּא מְזַבֵּחַ וּמַקְטִיר׃ [4]וַיֵּלֶךְ הַמֶּלֶךְ גִּבְעֹנָה
לִזְבֹּחַ שָׁם כִּי הִיא הַבָּמָה הַגְּדוֹלָה אֶלֶף עֹלוֹת יַעֲלֶה
שְׁלֹמֹה עַל הַמִּזְבֵּחַ הַהוּא׃ [5]בְּגִבְעוֹן נִרְאָה יְהוָה
אֶל־שְׁלֹמֹה בַּחֲלוֹם הַלָּיְלָה וַיֹּאמֶר אֱלֹהִים שְׁאַל מָה
אֶתֶּן־לָךְ׃ [6]וַיֹּאמֶר שְׁלֹמֹה אַתָּה עָשִׂיתָ

[3]וַיֶּאֱהַב שְׁלֹמֹה אֶת־יְהוָה	Now Solomon loved the LORD,
לָלֶכֶת בְּחֻקּוֹת	going according to the statutes
דָּוִד אָבִיו רַק בַּבָּמוֹת	of his father David; but upon the high places
הוּא מְזַבֵּחַ וּמַקְטִיר׃	he sacrificed and burnt incense.
[4]וַיֵּלֶךְ הַמֶּלֶךְ גִּבְעֹנָה לִזְבֹּחַ שָׁם	So the king went to Gibeon to sacrifice there,
כִּי הִיא הַבָּמָה הַגְּדוֹלָה	because that was the great high place;
אֶלֶף עֹלוֹת יַעֲלֶה שְׁלֹמֹה	Solomon sent up a thousand burnt offerings
עַל הַמִּזְבֵּחַ הַהוּא׃	upon that altar.
[5]בְּגִבְעוֹן נִרְאָה יְהוָה אֶל־שְׁלֹמֹה	At Gibeon the LORD appeared to Solomon
בַּחֲלוֹם הַלָּיְלָה	in a dream by night.
וַיֹּאמֶר אֱלֹהִים שְׁאַל מָה אֶתֶּן־לָךְ׃	And God said, “Ask, what shall I give you?”
[6]וַיֹּאמֶר שְׁלֹמֹה אַתָּה עָשִׂיתָ	And Solomon said, “You showed (lit. did)

NEW VOCABULARY

שְׁלֹמֹה	Solomon	גִּבְעֹנָה	to Gibeon
בְּחֻקּוֹת	according to the statutes	לִזְבֹּחַ	to sacrifice
בַּבָּמוֹת	upon the high places	עֹלוֹת	burnt offerings
מְזַבֵּחַ	(he) sacrificed	בַּחֲלוֹם	in a dream
וּמַקְטִיר	(he) burnt incense	שְׁאַל	(you) ask

VERB ANALYSIS

VERB	ROOT	PATTERN	MEANING	TENSE	P/G/N	SUFFIX
וַיֶּאֱהַב	א.ה.ב	פָּעַל	love	rv imperfect	3ms	
לָלֶכֶת	ה.ל.ך	פָּעַל	walk, go	infinitive		
מְזַבֵּחַ	ז.ב.ח	פִּעֵל	sacrifice	participle	ms	
וּמַקְטִיר	ק.ט.ר	הִפְעִיל	burn incense	participle	ms	
וַיֵּלֶךְ	ה.ל.ך	פָּעַל	walk, go	rv imperfect	3ms	
לִזְבֹּחַ	ז.ב.ח	פָּעַל	sacrifice	infinitive		
יַעֲלֶה	ע.ל.ה	הִפְעִיל	bring up, offer	imperfect	3ms	
נִרְאָה	ר.א.ה	נִפְעַל	appear	perfect	3ms	
וַיֹּאמֶר	א.מ.ר	פָּעַל	say	rv imperfect	3ms	
שְׁאַל	שׁ.א.ל	פָּעַל	ask	command	2ms	
אֶתֶּן	נ.ת.ן	פָּעַל	give, set	imperfect	1cs	
עָשִׂיתָ	ע.שׂ.ה	פָּעַל	make, do	perfect	2ms	

GRAMMATICAL NOTES

3:3 High places (בָּמוֹת) are natural or manufactured heights on which sacrifices were offered throughout the ancient Middle East. High places could include mountains, artificial mounds, platforms, and buildings erected on top of any of these.

3:4 The verb יַעֲלֶה is an imperfect, yet the action takes place in the past. Sometimes the imperfect signals regular or customary action that takes place in the past, present, or future.

3:4 You should not interpret the number **a thousand** literally. As in English, sometimes large numbers in Hebrew are figures of speech for **many**.

עִם־עַבְדְּךָ דָוִד אָבִי חֶסֶד גָּדוֹל כַּאֲשֶׁר הָלַךְ לְפָנֶיךָ
בֶּאֱמֶת וּבִצְדָקָה וּבְיִשְׁרַת לֵבָב עִמָּךְ וַתִּשְׁמָר־לוֹ
אֶת־הַחֶסֶד הַגָּדוֹל הַזֶּה וַתִּתֶּן־לוֹ בֵן יֹשֵׁב עַל־כִּסְאוֹ
כַּיּוֹם הַזֶּה׃ 7 וְעַתָּה יְהוָה אֱלֹהָי אַתָּה הִמְלַכְתָּ
אֶת־עַבְדְּךָ תַּחַת דָּוִד אָבִי וְאָנֹכִי נַעַר קָטֹן לֹא אֵדַע
צֵאת וָבֹא׃

עִם־עַבְדְּךָ דָוִד אָבִי חֶסֶד גָּדוֹל	your servant David, my father, great kindness
כַּאֲשֶׁר הָלַךְ לְפָנֶיךָ בֶּאֱמֶת	when he walked before you in truth
וּבִצְדָקָה וּבְיִשְׁרַת לֵבָב עִמָּךְ	and righteousness and uprightness of heart.
וַתִּשְׁמָר־לוֹ	And you preserved for him
אֶת־הַחֶסֶד הַגָּדוֹל הַזֶּה	this great kindness,
וַתִּתֶּן־לוֹ בֵן	and gave him a son
יֹשֵׁב עַל־כִּסְאוֹ כַּיּוֹם הַזֶּה׃	who sits upon his throne this day.
7 וְעַתָּה יְהוָה אֱלֹהָי	And now, O LORD my God,
אַתָּה הִמְלַכְתָּ אֶת־עַבְדְּךָ	you have made your servant (me) reign
תַּחַת דָּוִד אָבִי	after my father David.
וְאָנֹכִי נַעַר קָטֹן	But I am a little boy
לֹא אֵדַע צֵאת וָבֹא׃	(and) do not know (how) to go out or come in.

NEW VOCABULARY

חֶסֶד kindness
וּבְיִשְׁרַת and uprightness
כִּסְאוֹ his throne

VERB ANALYSIS

VERB	ROOT	PATTERN	MEANING	TENSE	P/G/N	SUFFIX
הָלַךְ	ה.ל.ך	פָּעַל	walk, go	perfect	3ms	
וַתִּשְׁמָר	ש.מ.ר	פָּעַל	keep, watch	rv imperfect	2ms	
וַתִּתֶּן	נ.ת.ן	פָּעַל	give, set	rv imperfect	2ms	
יֹשֵׁב	י.ש.ב	פָּעַל	sit, dwell	participle	ms	
הִמְלַכְתָּ	מ.ל.ך	הִפְעִיל	make reign	perfect	2ms	
אֵדַע	י.ד.ע	פָּעַל	know	imperfect	1cs	
צֵאת	י.צ.ה	פָּעַל	go out	infinitive		
וָבֹא	ב.ו.א	פָּעַל	come	infinitive		

GRAMMATICAL NOTES

3:6 You may have translated part of verse 6 as **You did with your servant . . . great kindness**. The words עָשָׂה, עִם and חֶסֶד make up a formula for **to deal kindly with** or **show kindness to**.

3:7 In this verse and others to follow, speakers refer to themselves as **your servant** or **your maidservant** instead of **I** or **me**. Such forms of address are marks of respect and humility before one's superior. In this verse, a king uses the term in God's presence; later (3:20), a subject uses the term before the king.

3:7 The regular infinitive can function as the subject or direct object of a verb. In verse 7, the infinitives צֵאת (**[how] to go out**) and וָבֹא (**or come in**) are the direct objects of the verb אֵדַע (**I know**).

8 וְעַבְדְּךָ בְּתוֹךְ עַמְּךָ אֲשֶׁר בָּחָרְתָּ עַם־רָב אֲשֶׁר
לֹא־יִמָּנֶה וְלֹא יִסָּפֵר מֵרֹב׃ 9 וְנָתַתָּ לְעַבְדְּךָ לֵב שֹׁמֵעַ
לִשְׁפֹּט אֶת־עַמְּךָ לְהָבִין בֵּין־טוֹב לְרָע כִּי מִי יוּכַל
לִשְׁפֹּט אֶת־עַמְּךָ הַכָּבֵד הַזֶּה׃ 10 וַיִּיטַב הַדָּבָר בְּעֵינֵי
אֲדֹנָי כִּי שָׁאַל שְׁלֹמֹה אֶת־הַדָּבָר הַזֶּה׃

8 וְעַבְדְּךָ בְּתוֹךְ עַמְּךָ	And your servant is in the midst of your people
אֲשֶׁר בָּחָרְתָּ עַם־רָב	whom you have chosen, a great people,
אֲשֶׁר לֹא־יִמָּנֶה וְלֹא יִסָּפֵר	who cannot be numbered or counted
מֵרֹב׃	on account of (its) multitude.
9 וְנָתַתָּ לְעַבְדְּךָ לֵב שֹׁמֵעַ	Give your servant (me) an understanding mind
לִשְׁפֹּט אֶת־עַמְּךָ	to govern (lit. judge) your people,
לְהָבִין בֵּין־טוֹב לְרָע	to discern good and evil,
כִּי מִי יוּכַל לִשְׁפֹּט	for who can govern
אֶת־עַמְּךָ הַכָּבֵד הַזֶּה׃	this vast people of yours?"
10 וַיִּיטַב הַדָּבָר	Now the speech was pleasing
בְּעֵינֵי אֲדֹנָי	in the eyes of the LORD,
כִּי שָׁאַל שְׁלֹמֹה אֶת־הַדָּבָר הַזֶּה׃	that Solomon had asked for this thing.

NEW VOCABULARY

בָּחַרְתָּ	you have chosen
יִמָּנֶה	be counted
מֵרֹב	on account of (its) multitude
לְהָבִין	to discern
הַכָּבֵד	(this) vast
וַיִּיטַב	(it) was pleasing
שָׁאַל	(he) had asked

VERB ANALYSIS

VERB	ROOT	PATTERN	MEANING	TENSE	P/G/N	SUFFIX
בָּחַרְתָּ	ב.ח.ר	פָּעַל	choose	perfect	2ms	
יִמָּנֶה	מ.נ.ה	נִפְעַל	be numbered	imperfect	3ms	
יִסָּפֵר	ס.פ.ר	נִפְעַל	be counted	imperfect	3ms	
וְנָתַתָּ	נ.ת.ן	פָּעַל	give, set	rv perfect	2ms	
שֹׁמֵעַ	ש.מ.ע	פָּעַל	hear	participle	ms	
לִשְׁפֹּט	ש.פ.ט	פָּעַל	judge	infinitive		
לְהָבִין	ב.י.ן	הִפְעִיל	understand	infinitive		
יוּכַל	י.כ.ל	פָּעַל	be able	imperfect	3ms	
וַיִּיטַב	י.ט.ב	פָּעַל	be pleasing	rv imperfect	3ms	
שָׁאַל	ש.א.ל	פָּעַל	ask	perfect	3ms	

GRAMMATICAL NOTES

3:9 Usually, if an rv perfect verb functions as a command, it follows a verb in the command tense; this is not the case with the verb וְנָתַתָּ. An inferior does not command a superior, so the king cannot command God. The rv perfect instead expresses a request and can be translated as **perhaps you would give**.

3:9 You learned that the word לֵב means **heart**. In fact, it means much more than that. לֵב refers to the inner person, in contrast to the physical body, and can be translated as **will**, **mind**, or **heart**. Once you have determined the sense of the Hebrew, translate according to what sounds the most natural in English.

11 וַיֹּאמֶר אֱלֹהִים אֵלָיו יַעַן אֲשֶׁר שָׁאַלְתָּ אֶת־הַדָּבָר
הַזֶּה וְלֹא־שָׁאַלְתָּ לְּךָ יָמִים רַבִּים וְלֹא־שָׁאַלְתָּ לְּךָ
עֹשֶׁר וְלֹא שָׁאַלְתָּ נֶפֶשׁ אֹיְבֶיךָ וְשָׁאַלְתָּ לְּךָ הָבִין
לִשְׁמֹעַ מִשְׁפָּט׃ 12 הִנֵּה עָשִׂיתִי כִדְבָרֶיךָ הִנֵּה נָתַתִּי לְךָ
לֵב חָכָם וְנָבוֹן אֲשֶׁר כָּמוֹךָ לֹא־הָיָה לְפָנֶיךָ וְאַחֲרֶיךָ
לֹא־יָקוּם כָּמוֹךָ׃ 13 וְגַם אֲשֶׁר לֹא־שָׁאַלְתָּ

11 וַיֹּאמֶר אֱלֹהִים אֵלָיו	And God said to him,
יַעַן אֲשֶׁר שָׁאַלְתָּ אֶת־הַדָּבָר הַזֶּה	"Because you asked for this thing—
וְלֹא־שָׁאַלְתָּ לְּךָ יָמִים רַבִּים	and did not ask for yourself many days,
וְלֹא־שָׁאַלְתָּ לְּךָ עֹשֶׁר	and did not ask for yourself riches,
וְלֹא שָׁאַלְתָּ נֶפֶשׁ אֹיְבֶיךָ	and did not ask for the life of your enemies—
וְשָׁאַלְתָּ לְּךָ הָבִין	but asked for (the) understanding
לִשְׁמֹעַ מִשְׁפָּט׃	to execute justice,
12 הִנֵּה עָשִׂיתִי כִדְבָרֶיךָ	see, now I act according to your words.
הִנֵּה נָתַתִּי לְךָ לֵב חָכָם וְנָבוֹן	Look, I give you a wise and discerning mind,
אֲשֶׁר כָּמוֹךָ לֹא־הָיָה לְפָנֶיךָ	so that there has been none like you before you,
וְאַחֲרֶיךָ לֹא־יָקוּם כָּמוֹךָ׃	and no one will rise up like you after you.
13 וְגַם אֲשֶׁר לֹא־שָׁאַלְתָּ	And also, what you did not ask for

NEW VOCABULARY

יַעַן אֲשֶׁר	because
שָׁאַלְתָּ	you asked
עֹשֶׁר	riches
אֹיְבֶיךָ	your enemies
הָבִין	(the) understanding
וְנָבוֹן	discerning

VERB ANALYSIS

VERB	ROOT	PATTERN	MEANING	TENSE	P/G/N	SUFFIX
וַיֹּאמֶר	א.מ.ר	פָּעַל	say	rv imperfect	3ms	
שָׁאַלְתָּ	ש.א.ל	פָּעַל	ask	perfect	2ms	
אֹיְבֶיךָ	א.י.ב	פָּעַל	be hostile to	participle	mp	2ms
וְשָׁאַלְתָּ	ש.א.ל	פָּעַל	ask	perfect	2ms	
הָבִין	ב.י.ן	הִפְעִיל	understand	infinitive		
לִשְׁמֹעַ	ש.מ.ע	פָּעַל	hear	infinitive		
עָשִׂיתִי	ע.ש.ה	פָּעַל	make, do	perfect	1cs	
נָתַתִּי	נ.ת.ן	פָּעַל	give, set	perfect	1cs	
וְנָבוֹן	ב.י.ן	נִפְעַל	be discerning	participle	ms	
הָיָה	ה.י.ה	פָּעַל	be, become	perfect	3ms	
יָקוּם	ק.ו.ם	פָּעַל	arise	imperfect	3ms	

GRAMMATICAL NOTES

3:11 For a discussion of יַעַן אֲשֶׁר, see the notes following Genesis 22:16 on page 21.

3:11 יָמִים רַבִּים is a figure of speech for **long life**.

3:12 שְׁמֹעַ מִשְׁפָּט is the Hebrew formula for **executing** or **carrying out** justice. It can also designate hearing a specific legal case.

3:12 ע.ש.ה and נ.ת.ן are conjugated in the perfect tense, but are translated as present tense. Hebrew uses the perfect tense for action that is completed once the speaker or author mentions it. Here God gives Solomon wisdom at the moment he proclaims his intention to do so.

נָתַתִּי לָךְ גַּם־עֹשֶׁר גַּם־כָּבוֹד אֲשֶׁר לֹא־הָיָה כָמוֹךָ
אִישׁ בַּמְּלָכִים כָּל־יָמֶיךָ׃ 14 וְאִם תֵּלֵךְ בִּדְרָכַי לִשְׁמֹר
חֻקַּי וּמִצְוֹתַי כַּאֲשֶׁר הָלַךְ דָּוִיד אָבִיךָ וְהַאֲרַכְתִּי
אֶת־יָמֶיךָ׃ 15 וַיִּקַץ שְׁלֹמֹה וְהִנֵּה חֲלוֹם וַיָּבוֹא
יְרוּשָׁלַםִ וַיַּעֲמֹד לִפְנֵי אֲרוֹן בְּרִית־אֲדֹנָי וַיַּעַל עֹלוֹת

נָתַתִּי לָךְ גַּם־עֹשֶׁר גַּם־כָּבוֹד	I grant you, both riches and honor,
אֲשֶׁר לֹא־הָיָה כָמוֹךָ אִישׁ בַּמְּלָכִים	so that there has not been any king like you
כָּל־יָמֶיךָ׃	for all of your days.
14 וְאִם תֵּלֵךְ בִּדְרָכַי	And if you walk in my ways
לִשְׁמֹר חֻקַּי וּמִצְוֹתַי	by keeping my statutes and commandments,
כַּאֲשֶׁר הָלַךְ דָּוִיד אָבִיךָ	as your father David walked,
וְהַאֲרַכְתִּי אֶת־יָמֶיךָ׃	then I will lengthen your days.”
15 וַיִּקַץ שְׁלֹמֹה וְהִנֵּה חֲלוֹם	Then Solomon awoke, and look, it was a dream.
וַיָּבוֹא יְרוּשָׁלַםִ וַיַּעֲמֹד	He came to Jerusalem and stood
לִפְנֵי אֲרוֹן בְּרִית־אֲדֹנָי	before the ark of the covenant of the LORD
וַיַּעַל עֹלוֹת	and sent up burnt offerings,

NEW VOCABULARY

עֹשֶׁר	riches
חֻקַּי	my statutes
וְהַאֲרַכְתִּי	then I will lengthen
וַיִּקַץ	then Solomon awoke
חֲלוֹם	a dream
עֹלוֹת	burnt offerings

VERB ANALYSIS

VERB	ROOT	PATTERN	MEANING	TENSE	P/G/N	SUFFIX
נָתַתִּי	נ.ת.ן	פָּעַל	give, set	perfect	1cs	
הָיָה	ה.י.ה	פָּעַל	be, become	perfect	3ms	
תֵּלֵךְ	ה.ל.ך	פָּעַל	walk, go	imperfect	2ms	
לִשְׁמֹר	ש.מ.ר	פָּעַל	keep, watch	infinitive		
הָלַךְ	ה.ל.ך	פָּעַל	walk, go	perfect	3ms	
וְהַאֲרַכְתִּי	א.ר.ך	הִפְעִיל	prolong	rv perfect	1cs	
וַיִּקַץ	י.ק.ץ	פָּעַל	awake	rv imperfect	3ms	
וַיָּבוֹא	ב.ו.א	פָּעַל	come	rv imperfect	3ms	
וַיַּעֲמֹד	ע.מ.ד	פָּעַל	stand	rv imperfect	3ms	
וַיַּעַל	ע.ל.ה	הִפְעִיל	bring up, offer	rv imperfect	3ms	

GRAMMATICAL NOTES

3:13 The Hebrew equivalent of the English construction **both . . . and** is **גַּם . . . גַּם**.

3:13 **אִישׁ בַּמְּלָכִים**, **a man among kings**, is better translated **any king**. Oftentimes **אִישׁ** precedes a noun that identifies a person's occupation, homeland, or people.

3:15 Note that we translated אֲדֹנָי as **the** LORD and not **my** LORD. As you know, the vowels for אֲדֹנָי are usually affixed to the Tetragrammaton so that the reader will not inadvertently pronounce the name of Israel's God. Here אֲדֹנָי replaces the Tetragrammaton in full; context suggests that **the** LORD is the best translation.

וַיַּעַשׂ שְׁלָמִים וַיַּעַשׂ מִשְׁתֶּה לְכָל־עֲבָדָיו׃ 16 אָז
תָּבֹאנָה שְׁתַּיִם נָשִׁים זֹנוֹת אֶל־הַמֶּלֶךְ וַתַּעֲמֹדְנָה
לְפָנָיו׃ 17 וַתֹּאמֶר הָאִשָּׁה הָאַחַת בִּי אֲדֹנִי אֲנִי וְהָאִשָּׁה
הַזֹּאת יֹשְׁבֹת בְּבַיִת אֶחָד וָאֵלֵד עִמָּהּ בַּבָּיִת׃ 18 וַיְהִי
בַּיּוֹם הַשְּׁלִישִׁי לְלִדְתִּי וַתֵּלֶד גַּם־הָאִשָּׁה הַזֹּאת
וַאֲנַחְנוּ יַחְדָּו

וַיַּעַשׂ שְׁלָמִים	and made peace offerings,
וַיַּעַשׂ מִשְׁתֶּה לְכָל־עֲבָדָיו׃	and prepared a feast for all of his servants.
16 אָז תָּבֹאנָה שְׁתַּיִם נָשִׁים זֹנוֹת	Then two prostitutes came
אֶל־הַמֶּלֶךְ וַתַּעֲמֹדְנָה לְפָנָיו׃	to the king and stood before him.
17 וַתֹּאמֶר הָאִשָּׁה הָאַחַת בִּי אֲדֹנִי	And the first woman said, “Excuse me, my Lord,
אֲנִי וְהָאִשָּׁה הַזֹּאת	this woman and I
יֹשְׁבֹת בְּבַיִת אֶחָד	live in one house,
וָאֵלֵד עִמָּהּ בַּבָּיִת׃	and I gave birth beside her in the house.
18 וַיְהִי בַּיּוֹם הַשְּׁלִישִׁי לְלִדְתִּי	And on the third day after I gave birth,
וַתֵּלֶד גַּם־הָאִשָּׁה הַזֹּאת	this woman also gave birth.
וַאֲנַחְנוּ יַחְדָּו	We were alone;

NEW VOCABULARY

שְׁלָמִים	peace offerings
מִשְׁתֶּה	a feast
זֹנוֹת	prostitutes
בִּי	excuse me
לָלִדְתִּי	I gave birth
יַחְדָּו	alone

VERB ANALYSIS

VERB	ROOT	PATTERN	MEANING	TENSE	P/G/N	SUFFIX
וַיַּעַשׂ	ע.שׂ.ה	פָּעַל	make, do	rv imperfect	3ms	
תָּבֹאנָה	ב.ו.א	פָּעַל	come	imperfect	3fp	
זֹנוֹת	ז.נ.ה	פָּעַל	fornicate	participle	fp	
וַתַּעֲמֹדְנָה	ע.מ.ד	פָּעַל	stand	rv imperfect	3fp	
וַתֹּאמֶר	א.מ.ר	פָּעַל	say	rv imperfect	3fs	
יֹשְׁבֹת	י.שׁ.ב	פָּעַל	sit, dwell	participle	fp	
וָאֵלֵד	י.ל.ד	פָּעַל	bear, beget	rv imperfect	1cs	
וַיְהִי	ה.י.ה	פָּעַל	be, become	rv imperfect	3ms	
לְלִדְתִּי	י.ל.ד	פָּעַל	bear, beget	infinitive		1cs
וַתֵּלֶד	י.ל.ד	פָּעַל	bear, beget	rv imperfect	3fs	

GRAMMATICAL NOTES

3:17 בִּי is a Hebrew interjection that begs forgiveness or requests pardon. It usually precedes אֲדֹנִי and can be translated as **excuse me**, **pray**, **a prayer**, **a petition** or **Oh**.

3:18 Examine the clause וַיְהִי בַּיּוֹם הַשְּׁלִישִׁי לְלִדְתִּי. This is an example of the infinitive used in a temporal clause. A discussion of past events usually begins with the word וַיְהִי, the first word in this clause. Next, the text tells how much time has passed from a past event to the present: three days. Finally, לְ attaches to the infinitive to indicate what the past event was. A literal translation of this clause reads, **it happened on the third day of my bearing a child**. Since this is not idiomatic English, we have adjusted the translation.

אֵין־זָר אִתָּנוּ בַּבַּיִת זוּלָתִי שְׁתַּיִם־אֲנַחְנוּ בַּבָּיִת׃
19 וַיָּמָת בֶּן־הָאִשָּׁה הַזֹּאת לָיְלָה אֲשֶׁר שָׁכְבָה עָלָיו׃
20 וַתָּקָם בְּתוֹךְ הַלַּיְלָה וַתִּקַּח אֶת־בְּנִי מֵאֶצְלִי
וַאֲמָתְךָ יְשֵׁנָה וַתַּשְׁכִּיבֵהוּ בְּחֵיקָהּ וְאֶת־בְּנָהּ הַמֵּת
הִשְׁכִּיבָה בְחֵיקִי׃ 21 וָאָקֻם בַּבֹּקֶר לְהֵינִיק אֶת־בְּנִי
וְהִנֵּה־מֵת וָאֶתְבּוֹנֵן אֵלָיו בַּבֹּקֶר

אֵין־זָר אִתָּנוּ בַּבַּיִת	there was no visitor with us in the house;
זוּלָתִי שְׁתַּיִם־אֲנַחְנוּ בַּבָּיִת׃	only the two of us were in the house.
19 וַיָּמָת בֶּן־הָאִשָּׁה הַזֹּאת לָיְלָה	This woman's son died by night
אֲשֶׁר שָׁכְבָה עָלָיו׃	because she lay on it.
20 וַתָּקָם בְּתוֹךְ הַלַּיְלָה	She got up in the middle of the night,
וַתִּקַּח אֶת־בְּנִי מֵאֶצְלִי	and took my son from beside me
וַאֲמָתְךָ יְשֵׁנָה	while I was sleeping.
וַתַּשְׁכִּיבֵהוּ בְּחֵיקָהּ	Then she laid him at her breast,
וְאֶת־בְּנָהּ הַמֵּת הִשְׁכִּיבָה בְחֵיקִי׃	and laid her dead son at my breast.
21 וָאָקֻם בַּבֹּקֶר לְהֵינִיק אֶת־בְּנִי	When I arose in the morning to nurse my son,
וְהִנֵּה־מֵת	there he was, dead!
וָאֶתְבּוֹנֵן אֵלָיו בַּבֹּקֶר	But I inspected him in the morning,

NEW VOCABULARY

יְשֵׁנָה	sleeping	זָר	visitor
בְּחֵיקָהּ	at her breast	זוּלָתִי	only
בְּחֵיקִי	at my breast	מֵאֶצְלִי	from beside me
לְהֵינִיק	to nurse	וַאֲמָתְךָ	I (lit. your maidservant)
וָאֶתְבּוֹנֵן	but I inspected		

VERB ANALYSIS

VERB	ROOT	PATTERN	MEANING	TENSE	P/G/N	SUFFIX
זָר	ז.ו.ר	פָּעַל	be a stranger	participle	ms	
וַיָּמָת	מ.ו.ת	פָּעַל	die	rv imperfect	3ms	
שָׁכְבָה	ש.כ.ב	פָּעַל	lie, lie down	perfect	3fs	
וַתָּקָם	ק.ו.ם	פָּעַל	arise	rv imperfect	3fs	
וַתִּקַּח	ל.ק.ח	פָּעַל	take	rv imperfect	3fs	
וַתַּשְׁכִּיבֵהוּ	ש.כ.ב	הִפְעִיל	lay down	rv imperfect	3fs	3ms
הַמֵּת	מ.ו.ת	פָּעַל	die	participle	ms	
הִשְׁכִּיבָה	ש.כ.ב	הִפְעִיל	lay down	perfect	3fs	
וָאָקֻם	ק.ו.ם	פָּעַל	arise	rv imperfect	1cs	
לְהֵינִיק	י.נ.ק	הִפְעִיל	nurse	infinitive		
מֵת	מ.ו.ת	פָּעַל	die	participle	ms	
וָאֶתְבּוֹנֵן	ב.י.ן	הִתְפּוֹלֵל	inspect	rv imperfect	1cs	

GRAMMATICAL NOTES

3:20 אֲמָתְךָ, **your maidservant**, functions the same way as עַבְדְּךָ, **your servant**, does in verse 7. The speaker calls herself this as a token of respect and humility before the king.

3:21 The הִתְפּוֹלֵל is another new, minor verb pattern. The הִתְפּוֹלֵל pattern replaces the הִתְפַּעֵל in hollow verbs. You do not need to learn this pattern at this time. See notes following Exodus 32:1 on page 25 for the פּוֹלֵל.

וְהִנֵּה לֹא־הָיָה בְנִי אֲשֶׁר יָלָדְתִּי׃ 22וַתֹּאמֶר הָאִשָּׁה
הָאַחֶרֶת לֹא כִי בְּנִי הַחַי וּבְנֵךְ הַמֵּת וְזֹאת אֹמֶרֶת לֹא
כִי בְּנֵךְ הַמֵּת וּבְנִי הֶחָי וַתְּדַבֵּרְנָה לִפְנֵי הַמֶּלֶךְ׃
23וַיֹּאמֶר הַמֶּלֶךְ זֹאת אֹמֶרֶת זֶה־בְּנִי הַחַי וּבְנֵךְ הַמֵּת
וְזֹאת אֹמֶרֶת

וְהִנֵּה לֹא־הָיָה בְנִי אֲשֶׁר יָלָדְתִּי׃	and see, he was not the son I had borne."
22וַתֹּאמֶר הָאִשָּׁה הָאַחֶרֶת	But the other woman said,
לֹא כִי בְּנִי הַחַי	"No, because my son is the living one,
וּבְנֵךְ הַמֵּת	and your son is the dead one."
וְזֹאת אֹמֶרֶת	But the first one said,
לֹא כִי בְּנֵךְ הַמֵּת	"No, because your son is the dead one,
וּבְנִי הֶחָי	and my son is the living one."
וַתְּדַבֵּרְנָה לִפְנֵי הַמֶּלֶךְ׃	Thus they spoke before the king.
23וַיֹּאמֶר הַמֶּלֶךְ זֹאת אֹמֶרֶת	Then the king said, "The one says,
זֶה־בְּנִי הַחַי	'This is my son, the living one,
וּבְנֵךְ הַמֵּת	and your son is the dead one.'
וְזֹאת אֹמֶרֶת	But the other one says,

VERB ANALYSIS

VERB	ROOT	PATTERN	MEANING	TENSE	P/G/N	SUFFIX
הָיָה	ה.י.ה	פָּעַל	be, become	perfect	3ms	
יָלָדְתִּי	י.ל.ד	פָּעַל	bear, beget	perfect	1cs	
וַתֹּאמֶר	א.מ.ר	פָּעַל	say	rv imperfect	3fs	
הַמֵּת	מ.ו.ת	פָּעַל	die	participle	ms	
אֹמֶרֶת	א.מ.ר	פָּעַל	say	participle	fs	
הַמֵּת	מ.ו.ת	פָּעַל	die	participle	ms	
וַתְּדַבֵּרְנָה	ד.ב.ר	פִּעֵל	speak	rv imperfect	3fp	
וַיֹּאמֶר	א.מ.ר	פָּעַל	say	rv imperfect	3ms	

GRAMMATICAL NOTES

3:22 The Hebrew word for **the living one** occurs twice in this verse. It is spelled הַחַי the first time and הֶחָי the second. הַחַי is the regular spelling; the irregular spelling הֶחָי is due to its position in the sentence. At the close of a verse or sentence, some words exhibit slight spelling changes; these alternate spellings are called **pausal forms**. For other pausal forms, see Ecclesiastes 1:4 and 1:7 on pages 155 and 157.

3:23 In this text, King Solomon refers to two women using the demonstrative pronoun **זֹאת** (**this**). When demonstrative pronouns are repeated in close succession, try translating them as **the one . . . the other**.

לֹא כִּי בְּנֵךְ הַמֵּת וּבְנִי הֶחָי׃ 24 וַיֹּאמֶר הַמֶּלֶךְ קְחוּ
לִי־חָרֶב וַיָּבִאוּ הַחֶרֶב לִפְנֵי הַמֶּלֶךְ׃ 25 וַיֹּאמֶר הַמֶּלֶךְ
גִּזְרוּ אֶת־הַיֶּלֶד הַחַי לִשְׁנָיִם וּתְנוּ אֶת־הַחֲצִי לְאַחַת
וְאֶת־הַחֲצִי לְאֶחָת׃ 26 וַתֹּאמֶר הָאִשָּׁה אֲשֶׁר־בְּנָהּ הַחַי
אֶל־הַמֶּלֶךְ כִּי־נִכְמְרוּ רַחֲמֶיהָ עַל־בְּנָהּ וַתֹּאמֶר בִּי
אֲדֹנִי

לֹא כִּי בְּנֵךְ הַמֵּת	'No, because your son is the dead one,
וּבְנִי הֶחָי׃	and my son is the living one.'"
24 וַיֹּאמֶר הַמֶּלֶךְ קְחוּ לִי־חָרֶב	So the king said, "Bring me a sword."
וַיָּבִאוּ הַחֶרֶב לִפְנֵי הַמֶּלֶךְ׃	And a sword was brought before the king.
25 וַיֹּאמֶר הַמֶּלֶךְ	And the king said,
גִּזְרוּ אֶת־הַיֶּלֶד הַחַי לִשְׁנָיִם	"Cut the living child in two,
וּתְנוּ אֶת־הַחֲצִי לְאַחַת	and give half to one
וְאֶת־הַחֲצִי לְאֶחָת׃	and the (other) half to the other."
26 וַתֹּאמֶר הָאִשָּׁה אֲשֶׁר־בְּנָהּ הַחַי	Then the woman whose son was alive said
אֶל־הַמֶּלֶךְ	to the king,
כִּי־נִכְמְרוּ רַחֲמֶיהָ עַל־בְּנָהּ	because her feelings grew tender for her son,
וַתֹּאמֶר בִּי אֲדֹנִי	"Please, my Lord,

NEW VOCABULARY

גִּזְרוּ	(you) cut in two
הַחֲצִי	the half
נִכְמְרוּ	(they) grew tender
רַחֲמֶיהָ	her feelings
בִּי	please

VERB ANALYSIS

VERB	ROOT	PATTERN	MEANING	TENSE	P/G/N	SUFFIX
הַמֵּת	מ.ו.ת	פָּעַל	die	participle	ms	
וַיֹּאמֶר	א.מ.ר	פָּעַל	say	rv imperfect	3ms	
קְחוּ	ל.ק.ח	פָּעַל	take	command	mp	
וַיָּבִאוּ	ב.ו.א	הִפְעִיל	bring	rv imperfect	3mp	
גִּזְרוּ	ג.ז.ר	פָּעַל	cut, divide	command	mp	
וּתְנוּ	נ.ת.ן	פָּעַל	give, set	command	mp	
וַתֹּאמֶר	א.מ.ר	פָּעַל	say	rv imperfect	3fs	
נִכְמְרוּ	כ.מ.ר	נִפְעַל	grow tender	perfect	3cp	

GRAMMATICAL NOTES

3:24 So far, this story features three characters: the king and the two women. Yet this verse reads, וַיָּבִאוּ הַחֶרֶב לִפְנֵי הַמֶּלֶךְ (**. . . they brought a sword before the king**). Who are the **they** in this passage? In fact, you need not supply a **they** at all. The mp subject of the verb ב.ו.א is not named, as these characters are not important to the story. When a Hebrew passage like this includes an unnamed 3mp subject, you may want to translate it as if the verb were in נִפְעַל or another passive construction. Notice that our translation does not specify the subject of וַיָּבִאוּ .

3:25 In this verse, the word אַחַת (**one**) functions as a pronoun and refers to each of the two women. As in 3:23, this pronoun is repeated within the verse and is best translated as **the one . . . the other one**. Also note that the Hebrew says **the half**, while the translation gives only **half** in Solomon's speech.

3:26 וַתֹּאמֶר (**and she said**) is redundant in this verse and should not be in your translation. Hebrew uses such repetition to resume the action of a main clause after a dependent one, but English does not.

תְּנוּ־לָהּ אֶת־הַיָּלוּד הַחַי וְהָמֵת אַל־תְּמִיתֻהוּ וְזֹאת
אֹמֶרֶת גַּם־לִי גַם־לָךְ לֹא יִהְיֶה גְּזֹרוּ׃ 27 וַיַּעַן הַמֶּלֶךְ
וַיֹּאמֶר תְּנוּ־לָהּ אֶת־הַיָּלוּד הַחַי וְהָמֵת לֹא תְמִיתֻהוּ
הִיא אִמּוֹ׃ 28 וַיִּשְׁמְעוּ כָל־יִשְׂרָאֵל אֶת־הַמִּשְׁפָּט אֲשֶׁר
שָׁפַט הַמֶּלֶךְ וַיִּרְאוּ מִפְּנֵי הַמֶּלֶךְ כִּי רָאוּ כִּי־חָכְמַת
אֱלֹהִים בְּקִרְבּוֹ לַעֲשׂוֹת מִשְׁפָּט׃

תְּנוּ־לָהּ אֶת־הַיָּלוּד הַחַי	give her the one born alive
וְהָמֵת אַל־תְּמִיתֻהוּ	and please, do not kill him."
וְזֹאת אֹמֶרֶת	But the other one said,
גַּם־לִי גַם־לָךְ לֹא יִהְיֶה גְּזֹרוּ׃	"It shall be neither mine nor yours; split it."
27 וַיַּעַן הַמֶּלֶךְ וַיֹּאמֶר	Then the king answered and said,
תְּנוּ־לָהּ אֶת־הַיָּלוּד הַחַי	"Give her the living child,
וְהָמֵת לֹא תְמִיתֻהוּ הִיא אִמּוֹ׃	and by no means kill it. She is his mother."
28 וַיִּשְׁמְעוּ כָל־יִשְׂרָאֵל	All of Israel heard
אֶת־הַמִּשְׁפָּט אֲשֶׁר שָׁפַט הַמֶּלֶךְ	the judgment that the king rendered.
וַיִּרְאוּ מִפְּנֵי הַמֶּלֶךְ	And they stood in awe of the king,
כִּי רָאוּ כִּי־חָכְמַת אֱלֹהִים בְּקִרְבּוֹ	for they saw that the wisdom of God was in him
לַעֲשׂוֹת מִשְׁפָּט׃	to impart justice.

NEW VOCABULARY

הַיִּלּוֹד	the one born
גִּזְרוּ	(you) split it

VERB ANALYSIS

VERB	ROOT	PATTERN	MEANING	TENSE	P/G/N	SUFFIX
תְּנוּ	נ.ת.ן	פָּעַל	give, set	command	mp	
הַיִּלּוֹד	י.ל.ד	פָּעַל	bear, beget	p. participle	ms	
וְהָמֵת	מ.ו.ת	הִפְעִיל	kill	emph. inf.		
תְּמִיתֻהוּ	מ.ו.ת	הִפְעִיל	kill	imperfect	2mp	3ms
אֹמֶרֶת	א.מ.ר	פָּעַל	say	participle	fs	
יִהְיֶה	ה.י.ה	פָּעַל	be, become	imperfect	3ms	
גְּזֹרוּ	ג.ז.ר	פָּעַל	cut, divide	command	mp	
וַיַּעַן	ע.נ.ה	פָּעַל	answer	rv imperfect	3ms	
וַיֹּאמֶר	א.מ.ר	פָּעַל	say	rv imperfect	3ms	
וַיִּשְׁמְעוּ	שׁ.מ.ע	פָּעַל	hear	rv imperfect	3mp	
שָׁפַט	שׁ.פ.ט	פָּעַל	judge	perfect	3ms	
וַיִּרְאוּ	י.ר.א	פָּעַל	fear	rv imperfect	3mp	
רָאוּ	ר.א.ה	פָּעַל	see	perfect	3cp	
לַעֲשׂוֹת	ע.שׂ.ה	פָּעַל	make, do	infinitive		

GRAMMATICAL NOTES

3:28 Notice that the noun **judgment** (מִשְׁפָּט) and the verb **to judge** (שָׁפַט) build from the same root and appear in the same clause. English speakers usually avoid such repetition whenever possible. However, it is good style in Hebrew to use related words for a verb and the object of that verb. The Bible frequently describes characters **fearing fears** and **dreaming dreams**. The technical term for this is the **cognate accusative**: **cognate** meaning related through root and **accusative** meaning the direct object of a verb. Look for this again in Ecclesiastes 1:3 on page 155.

3:28 **To fear before** (י.ר.א. מִן־) is the Hebrew formula for to **stand in awe of**.

1 [1]וַיְהִי דְּבַר־יְהוָה אֶל־יוֹנָה בֶן־אֲמִתַּי לֵאמֹר׃ [2]קוּם
לֵךְ אֶל־נִינְוֵה הָעִיר הַגְּדוֹלָה וּקְרָא עָלֶיהָ כִּי־עָלְתָה
רָעָתָם לְפָנָי׃ [3]וַיָּקָם יוֹנָה לִבְרֹחַ תַּרְשִׁישָׁה מִלִּפְנֵי
יְהוָה וַיֵּרֶד יָפוֹ וַיִּמְצָא אֳנִיָּה בָּאָה תַרְשִׁישׁ וַיִּתֵּן
שְׂכָרָהּ וַיֵּרֶד בָּהּ לָבוֹא עִמָּהֶם תַּרְשִׁישָׁה מִלִּפְנֵי יְהוָה׃

[1]וַיְהִי דְּבַר־יְהוָה אֶל־יוֹנָה	Now the word of the LORD came to Jonah,
בֶן־אֲמִתַּי לֵאמֹר׃	the son of Amittai,
[2]קוּם לֵךְ אֶל־נִינְוֵה הָעִיר הַגְּדוֹלָה	"Arise! Go to Nineveh, the great city,
וּקְרָא עָלֶיהָ	and call out against it,
כִּי־עָלְתָה רָעָתָם לְפָנָי׃	for their wickedness has come up before me."
[3]וַיָּקָם יוֹנָה לִבְרֹחַ תַּרְשִׁישָׁה	So Jonah arose to flee to Tarshish,
מִלִּפְנֵי יְהוָה	away from the LORD.
וַיֵּרֶד יָפוֹ וַיִּמְצָא אֳנִיָּה	He went down to Joppa and found a ship
בָּאָה תַרְשִׁישׁ	going to Tarshish,
וַיִּתֵּן שְׂכָרָהּ וַיֵּרֶד בָּהּ	paid (lit. gave) its fare, and went down in it
לָבוֹא עִמָּהֶם תַּרְשִׁישָׁה	to go with them to Tarshish,
מִלִּפְנֵי יְהוָה׃	away from the LORD.

NEW VOCABULARY

יוֹנָה	Jonah	תַּרְשִׁישָׁה	to Tarshish
אֲמִתַּי	Amittai	מִלִּפְנֵי	away from
נִינְוֵה	Nineveh	יָפוֹ	Joppa
רָעָתָם	their wickedness	אֳנִיָּה	a ship
לִבְרֹחַ	to flee	שְׂכָרָהּ	its fare

VERB ANALYSIS

VERB	ROOT	PATTERN	MEANING	TENSE	P/G/N	SUFFIX
וַיְהִי	ה.י.ה	פָּעַל	be, become	rv imperfect	3ms	
לֵאמֹר	א.מ.ר	פָּעַל	say	infinitive		
קוּם	ק.ו.ם	פָּעַל	arise	command	ms	
לֵךְ	ה.ל.ך	פָּעַל	walk, go	command	ms	
וּקְרָא	ק.ר.א	פָּעַל	call, proclaim	command	ms	
עָלְתָה	ע.ל.ה	פָּעַל	go up	perfect	3fs	
וַיָּקָם	ק.ו.ם	פָּעַל	arise	rv imperfect	3ms	
לִבְרֹחַ	ב.ר.ח	פָּעַל	flee	infinitive		
וַיֵּרֶד	י.ר.ד	פָּעַל	go down	rv imperfect	3ms	
וַיִּמְצָא	מ.צ.א	פָּעַל	find	rv imperfect	3ms	
בָּאָה	ב.ו.א	פָּעַל	come	participle	fs	
וַיִּתֵּן	נ.ת.ן	פָּעַל	give, set	rv imperfect	3ms	
לָבוֹא	ב.ו.א	פָּעַל	come	infinitive		

GRAMMATICAL NOTES

1:2 The pronouns **it** and **their** both refer to the city Nineveh. Notice that the first is singular and the second is plural. עִיר (**city**) is a collective plural, a singular noun made up of many parts. **It** refers to the city as a whole, while **their** refers to the residents of Nineveh.

1:3 Jonah flees to the city תַּרְשִׁישׁ (**Tarshish**). The **אָה** attached to this name is the **ה of direction.** See page 86 in *The First Hebrew Primer.*

1:3 מִלִּפְנֵי is made up of מִן (**from**) and לִפְנֵי (**before**).

4 וַיהוָה הֵטִיל רוּחַ־גְּדוֹלָה אֶל־הַיָּם וַיְהִי סַעַר־גָּדוֹל
בַּיָּם וְהָאֳנִיָּה חִשְּׁבָה לְהִשָּׁבֵר׃ 5 וַיִּירְאוּ הַמַּלָּחִים
וַיִּזְעֲקוּ אִישׁ אֶל־אֱלֹהָיו וַיָּטִלוּ אֶת־הַכֵּלִים אֲשֶׁר
בָּאֳנִיָּה אֶל־הַיָּם לְהָקֵל מֵעֲלֵיהֶם וְיוֹנָה יָרַד
אֶל־יַרְכְּתֵי הַסְּפִינָה וַיִּשְׁכַּב וַיֵּרָדַם׃ 6 וַיִּקְרַב אֵלָיו רַב
הַחֹבֵל וַיֹּאמֶר לוֹ

4 וַיהוָה הֵטִיל רוּחַ־גְּדוֹלָה אֶל־הַיָּם	But the LORD hurled a great wind upon the sea,
וַיְהִי סַעַר־גָּדוֹל בַּיָּם	and there was a great storm on the sea,
וְהָאֳנִיָּה חִשְּׁבָה לְהִשָּׁבֵר׃	and the ship was about to be broken up.
5 וַיִּירְאוּ הַמַּלָּחִים	And the sailors were afraid
וַיִּזְעֲקוּ אִישׁ אֶל־אֱלֹהָיו	and cried out, each to his god,
וַיָּטִלוּ אֶת־הַכֵּלִים	and they cast out their cargo,
אֲשֶׁר בָּאֳנִיָּה אֶל־הַיָּם	which was on the ship, to the sea
לְהָקֵל מֵעֲלֵיהֶם	to make (it) light for them.
וְיוֹנָה יָרַד אֶל־יַרְכְּתֵי הַסְּפִינָה	And Jonah went down to the bowels of the ship
וַיִּשְׁכַּב וַיֵּרָדַם׃	and lay down and was fast asleep.
6 וַיִּקְרַב אֵלָיו רַב הַחֹבֵל	The captain approached him
וַיֹּאמֶר לוֹ	and said to him,

NEW VOCABULARY

חֵטִיל	hurled
סַעַר	storm
וְהָאֳנִיָּה	and the ship
חִשְּׁבָה	was about to
הַמַּלָּחִים	the sailors
וַיִּזְעֲקוּ	and (they) cried out
וַיָּטִלוּ	they cast out
לְהָקֵל	to make (it) light
מֵעֲלֵיהֶם	from upon them
יַרְכְּתֵי	the bowels of
הַסְּפִינָה	the ship
וַיֵּרָדַם	was fast asleep
וַיִּקְרַב	and (he) approached
רַב הַחֹבֵל	the captain

VERB ANALYSIS

VERB	ROOT	PATTERN	MEANING	TENSE	P/G/N	SUFFIX
הֵטִיל	ט.ו.ל	הִפְעִיל	cast, hurl	perfect	3ms	
וַיְהִי	ה.י.ה	פָּעַל	be, become	rv imperfect	3ms	
חִשְּׁבָה	ח.ש.ב	פִּעֵל	think, plan	perfect	3fs	
לְהִשָּׁבֵר	ש.ב.ר	נִפְעַל	be broken	infinitive		
וַיִּירְאוּ	י.ר.א	פָּעַל	fear	rv imperfect	3mp	
וַיִּזְעֲקוּ	ז.ע.ק	פָּעַל	cry, cry out	rv imperfect	3mp	
וַיָּטִלוּ	ט.ו.ל	הִפְעִיל	cast, hurl	rv imperfect	3mp	
לְהָקֵל	ק.ל.ל	הִפְעִיל	make light	infinitive		
יָרַד	י.ר.ד	פָּעַל	go down	perfect	3ms	
וַיִּשְׁכַּב	ש.כ.ב	פָּעַל	lie, lie down	rv imperfect	3ms	
וַיֵּרָדַם	ר.ד.ם	נִפְעַל	be fast asleep	rv imperfect	3ms	
וַיִּקְרַב	ק.ר.ב	פָּעַל	come near	rv imperfect	3ms	
וַיֹּאמֶר	א.מ.ר	פָּעַל	say	rv imperfect	3ms	

GRAMMATICAL NOTES

1:4 ח.ש.ב usually means to **think**, **reckon**, or **invent**. Here the text anthropomorphizes the boat and says that it was **planning to break up**.

1:5 The word for **sailor** (מַלָּח) derives from **to salt** (מ.ל.ח).

מַה־לְּךָ נִרְדָּם קוּם קְרָא אֶל־אֱלֹהֶיךָ אוּלַי יִתְעַשֵּׁת
הָאֱלֹהִים לָנוּ וְלֹא נֹאבֵד׃ 7 וַיֹּאמְרוּ אִישׁ אֶל־רֵעֵהוּ
לְכוּ וְנַפִּילָה גוֹרָלוֹת וְנֵדְעָה בְּשֶׁלְּמִי הָרָעָה הַזֹּאת
לָנוּ וַיַּפִּלוּ גּוֹרָלוֹת וַיִּפֹּל הַגּוֹרָל עַל־יוֹנָה׃ 8 וַיֹּאמְרוּ
אֵלָיו הַגִּידָה־נָּא לָנוּ בַּאֲשֶׁר לְמִי־הָרָעָה הַזֹּאת לָנוּ

מַה־לְּךָ נִרְדָּם	"What is with you, sleeper?
קוּם קְרָא אֶל־אֱלֹהֶיךָ	Get up, call to your God;
אוּלַי יִתְעַשֵּׁת הָאֱלֹהִים לָנוּ	perhaps God will consider us
וְלֹא נֹאבֵד׃	and we will not perish."
7 וַיֹּאמְרוּ אִישׁ אֶל־רֵעֵהוּ	And they said, each to his friend,
לְכוּ וְנַפִּילָה גוֹרָלוֹת	"Come, let us cast lots
וְנֵדְעָה בְּשֶׁלְּמִי	so we will know on account of whom
הָרָעָה הַזֹּאת לָנוּ	this evil thing (is) on us."
וַיַּפִּלוּ גּוֹרָלוֹת	So they cast lots
וַיִּפֹּל הַגּוֹרָל עַל־יוֹנָה׃	and the lot fell on Jonah.
8 וַיֹּאמְרוּ אֵלָיו הַגִּידָה־נָּא לָנוּ	And they said to him, "Tell us,
בַּאֲשֶׁר לְמִי־הָרָעָה הַזֹּאת לָנוּ	on account of whom (is) this evil thing on us?

NEW VOCABULARY

וְנַפִּילָה גוֹרָלוֹת	let us cast lots	נִרְדָּם	sleeper
בְּשֶׁלְּמִי	on account of whom	אוּלַי	perhaps
וַיַּפִּלוּ גּוֹרָלוֹת	so they cast lots	יִתְעַשֵּׁת	(he) will consider
וַיִּפֹּל הַגּוֹרָל	and the lot fell	נֹאבֵד	we will perish

בַּאֲשֶׁר לְמִי־ on account of whom?

VERB ANALYSIS

VERB	ROOT	PATTERN	MEANING	TENSE	P/G/N	SUFFIX
נִרְדָּם	ר.ד.ם	נִפְעַל	be fast asleep	participle	ms	
קוּם	ק.ו.ם	פָּעַל	arise	command	ms	
קְרָא	ק.ר.א	פָּעַל	call, proclaim	command	ms	
יִתְעַשֵּׁת	ע.ש.ת	הִתְפַּעֵל	think	imperfect	3ms	
נֹאבֵד	א.ב.ד	פָּעַל	lose, perish	imperfect	1cp	
וַיֹּאמְרוּ	א.מ.ר	פָּעַל	say	rv imperfect	3mp	
לְכוּ	ה.ל.ך	פָּעַל	walk, go	command	mp	
וְנַפִּילָה	נ.פ.ל	הִפְעִיל	cast	cohortative	1cp	
וְנֵדְעָה	י.ד.ע	פָּעַל	know	cohortative	1cp	
וַיַּפִּלוּ	נ.פ.ל	הִפְעִיל	cast	rv imperfect	3mp	
וַיִּפֹּל	נ.פ.ל	פָּעַל	fall	rv imperfect	3ms	
הַגִּידָה	נ.ג.ד	הִפְעִיל	declare, tell	command	ms	

GRAMMATICAL NOTES

1:6 רַב (**many, much, a lot of**) also can mean **chief** or **head**. Here, רַב works with חֹבֵל (**sailor**) and designates the captain.

1:7 אִישׁ . . . אֶל־רֵעֵהוּ is a way to express **to one another.**

1:8 Look at the command הַגִּידָה־נָּא. First, remember that אָה may be attached to any ms command (see Exodus 32:10 on page 31). Second, notice the particle נָא at the end of the word. נָא can be found after commands, jussives, and cohortatives. It expresses urgency, entreaty, or encouragement.

מַה־מְּלַאכְתְּךָ וּמֵאַיִן תָּבוֹא מָה אַרְצֶךָ וְאֵי־מִזֶּה עַם
אָתָּה׃ 9 וַיֹּאמֶר אֲלֵיהֶם עִבְרִי אָנֹכִי וְאֶת־יְהוָה אֱלֹהֵי
הַשָּׁמַיִם אֲנִי יָרֵא אֲשֶׁר־עָשָׂה אֶת־הַיָּם וְאֶת־הַיַּבָּשָׁה׃
10 וַיִּירְאוּ הָאֲנָשִׁים יִרְאָה גְדוֹלָה וַיֹּאמְרוּ אֵלָיו
מַה־זֹּאת עָשִׂיתָ כִּי־יָדְעוּ הָאֲנָשִׁים כִּי־מִלִּפְנֵי יְהוָה
הוּא בֹרֵחַ כִּי הִגִּיד לָהֶם׃

מַה־מְּלַאכְתְּךָ	What is your occupation?
וּמֵאַיִן תָּבוֹא	From where do you come?
מָה אַרְצֶךָ	What is your land
וְאֵי־מִזֶּה עַם אָתָּה׃	and from which people are you?"
9 וַיֹּאמֶר אֲלֵיהֶם עִבְרִי אָנֹכִי	And he (Jonah) said to them, "I am a Hebrew,
וְאֶת־יְהוָה אֱלֹהֵי הַשָּׁמַיִם אֲנִי יָרֵא	and I fear the LORD, the God of heaven,
אֲשֶׁר־עָשָׂה אֶת־הַיָּם וְאֶת־הַיַּבָּשָׁה׃	who made the sea and the dry land."
10 וַיִּירְאוּ הָאֲנָשִׁים יִרְאָה גְדוֹלָה	And the men were very afraid
וַיֹּאמְרוּ אֵלָיו מַה־זֹּאת עָשִׂיתָ	and said to him, "What is this you have done?"
כִּי־יָדְעוּ הָאֲנָשִׁים	For the men knew
כִּי־מִלִּפְנֵי יְהוָה הוּא בֹרֵחַ	that he was running away from the LORD,
כִּי הִגִּיד לָהֶם׃	because (Jonah) had told them.

NEW VOCABULARY

מְלַאכְתְּךָ	your occupation
וּמֵאַיִן	from where
וְאֵי־מִזֶּה	and from which
עִבְרִי	a Hebrew
הַיַּבָּשָׁה	the dry land
מִלִּפְנֵי	away from
בֹּרֵחַ	was running away

VERB ANALYSIS

VERB	ROOT	PATTERN	MEANING	TENSE	P/G/N	SUFFIX
תָּבוֹא	ב.ו.א	פָּעַל	come	imperfect	2ms	
וַיֹּאמֶר	א.מ.ר	פָּעַל	say	rv imperfect	3ms	
יָרֵא	י.ר.א	פָּעַל	fear	participle	ms	
עָשָׂה	ע.שׂ.ה	פָּעַל	make, do	perfect	3ms	
וַיִּירְאוּ	י.ר.א	פָּעַל	fear	rv imperfect	3mp	
וַיֹּאמְרוּ	א.מ.ר	פָּעַל	say	rv imperfect	3mp	
עָשִׂיתָ	ע.שׂ.ה	פָּעַל	make, do	perfect	2ms	
יָדְעוּ	י.ד.ע	פָּעַל	know	perfect	3cp	
בֹּרֵחַ	ב.ר.ח	פָּעַל	flee	participle	ms	
הִגִּיד	נ.ג.ד	הִפְעִיל	declare, tell	perfect	3ms	

GRAMMATICAL NOTE

1:10 We translated כִּי הִגִּיד לָהֶם as **because Jonah had told them**. When you translate a perfect verb into the English past tense, you have three main options.

1. Simple past: Jonah **told** them.
2. Present perfect: Jonah **has told** them.
3. Past perfect: Jonah **had told** them.

The first choice indicates that the action is complete. The second choice suggests that the action is complete but affects the present. The third choice is used when the verbal action precedes that of another verb. The past perfect is the best choice for this sentence because Jonah told the men about his plan in the past and continues to flee in the present.

11 וַיֹּאמְרוּ אֵלָיו מַה־נַּעֲשֶׂה לָּךְ וְיִשְׁתֹּק הַיָּם מֵעָלֵינוּ
כִּי הַיָּם הוֹלֵךְ וְסֹעֵר׃ 12 וַיֹּאמֶר אֲלֵיהֶם שָׂאוּנִי וַהֲטִילֻנִי
אֶל־הַיָּם וְיִשְׁתֹּק הַיָּם מֵעֲלֵיכֶם כִּי יוֹדֵעַ אָנִי כִּי בְשֶׁלִּי
הַסַּעַר הַגָּדוֹל הַזֶּה עֲלֵיכֶם׃ 13 וַיַּחְתְּרוּ הָאֲנָשִׁים
לְהָשִׁיב אֶל־הַיַּבָּשָׁה וְלֹא יָכֹלוּ כִּי הַיָּם הוֹלֵךְ וְסֹעֵר
עֲלֵיהֶם׃

11 וַיֹּאמְרוּ אֵלָיו מַה־נַּעֲשֶׂה לָּךְ	So they said to him, "What shall we do to you
וְיִשְׁתֹּק הַיָּם מֵעָלֵינוּ	so that the sea will be quiet for us?"
כִּי הַיָּם הוֹלֵךְ וְסֹעֵר׃	For the sea grew more and more stormy.
12 וַיֹּאמֶר אֲלֵיהֶם שָׂאוּנִי	And he said to them, "Lift me
וַהֲטִילֻנִי אֶל־הַיָּם	and cast me into the sea,
וְיִשְׁתֹּק הַיָּם מֵעֲלֵיכֶם	and the sea will be quiet for you.
כִּי יוֹדֵעַ אָנִי כִּי בְשֶׁלִּי	For I know that (it is) on my account
הַסַּעַר הַגָּדוֹל הַזֶּה עֲלֵיכֶם׃	(that) this great storm (has come) against you."
13 וַיַּחְתְּרוּ הָאֲנָשִׁים	But the men rowed
לְהָשִׁיב אֶל־הַיַּבָּשָׁה וְלֹא יָכֹלוּ	to return to dry land, but they could not,
כִּי הַיָּם	because the sea
הוֹלֵךְ וְסֹעֵר עֲלֵיהֶם׃	grew more and more stormy around them.

NEW VOCABULARY

וְיִשְׁתֹּק	(it) will be quiet
וְסֹעֵר	and stormy
וַהֲטִילֻנִי	and cast me
בְּשֶׁלִּי	(it is) on my account
הַסַּעַר	the storm
וַיַּחְתְּרוּ	but (they) rowed
הַיַּבָּשָׁה	to dry land

VERB ANALYSIS

VERB	ROOT	PATTERN	MEANING	TENSE	P/G/N	SUFFIX
וַיֹּאמְרוּ	א.מ.ר	פָּעַל	say	rv imperfect	3mp	
נַעֲשֶׂה	ע.שׂ.ה	פָּעַל	make, do	imperfect	1cp	
וְיִשְׁתֹּק	שׁ.ת.ק	פָּעַל	be quiet	imperfect	3ms	
הוֹלֵךְ	ה.ל.ךְ	פָּעַל	walk, go	participle	ms	
וְסֹעֵר	ס.ע.ר	פָּעַל	storm, rage	participle	ms	
וַיֹּאמֶר	א.מ.ר	פָּעַל	say	rv imperfect	3ms	
שָׂאוּנִי	נ.שׂ.א	פָּעַל	lift, carry	command	mp	1cs
וַהֲטִילֻנִי	ט.ו.ל	הִפְעִיל	cast, hurl	command	mp	1cs
יוֹדֵעַ	י.ד.ע	פָּעַל	know	participle	ms	
וַיַּחְתְּרוּ	ח.ת.ר	פָּעַל	dig, row	rv imperfect	3mp	
לְהָשִׁיב	שׁ.ו.ב	הִפְעִיל	restore	infinitive		
יָכֹלוּ	י.כ.ל	פָּעַל	be able	perfect	3cp	

GRAMMATICAL NOTES

1:11, 1:12 When ה.ל.ךְ is the first of two participles, it is an idiom expressing something growing or increasing. Do not translate וְסֹעֵר הַיָּם הוֹלֵךְ as **the sea was going and storming.**

1:13 שׁ.ו.ב in the הִפְעִיל means **restore**, **bring back**, or **cause to return.** If you choose the first meaning, the men rowed to **regain** the dry land. If you choose the second or third, the men rowed to **return the boat** to dry land. We translated the verb as a פָּעַל.

14 וַיִּקְרְאוּ אֶל־יְהוָה וַיֹּאמְרוּ אָנָּה יְהוָה אַל־נָא
נֹאבְדָה בְּנֶפֶשׁ הָאִישׁ הַזֶּה וְאַל־תִּתֵּן עָלֵינוּ דָּם נָקִיא
כִּי־אַתָּה יְהוָה כַּאֲשֶׁר חָפַצְתָּ עָשִׂיתָ׃ 15 וַיִּשְׂאוּ
אֶת־יוֹנָה וַיְטִלֻהוּ אֶל־הַיָּם וַיַּעֲמֹד הַיָּם מִזַּעְפּוֹ׃
16 וַיִּירְאוּ הָאֲנָשִׁים יִרְאָה גְדוֹלָה אֶת־יְהוָה
וַיִּזְבְּחוּ־זֶבַח לַיהוָה וַיִּדְּרוּ נְדָרִים׃

14 וַיִּקְרְאוּ אֶל־יְהוָה וַיֹּאמְרוּ	They called to the LORD and said,
אָנָּה יְהוָה אַל־נָא נֹאבְדָה	"We beg you, LORD, do not let us perish
בְּנֶפֶשׁ הָאִישׁ הַזֶּה	for the life of this man
וְאַל־תִּתֵּן עָלֵינוּ דָּם נָקִיא	and do not lay innocent blood on us,
כִּי־אַתָּה יְהוָה	for you, LORD,
כַּאֲשֶׁר חָפַצְתָּ עָשִׂיתָ׃	have done as you pleased."
15 וַיִּשְׂאוּ אֶת־יוֹנָה	And they lifted Jonah
וַיְטִלֻהוּ אֶל־הַיָּם	and cast him into the sea,
וַיַּעֲמֹד הַיָּם מִזַּעְפּוֹ׃	and the sea ceased from its raging.
16 וַיִּירְאוּ הָאֲנָשִׁים יִרְאָה גְדוֹלָה	The men greatly feared
אֶת־יְהוָה וַיִּזְבְּחוּ־זֶבַח לַיהוָה	the LORD, and they sacrificed to the LORD
וַיִּדְּרוּ נְדָרִים׃	and made vows.

NEW VOCABULARY

מִזַּעְפּוֹ	from its raging	אָנָּה	we beg you
וַיִּזְבְּחוּ	they sacrificed	נֹאבְדָה	let us perish
זֶבַח	sacrifice	נָקִיא	innocent
וַיִּדְּרוּ	and they vowed	חָפַצְתָּ	you pleased
נְדָרִים	vows	וַיְטִלֻהוּ	and they cast him

VERB ANALYSIS

VERB	ROOT	PATTERN	MEANING	TENSE	P/G/N	SUFFIX
וַיִּקְרְאוּ	ק.ר.א	פָּעַל	call, proclaim	rv imperfect	3mp	
וַיֹּאמְרוּ	א.מ.ר	פָּעַל	say	rv imperfect	3mp	
נֹאבְדָה	א.ב.ד	פָּעַל	lose, perish	cohortative	1cp	
תִּתֵּן	נ.ת.ן	פָּעַל	give, set	imperfect	2ms	
חָפַצְתָּ	ח.פ.ץ	פָּעַל	please, delight	perfect	2ms	
עָשִׂיתָ	ע.שׂ.ה	פָּעַל	make, do	perfect	2ms	
וַיִּשְׂאוּ	נ.שׂ.א	פָּעַל	lift, carry	rv imperfect	3mp	
וַיְטִלֻהוּ	ט.ו.ל	הִפְעִיל	cast, hurl	rv imperfect	3mp	3ms
וַיַּעֲמֹד	ע.מ.ד	פָּעַל	stand	rv imperfect	3ms	
וַיִּירְאוּ	י.ר.א	פָּעַל	fear	rv imperfect	3mp	
וַיִּזְבְּחוּ	ז.ב.ח	פָּעַל	sacrifice	rv imperfect	3mp	
וַיִּדְּרוּ	נ.ד.ר	פָּעַל	vow	rv imperfect	3mp	

GRAMMATICAL NOTES

1:14 אָנָּה (**we beg you**) is a variant of אָנָּא, which is a composite of אָהּ (**ah, alas**) and the particle נָא. אָנָּה precedes an urgent request or command.

1:15 ע.מ.ד (**stand**) can also mean **stand still** or **stop**.

1:16 This verse contains three **cognate accusatives.** (For an explanation of the term, see I Kings 3:28 on page 103.) To make the English sound natural, do not let the verb and direct object repeat. In place of **they feared great fears**, write **they greatly feared**. For **they sacrificed a sacrifice**, try **they sacrificed** or **they offered a sacrifice**, and for **they vowed vows**, translate **they made vows**.

2 1 וַיְמַן יְהוָה דָּג גָּדוֹל לִבְלֹעַ אֶת־יוֹנָה וַיְהִי יוֹנָה
בִּמְעֵי הַדָּג שְׁלֹשָׁה יָמִים וּשְׁלֹשָׁה לֵילוֹת׃ 2 וַיִּתְפַּלֵּל
יוֹנָה אֶל־יְהוָה אֱלֹהָיו מִמְּעֵי הַדָּגָה׃

1 וַיְמַן יְהוָה דָּג גָּדוֹל	The LORD appointed a big fish
לִבְלֹעַ אֶת־יוֹנָה	to swallow Jonah,
וַיְהִי יוֹנָה בִּמְעֵי הַדָּג	and Jonah was in the belly of the fish
שְׁלֹשָׁה יָמִים וּשְׁלֹשָׁה לֵילוֹת׃	three days and three nights.
2 וַיִּתְפַּלֵּל יוֹנָה אֶל־יְהוָה אֱלֹהָיו	And Jonah prayed to the LORD his God
מִמְּעֵי הַדָּגָה׃	from the belly of the fish.

NEW VOCABULARY

בִּמְעֵי	in the belly of	וַיְמַן	(he) appointed
וַיִּתְפַּלֵּל	and (he) prayed	דָּג	fish
מִמְּעֵי	from the belly of	לִבְלֹעַ	to swallow

VERB ANALYSIS

VERB	ROOT	PATTERN	MEANING	TENSE	P/G/N	SUFFIX
וַיְמַן	מ.נ.ה	פִּעֵל	appoint	rv imperfect	3ms	
לִבְלֹעַ	ב.ל.ע	פָּעַל	swallow	infinitive		
וַיְהִי	ה.י.ה	פָּעַל	be, become	rv imperfect	3ms	
וַיִּתְפַּלֵּל	פ.ל.ל	הִתְפַּעֵל	pray	rv imperfect	3ms	

GRAMMATICAL NOTES

What happens next? Jonah does not stay in the fish. He offers his prayer to God, and at the end of chapter two the text reports:

וַיֹּאמֶר יְהוָה לַדָּג וַיָּקֵא אֶת־יוֹנָה אֶל־הַיַּבָּשָׁה׃

And the LORD spoke to the fish, and it (the fish) spewed Jonah out onto dry land.

In chapters three and four Jonah travels to Nineveh, the Ninevite king repents, the LORD decides to spare Nineveh, and Jonah and the LORD have a conversation about salvation and mercy.

Jonah is a late biblical composition. Evidence for this is in the Late Hebrew and Aramaic words. These include ע.שׁ.ת (1:6), שׁ.ת.ק (1:11), ח.ת.ר (1:13), ז.ע.ף (1:15), and מ.נ.ה in the פִּעֵל (2:1).

4 1 וְהָיָה בְּאַחֲרִית הַיָּמִים יִהְיֶה הַר בֵּית־יְהוָה נָכוֹן
בְּרֹאשׁ הֶהָרִים וְנִשָּׂא הוּא מִגְּבָעוֹת וְנָהֲרוּ עָלָיו
עַמִּים׃ 2 וְהָלְכוּ גּוֹיִם רַבִּים וְאָמְרוּ לְכוּ וְנַעֲלֶה
אֶל־הַר־יְהוָה וְאֶל־בֵּית אֱלֹהֵי יַעֲקֹב וְיוֹרֵנוּ מִדְּרָכָיו
וְנֵלְכָה בְּאֹרְחֹתָיו כִּי מִצִּיּוֹן תֵּצֵא תוֹרָה וּדְבַר־יְהוָה
מִירוּשָׁלִָם׃

1 וְהָיָה בְּאַחֲרִית הַיָּמִים	In the end of the days
יִהְיֶה הַר בֵּית־יְהוָה	the mountain of the LORD's house will be
נָכוֹן בְּרֹאשׁ הֶהָרִים	established at the top of the mountains
וְנִשָּׂא הוּא מִגְּבָעוֹת	and (will be) raised above the hills.
וְנָהֲרוּ עָלָיו עַמִּים׃	Peoples will stream to it,
2 וְהָלְכוּ גּוֹיִם רַבִּים וְאָמְרוּ	and many nations will go and say,
לְכוּ וְנַעֲלֶה אֶל־הַר־יְהוָה	"Come, let us go up to the mountain of the LORD,
וְאֶל־בֵּית אֱלֹהֵי יַעֲקֹב	to the house of the God of Jacob,
וְיוֹרֵנוּ מִדְּרָכָיו	so that he may teach us his ways
וְנֵלְכָה בְּאֹרְחֹתָיו	and we may walk in his paths."
כִּי מִצִּיּוֹן תֵּצֵא תוֹרָה	For from Zion shall come forth instruction,
וּדְבַר־יְהוָה מִירוּשָׁלִָם׃	and the word of the LORD from Jerusalem.

NEW VOCABULARY

בְּאַחֲרִית	in the end of
מִגְּבָעוֹת	above the hills
וְנָהֲרוּ	and (they) will stream
וְיוֹרֵנוּ	so that he may teach us
בְּאֹרְחֹתָיו	in his paths
מִצִּיּוֹן	from Zion

VERB ANALYSIS

VERB	ROOT	PATTERN	MEANING	TENSE	P/G/N	SUFFIX
וְהָיָה	ה.י.ה	פָּעַל	be, become	rv perfect	3ms	
יִהְיֶה	ה.י.ה	פָּעַל	be, become	imperfect	3ms	
נָכוֹן	כ.ו.ן	נִפְעַל	be established	participle	ms	
וְנִשָּׂא	נ.שׂ.א	נִפְעַל	be raised	participle	ms	
וְנָהֲרוּ	נ.ה.ר	פָּעַל	stream	rv perfect	3cp	
וְהָלְכוּ	ה.ל.ך	פָּעַל	walk, go	rv perfect	3cp	
וְאָמְרוּ	א.מ.ר	פָּעַל	say	rv perfect	3cp	
לְכוּ	ה.ל.ך	פָּעַל	walk, go	command	mp	
וְנַעֲלֶה	ע.ל.ה	פָּעַל	go up	imperfect	1cp	
וְיוֹרֵנוּ	י.ר.ה	הִפְעִיל	teach	imperfect	3ms	1cp
וְנֵלְכָה	ה.ל.ך	פָּעַל	walk, go	cohortative	1cp	
תֵּצֵא	י.צ.א	פָּעַל	go out	imperfect	3fs	

GRAMMATICAL NOTES

4:1 בְּאַחֲרִית הַיָּמִים is a prophetic idiom referring to the end of days or the final period of history as far as the author's perspective reaches. Thus, the meaning of בְּאַחֲרִית הַיָּמִים will change from one text to another. In Micah, the term probably describes an ideal future in which Israel is restored after its destruction by the Assyrians and Persians.

4:2 Recall that cohortatives occur in the first person singular and plural.

3 וְשָׁפַט בֵּין עַמִּים רַבִּים וְהוֹכִיחַ לְגוֹיִם
עֲצֻמִים עַד־רָחוֹק וְכִתְּתוּ חַרְבֹתֵיהֶם לְאִתִּים
וַחֲנִיתֹתֵיהֶם לְמַזְמֵרוֹת לֹא־יִשְׂאוּ גּוֹי אֶל־גּוֹי חֶרֶב
וְלֹא־יִלְמְדוּן עוֹד מִלְחָמָה׃ 4 וְיָשְׁבוּ אִישׁ תַּחַת גַּפְנוֹ
וְתַחַת תְּאֵנָתוֹ וְאֵין מַחֲרִיד

3 וְשָׁפַט בֵּין עַמִּים רַבִּים	He will judge among many peoples
וְהוֹכִיחַ לְגוֹיִם עֲצֻמִים	and arbitrate for mighty nations
עַד־רָחוֹק	far away.
וְכִתְּתוּ חַרְבֹתֵיהֶם לְאִתִּים	They shall beat their swords into ploughshares,
וַחֲנִיתֹתֵיהֶם לְמַזְמֵרוֹת	and their spears into pruning hooks.
לֹא־יִשְׂאוּ גּוֹי אֶל־גּוֹי חֶרֶב	Nation shall not raise up sword against nation,
וְלֹא־יִלְמְדוּן עוֹד מִלְחָמָה׃	and they shall not learn war any more.
4 וְיָשְׁבוּ אִישׁ תַּחַת גַּפְנוֹ	But every man shall sit under his grapevine
וְתַחַת תְּאֵנָתוֹ	and beneath his fig tree,
וְאֵין מַחֲרִיד	and none shall terrify (him),

NEW VOCABULARY

וְהוֹכִיחַ	and arbitrate	וַחֲנִיתֹתֵיהֶם	and their spears
עֲצֻמִים	mighty	לְמַזְמֵרוֹת	into pruning hooks
עַד־רָחוֹק	far away	יִלְמְדוּן	they shall learn
וְכִתְּתוּ	they shall beat	גַּפְנוֹ	his grapevine
לְאִתִּים	into ploughshares	תְּאֵנָתוֹ	his fig tree
מַחֲרִיד	terrify (him)		

VERB ANALYSIS

VERB	ROOT	PATTERN	MEANING	TENSE	P/G/N	SUFFIX
וְשָׁפַט	ש.פ.ט	פָּעַל	judge	rv perfect	3ms	
וְהוֹכִיחַ	י.כ.ח	הִפְעִיל	judge, reprove	rv perfect	3ms	
וְכִתְּתוּ	כ.ת.ת	פִּעֵל	beat, crush	rv perfect	3cp	
יִשְׂאוּ	נ.שׂ.א	פָּעַל	lift, carry	imperfect	3mp	
יִלְמְדוּן	ל.מ.ד	פָּעַל	learn	imperfect	3mp	
וְיָשְׁבוּ	י.שׁ.ב	פָּעַל	sit, dwell	rv perfect	3cp	
מַחֲרִיד	ח.ר.ד	הִפְעִיל	terrify	participle	ms	

GRAMMATICAL NOTE

4:3 יִלְמְדוּן has an extra **nun** at the end. The expected 3mp form is יִלְמְדוּ. This additional letter is called the **paragogic nun**. It can appear at the end of several types of verbs, but occurs most often at the end of 3mp imperfects. The paragogic nun should not affect your translation.

5 כִּֽי־פִּ֛י יְהוָ֥ה צְבָא֖וֹת דִּבֵּֽר׃ כִּ֚י כָּל־הָ֣עַמִּ֔ים יֵלְכ֕וּ
אִ֖ישׁ בְּשֵׁ֣ם אֱלֹהָ֑יו וַאֲנַ֗חְנוּ נֵלֵ֛ךְ בְּשֵׁם־יְהוָ֥ה אֱלֹהֵ֖ינוּ
לְעוֹלָ֥ם וָעֶֽד׃

5 כִּֽי־פִּ֛י יְהוָ֥ה צְבָא֖וֹת דִּבֵּֽר׃	for the mouth of the LORD of hosts has spoken.
כִּ֚י כָּל־הָ֣עַמִּ֔ים יֵלְכ֕וּ	For all peoples walk,
אִ֖ישׁ בְּשֵׁ֣ם אֱלֹהָ֑יו	each in the name of their god.
וַאֲנַ֗חְנוּ נֵלֵ֛ךְ בְּשֵׁם־יְהוָ֥ה	and we will go in the name of the LORD
אֱלֹהֵ֖ינוּ לְעוֹלָ֥ם וָעֶֽד׃	our God, forever and ever.

VERB ANALYSIS

VERB	ROOT	PATTERN	MEANING	TENSE	P/G/N	SUFFIX
דִּבֵּר	ד.ב.ר	פִּעֵל	speak	perfect	3ms	
יֵלְכוּ	ה.ל.ך	פָּעַל	walk, go	imperfect	3mp	
נֵלֵךְ	ה.ל.ך	פָּעַל	walk, go	imperfect	1cp	

GRAMMATICAL NOTE

You can find a slightly different version of this passage in Isaiah 2:2–4.

SELECTIONS FROM

כְּתוּבִים
THE WRITINGS

תְּהִלָּה כג	126	Psalm 23:1–6
תְּהִלָּה כט	130	Psalm 29:1–11
תְּהִלָּה סז	136	Psalm 67:1–8
תְּהִלָּה קלו	140	Psalm 136:1–26
שִׁיר הַשִּׁירִים	150	Song of Songs 3:1–5
קֹהֶלֶת	154	Ecclesiastes 1:1–9
קֹהֶלֶת	160	Ecclesiastes 3:1–22

23 ¹מִזְמוֹר לְדָוִד יְהוָה רֹעִי לֹא אֶחְסָר׃ ²בִּנְאוֹת דֶּשֶׁא
יַֽרְבִּיצֵנִי עַל־מֵי מְנֻחוֹת יְנַהֲלֵנִי׃ ³נַפְשִׁי יְשׁוֹבֵב יַֽנְחֵנִי
בְמַעְגְּלֵי־צֶדֶק לְמַעַן שְׁמוֹ׃ ⁴גַּם כִּי־אֵלֵךְ בְּגֵיא
צַלְמָוֶת לֹא־אִירָא רָע

1 מִזְמוֹר לְדָוִד	A psalm of David.
יְהוָה רֹעִי לֹא אֶחְסָר׃	The LORD is my shepherd; I lack nothing.
2 בִּנְאוֹת דֶּשֶׁא יַֽרְבִּיצֵנִי	He makes me lie down in green pastures;
עַל־מֵי מְנֻחוֹת יְנַהֲלֵנִי׃	he leads me beside peaceful waters.
3 נַפְשִׁי יְשׁוֹבֵב	He restores my life;
יַֽנְחֵנִי בְמַעְגְּלֵי־צֶדֶק	he leads me in right paths
לְמַעַן שְׁמוֹ׃	for the sake of his name.
4 גַּם כִּי־אֵלֵךְ	Even though I walk
בְּגֵיא צַלְמָוֶת	through a valley of deep darkness,
לֹא־אִירָא רָע	I fear no harm

NEW VOCABULARY

מִזְמוֹר a psalm	יְנַהֲלֵנִי he leads me
רֹעִי my shepherd	יְשׁוֹבֵב he restores
אֶחְסָר I lack	יַנְחֵנִי he leads me
בִּנְאוֹת in pastures	בְמַעְגְּלֵי-צֶדֶק in right paths
דֶּשֶׁא green	גַּם כִּי even though
יַרְבִּיצֵנִי he makes me lie down	בְּגֵיא a valley
מְנֻחוֹת peaceful	צַלְמָוֶת deep darkness

VERB ANALYSIS

VERB	ROOT	PATTERN	MEANING	TENSE	P/G/N	SUFFIX
רֹעִי	ר.ע.ה	פָּעַל	shepherd	participle	ms	1cs
אֶחְסָר	ח.ס.ר	פָּעַל	lack, need	imperfect	1cs	
יַרְבִּיצֵנִי	ר.ב.ץ	הִפְעִיל	make lie down	imperfect	3ms	1cs
יְנַהֲלֵנִי	נ.ה.ל	פִּעֵל	lead, guide	imperfect	3ms	1cs
יְשׁוֹבֵב	שׁ.ו.ב	פּוֹלֵל	restore	imperfect	3ms	
יַנְחֵנִי	נ.ח.ה	הִפְעִיל	guide	imperfect	3ms	1cs
אֵלֵךְ	ה.ל.ך	פָּעַל	walk, go	imperfect	1cs	
אִירָא	י.ר.א	פָּעַל	fear	imperfect	1cs	

GRAMMATICAL NOTES

Psalm 23 is a personal prayer of thanksgiving and faith.

23:1 The לְ in לְדָוִד is called the לְ of authorship.

23:1 Take care not to confuse רֹעֶה (**shepherd**) with רֵעַ (**friend, neighbor**).

23:2 דֶּשֶׁא signifies the type of greenness associated with springtime vegetation.

23:3 יְשׁוֹבֵב is in the פּוֹלֵל. For a full explanation, see Exodus 32:1 on page 25.

23:3 צַדִּיק, a word you know, is the adjective for **righteous**. צֶדֶק, a new word, is the noun for **righteousness**.

כִּי־אַתָּה עִמָּדִי שִׁבְטְךָ וּמִשְׁעַנְתֶּךָ הֵמָּה יְנַחֲמֻנִי׃
5 תַּעֲרֹךְ לְפָנַי שֻׁלְחָן נֶגֶד צֹרְרָי דִּשַּׁנְתָּ בַשֶּׁמֶן רֹאשִׁי
כּוֹסִי רְוָיָה׃ 6 אַךְ טוֹב וָחֶסֶד יִרְדְּפוּנִי כָּל־יְמֵי חַיָּי
וְשַׁבְתִּי בְּבֵית־יְהוָה לְאֹרֶךְ יָמִים׃

כִּי־אַתָּה עִמָּדִי	because you are with me;
שִׁבְטְךָ וּמִשְׁעַנְתֶּךָ הֵמָּה יְנַחֲמֻנִי׃	your rod and your staff, they comfort me.
5 תַּעֲרֹךְ לְפָנַי שֻׁלְחָן	You prepare a table for me
נֶגֶד צֹרְרָי	in sight of my adversaries;
דִּשַּׁנְתָּ בַשֶּׁמֶן רֹאשִׁי	you anoint my head with oil;
כּוֹסִי רְוָיָה׃	my cup is full.
6 אַךְ טוֹב וָחֶסֶד יִרְדְּפוּנִי	Only goodness and kindness will follow me
כָּל־יְמֵי חַיָּי	all the days of my life,
וְשַׁבְתִּי בְּבֵית־יְהוָה	and I will dwell in the LORD's house
לְאֹרֶךְ יָמִים׃	for (the) length of (my) days.

NEW VOCABULARY

עִמָּדִי	with me	דִּשַּׁנְתָּ	you anoint
שִׁבְטְךָ	your rod	בַשֶּׁמֶן	with oil
וּמִשְׁעַנְתֶּךָ	and your staff	כּוֹסִי	my cup
יְנַחֲמֻנִי	they comfort me	רְוָיָה	is full
תַּעֲרֹךְ	you prepare	וָחֶסֶד	and kindness
שֻׁלְחָן	a table	יִרְדְּפוּנִי	(they) will follow me
צֹרְרָי	my adversaries	לְאֹרֶךְ	for (the) length

VERB ANALYSIS

VERB	ROOT	PATTERN	MEANING	TENSE	P/G/N	SUFFIX
יְנַחֲמֻנִי	נ.ח.ם	פִּעֵל	comfort	imperfect	3ms	1cs
תַּעֲרֹךְ	ע.ר.ך	פָּעַל	arrange	imperfect	2ms	
צֹרְרָי	צ.ר.ר	פָּעַל	be hostile to	participle	mp	1cs
דִּשַּׁנְתָּ	ד.שׁ.ן	פִּעֵל	make fat	perfect	2ms	
יִרְדְּפוּנִי	ר.ד.ף	פָּעַל	pursue	imperfect	3mp	1cs
וְשַׁבְתִּי	שׁ.ו.ב	פָּעַל	turn, return	rv perfect	1cs	

GRAMMATICAL NOTES

Shepherd imagery—including references to a rod, a staff, pastures, spring growth, and being led to drink—is the hallmark of this psalm.

23:4 רָע (**evil**), does not always imply wickedness. Sometimes the word simply means **harmful** or **unpleasant**.

23:4 עִמָּדִי is another way to write עִמִּי (**with me**).

23:5 **My cup** is a metaphor for physical sustenance and salvation. It is used similarly in Psalm 16:5 and 116:13.

23:5 ד.שׁ.ן רֹאשׁ is a formula meaning **to anoint**.

23:6 וְשַׁבְתִּי is the rv perfect for שׁ.ו.ב. We emended the text to יָשַׁבְתִּי, the rv perfect for י.שׁ.ב, following a similar phrase in Psalm 27:4.

23:6 **Length of days**, or **long days**, signifies all the days in one's life.

29 [1] מִזְמוֹר לְדָוִד הָבוּ לַיהוָה בְּנֵי אֵלִים הָבוּ לַיהוָה
כָּבוֹד וָעֹז׃ [2] הָבוּ לַיהוָה כְּבוֹד שְׁמוֹ הִשְׁתַּחֲווּ לַיהוָה
בְּהַדְרַת־קֹדֶשׁ׃ [3] קוֹל יְהוָה עַל־הַמָּיִם אֵל־הַכָּבוֹד
הִרְעִים יְהוָה עַל־מַיִם רַבִּים׃ [4] קוֹל־יְהוָה בַּכֹּחַ קוֹל
יְהוָה בֶּהָדָר׃

[1] מִזְמוֹר לְדָוִד	A psalm of David.
הָבוּ לַיהוָה בְּנֵי אֵלִים	Credit to the LORD, sons of gods
הָבוּ לַיהוָה כָּבוֹד וָעֹז׃	Credit to the LORD, glory and strength.
[2] הָבוּ לַיהוָה כְּבוֹד שְׁמוֹ	Credit to the LORD, the glory of his name;
הִשְׁתַּחֲווּ לַיהוָה בְּהַדְרַת־קֹדֶשׁ׃	bow down to the LORD in holy splendor.
[3] קוֹל יְהוָה עַל־הַמָּיִם	The voice of the LORD is over the waters,
אֵל־הַכָּבוֹד הִרְעִים	the God of glory thunders;
יְהוָה עַל־מַיִם רַבִּים׃	the LORD (thunders) over many waters.
[4] קוֹל־יְהוָה בַּכֹּחַ	The voice of the LORD is in power;
קוֹל יְהוָה בֶּהָדָר׃	the voice of the LORD is in splendor.

NEW VOCABULARY

מִזְמוֹר	a psalm	הִשְׁתַּחֲווּ	(you) bow down
הָבוּ	credit	בְּהַדְרַת	in splendor
אֵלִים	gods	הִרְעִים	thunders
וָעֹז	and strength	בֶּהָדָר	in splendor

VERB ANALYSIS

VERB	ROOT	PATTERN	MEANING	TENSE	P/G/N	SUFFIX
הָבוּ	י.ה.ב	פָּעַל	credit, attribute	command	mp	
הִשְׁתַּחֲווּ	ח.ו.ה	הִשְׁתָּפֵל	worship	command	mp	
הִרְעִים	ר.ע.ם	הִפְעִיל	thunder	perfect	3ms	

GRAMMATICAL NOTES

Psalm 29 is best described as a song of praise, but its meter and imagery differ greatly from other psalms. Most scholars agree that Israel borrowed parts of Psalm 29 from its Canaanite neighbors and adapted it to the worship of the LORD. In the Canaanite sphere, this song described the appearance of the god Baal in a thunderstorm. We will discuss Canaanite features of this psalm as we continue.

29:1 בְּנֵי אֵלִים literally translates as **the sons of the gods**. The Canaanites worshipped more than one god in a hierarchical pantheon. A king god or "father" god sat at the highest level, and his subordinates or "sons" sat below him. Monotheists understand בְּנֵי אֵלִים as divine beings but not gods, much like the מַלְאָכִים (**messengers** or **angels**). The word אֵלִים is a rare plural form of אֵל that appears only in Hebrew poetry.

29:3 The voice of God *is* the thunder, and this verse begins a description of God's visible manifestation on earth.

29:3 Note that הַמָּיִם is in pause; the expected form is הַמַּיִם.

5קוֹל יְהוָה שֹׁבֵר אֲרָזִים וַיְשַׁבֵּר יְהוָה אֶת־אַרְזֵי
הַלְּבָנוֹן׃ 6וַיַּרְקִידֵם כְּמוֹ־עֵגֶל לְבָנוֹן וְשִׂרְיֹן כְּמוֹ
בֶן־רְאֵמִים׃ 7קוֹל־יְהוָה חֹצֵב לַהֲבוֹת אֵשׁ׃ 8קוֹל יְהוָה
יָחִיל מִדְבָּר יָחִיל יְהוָה מִדְבַּר קָדֵשׁ׃ 9קוֹל יְהוָה
יְחוֹלֵל אַיָּלוֹת וַיֶּחֱשֹׂף יְעָרוֹת

5קוֹל יְהוָה שֹׁבֵר אֲרָזִים	the voice of the LORD breaks the cedars;
וַיְשַׁבֵּר יְהוָה אֶת־אַרְזֵי הַלְּבָנוֹן׃	the LORD shatters the cedars of Lebanon.
6וַיַּרְקִידֵם כְּמוֹ־עֵגֶל	He makes them skip like a calf,
לְבָנוֹן וְשִׂרְיֹן	Lebanon and Sirion,
כְּמוֹ בֶן־רְאֵמִים׃	like the young of wild oxen.
7קוֹל־יְהוָה חֹצֵב לַהֲבוֹת אֵשׁ׃	The voice of the LORD divides the flames of fire.
8קוֹל יְהוָה יָחִיל מִדְבָּר	The voice of the LORD shakes the wilderness;
יָחִיל יְהוָה מִדְבַּר קָדֵשׁ׃	the LORD shakes the wilderness of Kadesh.
9קוֹל יְהוָה יְחוֹלֵל אַיָּלוֹת	The voice of the LORD makes the does calve
וַיֶּחֱשֹׂף יְעָרוֹת	and strips the forests bare;

NEW VOCABULARY

לַהֲבוֹת	the flames of	אֲרָזִים	the cedars
אֵשׁ	fire	אַרְזֵי	the cedars of
יָחִיל	shakes	לְבָנוֹן	Lebanon
קָדֵשׁ	Kadesh	וַיַּרְקִידֵם	he makes them skip
יְחוֹלֵל	makes calve	עֵגֶל	a calf
אַיָּלוֹת	does	וְשִׂרְיֹן	and Sirion
וַיֶּחֱשֹׂף	strips bare	רְאֵמִים	wild oxen
יְעָרוֹת	the forests	חֹצֵב	divides

VERB ANALYSIS

VERB	ROOT	PATTERN	MEANING	TENSE	P/G/N	SUFFIX
שֹׁבֵר	ש.ב.ר	פָּעַל	break	participle	ms	
וַיְשַׁבֵּר	ש.ב.ר	פִּעֵל	break, shatter	rv imperfect	3ms	
וַיַּרְקִידֵם	ר.ק.ד	הִפְעִיל	make skip	rv imperfect	3ms	3mp
חֹצֵב	ח.צ.ב	פָּעַל	cleave, divide	participle	ms	
יָחִיל	ח.ו.ל	הִפְעִיל	make tremble	imperfect	3ms	
יְחוֹלֵל	ח.ו.ל	פּוֹלֵל	bring forth	imperfect	3ms	
וַיֶּחֱשֹׂף	ח.שׂ.ף	פָּעַל	strip bare	rv imperfect	3ms	

GRAMMATICAL NOTES

29:5–6 The manifestation of God continues with a show of destructive force. Lebanon and Sirion are mountain ranges; the Lebanon range runs along the coast of Syria and Lebanon, and Sirion is probably Mount Hermon, the highest mountain in a range between Lebanon and Syria. The language parallels descriptions of Baal's making "the mountain quake."

29:8 This Kadesh is likely the Syrian desert north of Israel.

29:9 It may seem odd that the root ח.ו.ל, which means **tremble** in פָּעַל, can mean **make calve**. In the פּוֹלֵל, ח.ו.ל can indicate writhing or trembling to bring forth something. In verse 9, the does writhe while delivering their young.

וּבְהֵיכָלוֹ כֻּלּוֹ אֹמֵר כָּבוֹד׃ 10 יְהוָה לַמַּבּוּל יָשָׁב וַיֵּשֶׁב
יְהוָה מֶלֶךְ לְעוֹלָם׃ 11 יְהוָה עֹז לְעַמּוֹ יִתֵּן יְהוָה יְבָרֵךְ
אֶת־עַמּוֹ בַשָּׁלוֹם׃

וּבְהֵיכָלוֹ כֻּלּוֹ אֹמֵר כָּבוֹד׃	and in his temple all say, "Glory!"
10 יְהוָה לַמַּבּוּל יָשָׁב	The LORD sat (enthroned) at the flood;
וַיֵּשֶׁב יְהוָה מֶלֶךְ לְעוֹלָם׃	the LORD sits (enthroned) (as) king forever.
11 יְהוָה עֹז לְעַמּוֹ יִתֵּן	May the LORD give strength to his people;
יְהוָה יְבָרֵךְ אֶת־עַמּוֹ בַשָּׁלוֹם׃	May the LORD bless his people with peace.

NEW VOCABULARY

וּבְהֵיכָלוֹ	and in his temple
לַמַּבּוּל	at the flood
עֹז	strength

VERB ANALYSIS

VERB	ROOT	PATTERN	MEANING	TENSE	P/G/N	SUFFIX
אֹמֵר	א.מ.ר	פָּעַל	say	participle	ms	
יָשָׁב	י.שׁ.ב	פָּעַל	sit, dwell	perfect	3ms	
וַיֵּשֶׁב	י.שׁ.ב	פָּעַל	sit, dwell	rv imperfect	3ms	
יִתֵּן	נ.ת.ן	פָּעַל	give, set	imperfect	3ms	
יְבָרֵךְ	ב.ר.ךְ	פִּעֵל	bless	imperfect	3ms	

GRAMMATICAL NOTES

29:9 One stylistic feature of this psalm is **balance** or **parallelism**. Most verses have two parts; the first part states an idea, and the second part repeats it using different language. Verse 9 seems to have three parts. **The voice of the LORD makes the does calv**e is balanced by **and strips the forests bare**. The next line, **and in his temple all say, "Glory!"**, stands alone. Some scholars suspect that a line balancing this one may have dropped out of the text.

29:10 This verse leaves the earthly realm behind and returns to heaven. In a polytheistic setting this verse would describe the subordinate gods recognizing the power of the head god and paying homage to him. In a monotheistic setting the verse draws a parallel between heavenly beings praising God in the heavenly temple and mortal beings praising God in the temple on earth. The objective is to recognize the supremacy and majesty of Israel's God.

29:11 The last verse of Psalm 29 is Israelite and was not borrowed from outside sources. It may express a patriotic wish that Israel be granted favor by its God.

67

1 לַמְנַצֵּחַ בִּנְגִינֹת מִזְמוֹר שִׁיר׃
2 אֱלֹהִים יְחָנֵּנוּ וִיבָרְכֵנוּ יָאֵר פָּנָיו אִתָּנוּ סֶלָה׃ 3 לָדַעַת
בָּאָרֶץ דַּרְכֶּךָ בְּכָל־גּוֹיִם יְשׁוּעָתֶךָ׃
4 יוֹדוּךָ עַמִּים אֱלֹהִים יוֹדוּךָ עַמִּים כֻּלָּם׃
5 יִשְׂמְחוּ וִירַנְּנוּ לְאֻמִּים

1 לַמְנַצֵּחַ בִּנְגִינֹת מִזְמוֹר שִׁיר׃	For the director, with music. A psalm. A song.
2 אֱלֹהִים יְחָנֵּנוּ וִיבָרְכֵנוּ	May God be gracious to us and bless us;
יָאֵר פָּנָיו אִתָּנוּ סֶלָה׃	may he make his face shine upon us. *Selah.*
3 לָדַעַת בָּאָרֶץ דַּרְכֶּךָ	That your way be known on earth,
בְּכָל־גּוֹיִם יְשׁוּעָתֶךָ׃	your salvation among all nations.
4 יוֹדוּךָ עַמִּים אֱלֹהִים	May the peoples praise you, God;
יוֹדוּךָ עַמִּים כֻּלָּם׃	may all the peoples praise you.
5 יִשְׂמְחוּ וִירַנְּנוּ לְאֻמִּים	The nations will be happy and sing for joy;

NEW VOCABULARY

לַמְנַצֵּחַ	for the director
בִּנְגִינֹת	with music
מִזְמוֹר	a psalm
שִׁיר	a song
יְחָנֵּנוּ	may (he) be gracious
יָאֵר	he make shine
יְשׁוּעָתֶךָ	your salvation
יוֹדוּךָ	may (they) praise you
יִשְׂמְחוּ	(they) will be happy
וִירַנְּנוּ	(they) will sing for joy
לְאֻמִּים	the nations

VERB ANALYSIS

VERB	ROOT	PATTERN	MEANING	TENSE	P/G/N	SUFFIX
לַמְנַצֵּחַ	נ.צ.ח	פִּעֵל	direct	participle	ms	
יְחָנֵּנוּ	ח.נ.ן	פָּעַל	be gracious	imperfect	3ms	1cp
וִיבָרְכֵנוּ	ב.ר.ך	פִּעֵל	bless	imperfect	3ms	1cp
יָאֵר	א.ו.ר	הִפְעִיל	make shine	jussive	3ms	
לָדַעַת	י.ד.ע	פָּעַל	know	infinitive		
יוֹדוּךָ	י.ד.ה	הִפְעִיל	praise	imperfect	3mp	2ms
יִשְׂמְחוּ	ש.מ.ח	פָּעַל	be happy	imperfect	3mp	
וִירַנְּנוּ	ר.נ.ן	פִּעֵל	shout with joy	imperfect	3mp	

GRAMMATICAL NOTES

Psalm 67 may be interpreted as a prayer song (asking for a blessing) or as a song of thanksgiving. Categorization depends on how certain verbs are analyzed. See the first note on page 139 for more information.

1:2 סֶלָה probably derives from the root ס.ל.ל, meaning **to lift up**. The word signals a pause or interruption in a psalm's recitation, coming at the end of a unit or stanza. As with אָמֵן (**amen**), it is difficult to exactly capture the sense of סֶלָה in English, and we do not translate the word in this text.

1:3 Notice the use of the regular infinitive in this verse. לָדַעַת expresses the purpose of the preceding action; the psalmist asks God to **make his face shine upon us** so that God's way will be known on earth. This is a common use of the infinitive when it stands after לְ.

כִּי־תִשְׁפֹּט עַמִּים מִישׁוֹר
וּלְאֻמִּים בָּאָרֶץ תַּנְחֵם סֶלָה׃
6 יוֹדוּךָ עַמִּים אֱלֹהִים יוֹדוּךָ עַמִּים כֻּלָּם׃
7 אֶרֶץ נָתְנָה יְבוּלָהּ יְבָרְכֵנוּ אֱלֹהִים אֱלֹהֵינוּ׃
8 יְבָרְכֵנוּ אֱלֹהִים וְיִירְאוּ אֹתוֹ כָּל־אַפְסֵי־אָרֶץ׃

כִּי־תִשְׁפֹּט עַמִּים מִישׁוֹר	for you judge peoples with fairness,
וּלְאֻמִּים בָּאָרֶץ תַּנְחֵם סֶלָה׃	and guide the nations upon the earth. *Selah.*
6 יוֹדוּךָ עַמִּים אֱלֹהִים	May the peoples praise you, God;
יוֹדוּךָ עַמִּים כֻּלָּם׃	may all the peoples praise you.
7 אֶרֶץ נָתְנָה יְבוּלָהּ	Earth has given its produce;
יְבָרְכֵנוּ אֱלֹהִים אֱלֹהֵינוּ׃	God, our God, has blessed us.
8 יְבָרְכֵנוּ אֱלֹהִים	God has blessed us;
וְיִירְאוּ אֹתוֹ כָּל־אַפְסֵי־אָרֶץ׃	may all the ends of the earth revere him.

NEW VOCABULARY

מִישׁוֹר	with fairness
וּלְאֻמִּים	the nations
תַּנְחֵם	(you) guide
יוֹדוּךָ	may (they) praise you
יְבוּלָהּ	its produce
אַפְסֵי	the ends of

VERB ANALYSIS

VERB	ROOT	PATTERN	MEANING	TENSE	P/G/N	SUFFIX
תִשְׁפֹּט	ש.פ.ט	פָּעַל	judge	imperfect	2ms	
תַּנְחֵם	נ.ח.ה	הִפְעִיל	guide	imperfect	2ms	3mp
יוֹדוּךָ	י.ד.ה	הִפְעִיל	praise	imperfect	3mp	2ms
נָתְנָה	נ.ת.ן	פָּעַל	give, set	perfect	3fs	
יְבָרְכֵנוּ	ב.ר.ך	פִּעֵל	bless	imperfect	3ms	1cp
וְיִירְאוּ	י.ר.א	פָּעַל	fear	imperfect	3mp	

GRAMMATICAL NOTES

How to translate many of the verbs in this section is a matter of interpretation. יָאֵר is jussive in form and meaning (see Genesis 22:12, page 19, for information about the jussive), but many of the verbs in Psalm 67 are regular imperfects translated as jussives. You may translate them as regular, present tense verbs if you wish. Notice how this changes the meaning of the poem and choose according to your understanding of the psalm.

67:7 יְבָרְכֵנוּ looks like a standard imperfect verb, yet we have translated it as a perfect. Notice that verse 7 has only two verbs, and that the first (נָתְנָה) is a perfect. Sometimes in poetry order alone determines the tense of a verb, so that if the first verb is past tense, the second one will be too. Other times an imperfect may represent the past tense, even if there is no perfect verb before it. The reasons for this are complicated. All you need to know is that verb tenses can be confusing in poetry; that the imperfect can be translated as future action, present action, past action, or wished-for action in poetry; and that your translation should rely on context.

136 1 הוֹדוּ לַיהוָה כִּי־טוֹב כִּי לְעוֹלָם חַסְדּוֹ׃
2 הוֹדוּ לֵאלֹהֵי הָאֱלֹהִים כִּי לְעוֹלָם חַסְדּוֹ׃
3 הוֹדוּ לַאֲדֹנֵי הָאֲדֹנִים כִּי לְעוֹלָם חַסְדּוֹ׃
4 לְעֹשֵׂה נִפְלָאוֹת גְּדֹלוֹת לְבַדּוֹ כִּי לְעוֹלָם חַסְדּוֹ׃
5 לְעֹשֵׂה הַשָּׁמַיִם בִּתְבוּנָה כִּי לְעוֹלָם חַסְדּוֹ׃
6 לְרֹקַע הָאָרֶץ עַל־הַמָּיִם כִּי לְעוֹלָם חַסְדּוֹ׃

1 הוֹדוּ לַיהוָה כִּי־טוֹב	Give thanks to the LORD for he is good,
כִּי לְעוֹלָם חַסְדּוֹ׃	for his kindness is everlasting;
2 הוֹדוּ לֵאלֹהֵי הָאֱלֹהִים	Give thanks to the God of gods,
כִּי לְעוֹלָם חַסְדּוֹ׃	for his kindness is everlasting;
3 הוֹדוּ לַאֲדֹנֵי הָאֲדֹנִים	Give thanks to the Lord of lords,
כִּי לְעוֹלָם חַסְדּוֹ׃	for his kindness is everlasting;
4 לְעֹשֵׂה נִפְלָאוֹת גְּדֹלוֹת לְבַדּוֹ	to him who alone does great wonders,
כִּי לְעוֹלָם חַסְדּוֹ׃	for his kindness is everlasting;
5 לְעֹשֵׂה הַשָּׁמַיִם בִּתְבוּנָה	to him who made the heavens with understanding,
כִּי לְעוֹלָם חַסְדּוֹ׃	for his kindness is everlasting;
6 לְרֹקַע הָאָרֶץ עַל־הַמָּיִם	to him who spread the earth over the water,
כִּי לְעוֹלָם חַסְדּוֹ׃	for his kindness is everlasting;

NEW VOCABULARY

הוֹדוּ	give thanks
חַסְדּוֹ	his kindness
נִפְלָאוֹת	wonders
לְבַדּוֹ	alone
בִּתְבוּנָה	with understanding
לְרֹקַע	to him who spread

VERB ANALYSIS

VERB	ROOT	PATTERN	MEANING	TENSE	P/G/N	SUFFIX
הוֹדוּ	י.ד.ה	הִפְעִיל	praise	command	mp	
לְעֹשֵׂה	ע.שׂ.ה	פָּעַל	make, do	participle	ms	
נִפְלָאוֹת	פ.ל.א	נִפְעַל	be wonderful	participle	fp	
לְרֹקַע	ר.ק.ע	פָּעַל	beat, spread	participle	ms	

GRAMMATICAL NOTES

Psalm 136 is a thanksgiving that summarizes God's work in creation and the history of Israel. If you find psalms difficult to translate, this selection should boost your confidence because it includes much repetition, has a simple vocabulary, and is written in a narrative style. The second half of each verse is a congregational response. Psalm 136 is also an excellent review of participles.

136:1 Since חַסְדּוֹ (**his kindness**) is part of the congregational response, we list it under new vocabulary only for this verse.

136:2 When deciding how to translate אֱלֹהִים (**God, gods**), let the context guide you. The sense of this verse is that Israel's God is the only true one among many other nations' gods. Therefore, the first אֱלֹהִים is singular and the second אֱלֹהִים is plural.

136:2,3 When a word pair repeats the same word—for example, מֶלֶךְ-מְלָכִים—the resulting form is the **superlative**, a degree of comparison denoting an unsurpassed level or the supremacy of something. **God of gods** means that Israel's God is the only true one, and **Lord of lords** indicates that Israel's God is the most majestic.

7 לְעֹשֵׂה אוֹרִים גְּדֹלִים כִּי לְעוֹלָם חַסְדּוֹ׃
8 אֶת־הַשֶּׁמֶשׁ לְמֶמְשֶׁלֶת בַּיּוֹם כִּי לְעוֹלָם חַסְדּוֹ׃
9 אֶת־הַיָּרֵחַ וְכוֹכָבִים
לְמֶמְשְׁלוֹת בַּלָּיְלָה כִּי לְעוֹלָם חַסְדּוֹ׃
10 לְמַכֵּה מִצְרַיִם בִּבְכוֹרֵיהֶם כִּי לְעוֹלָם חַסְדּוֹ׃
11 וַיּוֹצֵא יִשְׂרָאֵל מִתּוֹכָם כִּי לְעוֹלָם חַסְדּוֹ׃

7 לְעֹשֵׂה אוֹרִים גְּדֹלִים	to him who made (the) great lights,
כִּי לְעוֹלָם חַסְדּוֹ׃	for his kindness is everlasting;
8 אֶת־הַשֶּׁמֶשׁ לְמֶמְשֶׁלֶת בַּיּוֹם	the sun for the rule of the day,
כִּי לְעוֹלָם חַסְדּוֹ׃	for his kindness is everlasting;
9 אֶת־הַיָּרֵחַ וְכוֹכָבִים	the moon and stars
לְמֶמְשְׁלוֹת בַּלָּיְלָה	for the rule of the night,
כִּי לְעוֹלָם חַסְדּוֹ׃	for his kindness is everlasting;
10 לְמַכֵּה מִצְרַיִם	to him who struck Egypt
בִּבְכוֹרֵיהֶם	through their firstborn,
כִּי לְעוֹלָם חַסְדּוֹ׃	for his kindness is everlasting;
11 וַיּוֹצֵא יִשְׂרָאֵל מִתּוֹכָם	and him who brought out Israel from its midst,
כִּי לְעוֹלָם חַסְדּוֹ׃	for his kindness is everlasting;

NEW VOCABULARY

לְמֶמְשֶׁלֶת	for the rule of
הַיָּרֵחַ	the moon
וְכוֹכָבִים	and stars
לְמֶמְשְׁלוֹת	for the rule of
בִּבְכוֹרֵיהֶם	their firstborn

VERB ANALYSIS

VERB	ROOT	PATTERN	MEANING	TENSE	P/G/N	SUFFIX
לְעֹשֵׂה	ע.שׂ.ה	פָּעַל	make, do	participle	ms	
לְמַכֵּה	נ.כ.ה	הִפְעִיל	strike, smite	participle	ms	
וַיּוֹצֵא	י.צ.א	הִפְעִיל	bring out	rv imperfect	3ms	

GRAMMATICAL ANALYSIS

136:5–9 You can find the story of God's creating the heaven, earth, sun, moon, and stars in Genesis 1:6–19.

136:10 Slaying of the firstborn, the tenth and final plague, occurs in Exodus 11:1–10 and Exodus 12:29–32.

136:9 מֶמְשְׁלוֹת **(rules, dominations)** is plural in form, but **the moon and the stars for the rules of the night** is not idiomatic English. There are many stars, but they rule together as a collective noun and therefore should be translated as a singular.

[12] בְּיָד חֲזָקָה וּבִזְרוֹעַ נְטוּיָה	כִּי לְעוֹלָם חַסְדּוֹ:
[13] לְגֹזֵר יַם־סוּף לִגְזָרִים	כִּי לְעוֹלָם חַסְדּוֹ:
[14] וְהֶעֱבִיר יִשְׂרָאֵל בְּתוֹכוֹ	כִּי לְעוֹלָם חַסְדּוֹ:
[15] וְנִעֵר פַּרְעֹה וְחֵילוֹ בְיַם־סוּף	כִּי לְעוֹלָם חַסְדּוֹ:
[16] לְמוֹלִיךְ עַמּוֹ בַּמִּדְבָּר	כִּי לְעוֹלָם חַסְדּוֹ:

[12] בְּיָד חֲזָקָה וּבִזְרוֹעַ נְטוּיָה	with a strong hand and an outstretched arm,
כִּי לְעוֹלָם חַסְדּוֹ:	for his kindness is everlasting;
[13] לְגֹזֵר יַם־סוּף לִגְזָרִים	to him who split the Sea of Reeds,
כִּי לְעוֹלָם חַסְדּוֹ:	for his kindness is everlasting;
[14] וְהֶעֱבִיר יִשְׂרָאֵל בְּתוֹכוֹ	and made Israel pass through the middle of it,
כִּי לְעוֹלָם חַסְדּוֹ:	for his kindness is everlasting;
[15] וְנִעֵר פַּרְעֹה וְחֵילוֹ	and shook off Pharaoh and his army
בְיַם־סוּף	in the Sea of Reeds,
כִּי לְעוֹלָם חַסְדּוֹ:	for his kindness is everlasting;
[16] לְמוֹלִיךְ עַמּוֹ בַּמִּדְבָּר	to him who led his people through the wilderness,
כִּי לְעוֹלָם חַסְדּוֹ:	for his kindness is everlasting;

NEW VOCABULARY

חֲזָקָה	strong
וּבִזְרוֹעַ	and an arm
נְטוּיָה	outstretched
לְגֹזֵר	to him who split
סוּף	reeds
לִגְזָרִים	in parts
וְנִעֵר	and (who) shook off Pharaoh
וְחֵילוֹ	and his army

VERB ANALYSIS

VERB	ROOT	PATTERN	MEANING	TENSE	P/G/N	SUFFIX
נְטוּיָה	נ.ט.ה	פָּעַל	stretch out	p. participle	fs	
לְגֹזֵר	ג.ז.ר	פָּעַל	cut, divide	participle	ms	
וְהֶעֱבִיר	ע.ב.ר	הִפְעִיל	make pass	perfect	3ms	
וְנִעֵר	נ.ע.ר	פִּעֵל	shake off	perfect	3ms	
לְמוֹלִיךְ	ה.ל.ך	הִפְעִיל	lead	participle	ms	

GRAMMATICAL NOTES

136:13 Scholars have long argued over the identity of the Sea of Reeds. The Gulf of Aqaba, the Gulf of Suez, and various lakes near the Nile delta have all been suggested. Meanwhile, you may have noticed that סוּף **(reeds)** lacks a plural ending; it is another collective plural.

136:13 We left לִגְזָרִים **(in parts)** out of our translation because it makes the sentence sound as if the sea were divided into several parts, and in this verse it is clear that the Sea of Reeds was divided in half.

136:15 Some scholars suggest that בְיַם־סוּף **(in the Sea of Reeds)**should be deleted in this verse.

136:16 מִדְבָּר **(wilderness)** is in pause; the regular form is מִדְבַּר.

136:13-15 The miracle at sea is detailed in Exodus 14 and 15.

17 לְמַכֵּה מְלָכִים גְּדֹלִים	כִּי לְעוֹלָם חַסְדּוֹ׃
18 וַיַּהֲרֹג מְלָכִים אַדִּירִים	כִּי לְעוֹלָם חַסְדּוֹ׃
19 לְסִיחוֹן מֶלֶךְ הָאֱמֹרִי	כִּי לְעוֹלָם חַסְדּוֹ׃
20 וּלְעוֹג מֶלֶךְ הַבָּשָׁן	כִּי לְעוֹלָם חַסְדּוֹ׃
21 וְנָתַן אַרְצָם לְנַחֲלָה	כִּי לְעוֹלָם חַסְדּוֹ׃
22 נַחֲלָה לְיִשְׂרָאֵל עַבְדּוֹ	כִּי לְעוֹלָם חַסְדּוֹ׃

17 לְמַכֵּה מְלָכִים גְּדֹלִים	to him who struck down great kings,
כִּי לְעוֹלָם חַסְדּוֹ׃	for his kindness is everlasting;
18 וַיַּהֲרֹג מְלָכִים אַדִּירִים	and slew mighty kings—
כִּי לְעוֹלָם חַסְדּוֹ׃	for his kindness is everlasting;
19 לְסִיחוֹן מֶלֶךְ הָאֱמֹרִי	Sihon, king of Amorites,
כִּי לְעוֹלָם חַסְדּוֹ׃	for his kindness is everlasting;
20 וּלְעוֹג מֶלֶךְ הַבָּשָׁן	and Og, king of Bashan—
כִּי לְעוֹלָם חַסְדּוֹ׃	for his kindness is everlasting;
21 וְנָתַן אַרְצָם לְנַחֲלָה	and gave their land as an inheritance,
כִּי לְעוֹלָם חַסְדּוֹ׃	for his kindness is everlasting;
22 נַחֲלָה לְיִשְׂרָאֵל עַבְדּוֹ	an inheritance for his servant Israel,
כִּי לְעוֹלָם חַסְדּוֹ׃	for his kindness is everlasting;

NEW VOCABULARY

וַיַּהֲרֹג	and (he) slew
אַדִּירִים	mighty
לְסִיחוֹן	Sihon
הָאֱמֹרִי	the Amorites
וּלְעוֹג	and Og
הַבָּשָׁן	Bashan

VERB ANALYSIS

VERB	ROOT	PATTERN	MEANING	TENSE	P/G/N	SUFFIX
לְמַכֵּה	נ.כ.ה	הִפְעִיל	strike, smite	participle	ms	
וַיַּהֲרֹג	ה.ר.ג	פָּעַל	kill, slay	rv imperfect	3ms	
וְנָתַן	נ.ת.ן	פָּעַל	give, set	perfect	3ms	

GRAMMATICAL NOTES

136:19–20 The לְ attached to Sihon and Og is the לְ of specification, meaning **with respect to**. It signifies that Sihon and Og are among the kings mentioned in the clause **and slew mighty kings**. You do not always need to translate this לְ.

136:19 In biblical tradition, the Amorites were one of the groups that inhabited Canaan before the Israelite invasion, and Bashan was a small kingdom north of the Jabbok River. Both were located east of the Jordan River in an area called the Transjordan. Numbers 21:21–25 describes the defeat of these and other Canaanite kingdoms.

23 שֶׁבְּשִׁפְלֵנוּ זָכַר־לָנוּ	כִּי לְעוֹלָם חַסְדּוֹ׃
24 וַיִּפְרְקֵנוּ מִצָּרֵינוּ	כִּי לְעוֹלָם חַסְדּוֹ׃
25 נֹתֵן לֶחֶם לְכָל־בָּשָׂר	כִּי לְעוֹלָם חַסְדּוֹ׃
26 הוֹדוּ לְאֵל הַשָּׁמָיִם	כִּי לְעוֹלָם חַסְדּוֹ׃

23 שֶׁבְּשִׁפְלֵנוּ זָכַר־לָנוּ	who remembered us in our degradation,
כִּי לְעוֹלָם חַסְדּוֹ׃	for his kindness is everlasting;
24 וַיִּפְרְקֵנוּ מִצָּרֵינוּ	and rescued us from our enemies,
כִּי לְעוֹלָם חַסְדּוֹ׃	for his kindness is everlasting;
25 נֹתֵן לֶחֶם לְכָל־בָּשָׂר	he who gives food to all flesh,
כִּי לְעוֹלָם חַסְדּוֹ׃	for his kindness is everlasting;
26 הוֹדוּ לְאֵל הַשָּׁמָיִם	give thanks to the God of heaven.
כִּי לְעוֹלָם חַסְדּוֹ׃	for his kindness is everlasting;

NEW VOCABULARY

שֶׁבְּשִׁפְלֵנוּ	who in our degradation
וַיִּפְרְקֵנוּ	and (who) rescued us
מִצָּרֵינוּ	from our enemies
הוֹדוּ	give thanks

VERB ANALYSIS

VERB	ROOT	PATTERN	MEANING	TENSE	P/G/N	SUFFIX
זָכַר	ז.כ.ר	פָּעַל	remember	perfect	3ms	
וַיִּפְרְקֵנוּ	פ.ר.ק	פָּעַל	rescue	rv perfect	3ms	1cp
נֹתֵן	נ.ת.ן	פָּעַל	give, set	participle	ms	
הוֹדוּ	י.ד.ה	הִפְעִיל	praise	command	mp	

GRAMMATICAL NOTE

Psalm 136 is a song of praise fashioned as a mild command; a community would have chanted this psalm during public worship. Psalm 136 may have originated in the spring Passover celebration, a holiday with which it is associated in modern times.

3 [1] עַל־מִשְׁכָּבִי בַּלֵּילוֹת בִּקַּשְׁתִּי אֵת שֶׁאָהֲבָה נַפְשִׁי
בִּקַּשְׁתִּיו וְלֹא מְצָאתִיו׃ [2] אָקוּמָה נָּא וַאֲסוֹבְבָה בָעִיר
בַּשְּׁוָקִים וּבָרְחֹבוֹת אֲבַקְשָׁה אֵת שֶׁאָהֲבָה נַפְשִׁי
בִּקַּשְׁתִּיו וְלֹא מְצָאתִיו׃ [3] מְצָאוּנִי הַשֹּׁמְרִים הַסֹּבְבִים
בָּעִיר אֵת שֶׁאָהֲבָה נַפְשִׁי רְאִיתֶם׃

[1] עַל־מִשְׁכָּבִי בַּלֵּילוֹת	Upon my bed at night
בִּקַּשְׁתִּי אֵת שֶׁאָהֲבָה נַפְשִׁי	I sought the one my soul loves.
בִּקַּשְׁתִּיו וְלֹא מְצָאתִיו׃	I sought him, but did not find him.
[2] אָקוּמָה נָּא וַאֲסוֹבְבָה בָעִיר	I will rise and go about in the city,
בַּשְּׁוָקִים וּבָרְחֹבוֹת	in the streets and in the squares.
אֲבַקְשָׁה אֵת שֶׁאָהֲבָה נַפְשִׁי	I will seek the one my soul loves.
בִּקַּשְׁתִּיו וְלֹא מְצָאתִיו׃	I sought him, but did not find him.
[3] מְצָאוּנִי הַשֹּׁמְרִים	The guards found me,
הַסֹּבְבִים בָּעִיר	the ones who go about in the city.
אֵת שֶׁאָהֲבָה נַפְשִׁי רְאִיתֶם׃	"Have you seen the one my soul loves?"

NEW VOCABULARY

וָאֲסוֹבְבָה	and go about	מִשְׁכָּבִי	my bed
בַּשְּׁוָקִים	in the streets	שֶׁ-	that, who, which, where
וּבָרְחֹבוֹת	and in the squares	אָקוּמָה	I will rise
הַסֹּבְבִים	the ones who go about		

VERB ANALYSIS

VERB	ROOT	PATTERN	MEANING	TENSE	P/G/N	SUFFIX
בִּקַּשְׁתִּי	ב.ק.ש	פִּעֵל	seek	perfect	1cs	
שֶׁאָהֲבָה	א.ה.ב	פָּעַל	love	perfect	3fs	
בִּקַּשְׁתִּיו	ב.ק.ש	פִּעֵל	seek	perfect	1cs	3ms
מְצָאתִיו	מ.צ.א	פָּעַל	find	perfect	1cs	3ms
אָקוּמָה	ק.ו.ם	פָּעַל	arise	cohortative	1cs	
וַאֲסוֹבְבָה	ס.ב.ב	פּוֹלֵל	go about	cohortative	1cs	
אֲבַקְשָׁה	ב.ק.ש	פִּעֵל	seek	cohortative	1cs	
מְצָאוּנִי	מ.צ.א	פָּעַל	find	perfect	3cp	1cs
הַשֹּׁמְרִים	ש.מ.ר	פָּעַל	keep, watch	participle	mp	
הַסֹּבְבִים	ס.ב.ב	פָּעַל	go around,turn	participle	mp	
רְאִיתֶם	ר.א.ה	פָּעַל	see	perfect	2mp	

GRAMMATICAL NOTES

Throughout this section, the particle שֶׁ appears in front of many words. In parts of the Hebrew Bible, including Song of Songs, שֶׁ is used in place of אֲשֶׁר with no change in meaning.

3:2 So far you have seen the פּוֹלֵל pattern for hollow verbs only; it is also used for some **geminate** verbs, ones in which the final two root letters are the same. Other examples of the פּוֹלֵל appear in Exodus 32:1, II Samuel 7:13, and Song of Songs 3:5.

4 כִּמְעַט שֶׁעָבַרְתִּי מֵהֶם עַד שֶׁמָּצָאתִי אֵת שֶׁאָהֲבָה
נַפְשִׁי אֲחַזְתִּיו וְלֹא אַרְפֶּנּוּ עַד־שֶׁהֲבֵיאתִיו אֶל־בֵּית
אִמִּי וְאֶל־חֶדֶר הוֹרָתִי׃ 5 הִשְׁבַּעְתִּי אֶתְכֶם בְּנוֹת
יְרוּשָׁלַם בִּצְבָאוֹת אוֹ בְּאַיְלוֹת הָדֶה אִם־תָּעִירוּ
וְאִם־תְּעוֹרְרוּ אֶת־הָאַהֲבָה עַד שֶׁתֶּחְפָּץ׃

4 כִּמְעַט שֶׁעָבַרְתִּי מֵהֶם	Scarcely had I passed them,
עַד שֶׁמָּצָאתִי אֵת שֶׁאָהֲבָה נַפְשִׁי	when I found the one my soul loves.
אֲחַזְתִּיו וְלֹא אַרְפֶּנּוּ	I held him and did not let him go
עַד־שֶׁהֲבֵיאתִיו	until I brought him
אֶל־בֵּית אִמִּי	to my mother's house,
וְאֶל־חֶדֶר הוֹרָתִי׃	and to the room of the one who conceived me.
5 הִשְׁבַּעְתִּי אֶתְכֶם	I make you promise,
בְּנוֹת יְרוּשָׁלַם	daughters of Jerusalem,
בִּצְבָאוֹת אוֹ בְּאַיְלוֹת הָדֶה	by gazelles or by does of the field,
אִם־תָּעִירוּ וְאִם־תְּעוֹרְרוּ	that you not stir up or rouse
אֶת־הָאַהֲבָה עַד שֶׁתֶּחְפָּץ׃	love until it pleases.

NEW VOCABULARY

הִשְׁבַּעְתִּי	I make promise	כִּמְעַט	scarcely
בִּצְבָאוֹת	by gazelles	אֲחַזְתִּיו	I held him
בְּאַיְלוֹת	by does	אַרְפֶּנּוּ	(I) let him go
תָּעִירוּ	you stir up	חֶדֶר	room
תְּעוֹרְרוּ	(you) rouse	הוֹרָתִי	the one who conceived me

שֶׁתֶּחְפָּץ it pleases

VERB ANALYSIS

VERB	ROOT	PATTERN	MEANING	TENSE	P/G/N	SUFFIX
שֶׁעָבַרְתִּי	ע.ב.ר	פָּעַל	pass over	perfect	1cs	
שֶׁמָּצָאתִי	מ.צ.א	פָּעַל	find	perfect	1cs	
שֶׁאָהֲבָה	א.ה.ב	פָּעַל	love	perfect	3fs	
אֲחַזְתִּיו	א.ח.ז	פָּעַל	grasp	perfect	1cs	3ms
אַרְפֶּנּוּ	ר.פ.ה	הִפְעִיל	let go	imperfect	1cs	3ms
שֶׁהֲבֵיאתִיו	ב.ו.א	הִפְעִיל	bring	perfect	1cs	3ms
הוֹרָתִי	ה.ר.ה	פָּעַל	conceive	participle	fs	1cs
הִשְׁבַּעְתִּי	ש.ב.ע	הִפְעִיל	make to swear	perfect	1cs	
תָּעִירוּ	ע.ו.ר	הִפְעִיל	stir up	imperfect	2mp	
תְּעוֹרְרוּ	ע.ו.ר	פּוֹלֵל	rouse	imperfect	2mp	
שֶׁתֶּחְפָּץ	ח.פ.ץ	פָּעַל	please, delight	imperfect	3fs	

GRAMMATICAL NOTES

3:4 עַד שֶׁ, like עַד אֲשֶׁר, is an idiom for **until**.

3:5 There is a special formula in Hebrew for an **adjuration**. You **adjure** someone when you insist that he or she make a promise in which there is a penalty for breaking one's word. Here the speaker adjures the reader using the הִפְעִיל of the root ש.ב.ע. When the word אִם follows an adjuration, it means **that not**. This verse does not say, **if you stir up or rouse love**; it says, **that you not stir up or rouse love**.

3:5 The verbs תָּעִירוּ and תְּעוֹרְרוּ have masculine endings, even though the subject (בְּנוֹת) is feminine. As the language developed, feminine verbal endings began to disappear.

1 [1] דִּבְרֵי קֹהֶלֶת בֶּן־דָּוִד מֶלֶךְ בִּירוּשָׁלָם׃ [2] הֲבֵל הֲבָלִים
אָמַר קֹהֶלֶת הֲבֵל הֲבָלִים הַכֹּל הָבֶל׃ [3] מַה־יִּתְרוֹן
לָאָדָם בְּכָל־עֲמָלוֹ שֶׁיַּעֲמֹל תַּחַת הַשָּׁמֶשׁ׃ [4] דּוֹר הֹלֵךְ
וְדוֹר בָּא וְהָאָרֶץ לְעוֹלָם עֹמָדֶת׃ [5] וְזָרַח הַשֶּׁמֶשׁ וּבָא
הַשָּׁמֶשׁ וְאֶל־מְקוֹמוֹ שׁוֹאֵף זוֹרֵחַ הוּא שָׁם׃

[1] דִּבְרֵי קֹהֶלֶת בֶּן־דָּוִד	The words of Kohelet, the son of David,
מֶלֶךְ בִּירוּשָׁלָם׃	king in Jerusalem.
[2] הֲבֵל הֲבָלִים אָמַר קֹהֶלֶת	"Vanity of vanities," Kohelet said.
הֲבֵל הֲבָלִים הַכֹּל הָבֶל׃	"Vanity of vanities, all is vanity.
[3] מַה־יִּתְרוֹן לָאָדָם בְּכָל־עֲמָלוֹ	What is the profit for man in all his labor
שֶׁיַּעֲמֹל תַּחַת הַשָּׁמֶשׁ׃	at which he labors under the sun?
[4] דּוֹר הֹלֵךְ וְדוֹר בָּא	A generation goes and a generation comes,
וְהָאָרֶץ לְעוֹלָם עֹמָדֶת׃	but the earth remains (lit. stands) forever.
[5] וְזָרַח הַשֶּׁמֶשׁ וּבָא הַשָּׁמֶשׁ	The sun rises and the sun sets (lit. goes),
וְאֶל־מְקוֹמוֹ שׁוֹאֵף	and to its place it hastens (lit. gasps)
זוֹרֵחַ הוּא שָׁם׃	where it rises.

NEW VOCABULARY

עֲמָלוֹ	his labor	קֹהֶלֶת	Kohelet
שֶׁיַּעֲמֹל	at which he labors	הֲבֵל הֲבָלִים	vanity of vanities
וְזָרַח	rises	הָבֶל	vanity
שׁוֹאֵף	it hastens	יִתְרוֹן	profit
זוֹרֵחַ	it rises		

VERB ANALYSIS

VERB	ROOT	PATTERN	MEANING	TENSE	P/G/N	SUFFIX
אָמַר	א.מ.ר	פָּעַל	say	perfect	3ms	
שֶׁיַּעֲמֹל	ע.מ.ל	פָּעַל	labor	imperfect	3ms	
הֹלֵךְ	ה.ל.ך	פָּעַל	walk, go	participle	ms	
בָּא	ב.ו.א	פָּעַל	come	participle	ms	
עֹמָדֶת	ע.מ.ד	פָּעַל	stand	participle	fs	
וְזָרַח	ז.ר.ח	פָּעַל	rise	rv perfect	3ms	
וּבָא	ב.ו.א	פָּעַל	come	rv perfect	3ms	
שׁוֹאֵף	ש.א.ף	פָּעַל	gasp	participle	ms	
זוֹרֵחַ	ז.ר.ח	פָּעַל	rise	participle	ms	

GRAMMATICAL NOTES

1:1 The word קֹהֶלֶת has an uncertain meaning. Some translate the word as **preacher**, and it is from this understanding that the title Ecclesiastes derives. Others suggest that the word means **assembler**, as in one who assembles prayers or worshippers.

1:3 Notice that this sentence contains a noun and verb, עֲמָלוֹ and שֶׁיַּעֲמֹל, derived from the same root. This is another example of the **cognate accusative**. See I Kings 3:28 on page 103 for a full explanation.

1:4 The regular fs participle for ע.מ.ד is עֹמֶדֶת; עֹמָדֶת is a **pausal form**. See I Kings 3:22 on page 99 for an explanation of pausal forms.

1:5 שָׁם **(there)** is a redundant adverb and should not be included in your translation.

6 הוֹלֵךְ אֶל־דָּרוֹם וְסוֹבֵב אֶל־צָפוֹן סוֹבֵב סֹבֵב הוֹלֵךְ
הָרוּחַ וְעַל־סְבִיבֹתָיו שָׁב הָרוּחַ׃ 7 כָּל־הַנְּחָלִים הֹלְכִים
אֶל־הַיָּם וְהַיָּם אֵינֶנּוּ מָלֵא אֶל־מְקוֹם שֶׁהַנְּחָלִים
הֹלְכִים שָׁם הֵם שָׁבִים לָלָכֶת׃ 8 כָּל־הַדְּבָרִים יְגֵעִים
לֹא־יוּכַל אִישׁ לְדַבֵּר

6 הוֹלֵךְ אֶל־דָּרוֹם	Going to the south,
וְסוֹבֵב אֶל־צָפוֹן סוֹבֵב סֹבֵב	and turning to the north, turning, turning,
הוֹלֵךְ הָרוּחַ	the wind goes,
וְעַל־סְבִיבֹתָיו שָׁב הָרוּחַ׃	and on its circuit the wind returns.
7 כָּל־הַנְּחָלִים הֹלְכִים אֶל־הַיָּם	All of the streams flow (lit. go) to the sea,
וְהַיָּם אֵינֶנּוּ מָלֵא	but the sea is not full.
אֶל־מְקוֹם שֶׁהַנְּחָלִים הֹלְכִים	To the place where the streams flow,
שָׁם הֵם שָׁבִים לָלָכֶת׃	there they return to flow.
8 כָּל־הַדְּבָרִים יְגֵעִים	All things are wearisome;
לֹא־יוּכַל אִישׁ לְדַבֵּר	a man cannot speak (of them).

NEW VOCABULARY

סְבִיבֹתָיו	its circuit	דָּרוֹם	south
הַנְּחָלִים	the streams	וְסוֹבֵב	and turning
מָלֵא	is full	צָפוֹן	north
שֶׁהַנְּחָלִים	where the streams	סֹבֵב	turning

יְגֵעִים wearisome

VERB ANALYSIS

VERB	ROOT	PATTERN	MEANING	TENSE	P/G/N	SUFFIX
הוֹלֵךְ	ה.ל.ך	פָּעַל	walk, go	participle	ms	
סוֹבֵב	ס.ב.ב	פָּעַל	go around,turn	participle	ms	
סֹבֵב	ס.ב.ב	פָּעַל	go around,turn	participle	ms	
שָׁב	שׁ.ו.ב	פָּעַל	turn, return	participle	ms	
הֹלְכִים	ה.ל.ך	פָּעַל	walk, go	participle	mp	
שָׁבִים	שׁ.ו.ב	פָּעַל	turn, return	participle	mp	
לָלָכֶת	ה.ל.ך	פָּעַל	walk, go	infinitive		
יוּכַל	י.כ.ל	פָּעַל	be able	imperfect	3ms	
לְדַבֵּר	ד.ב.ר	פִּעֵל	speak	infinitive		

GRAMMATICAL NOTES

Throughout Ecclesiastes שֶׁ replaces אֲשֶׁר. You saw the same pattern in Song of Songs 3:1-5. שֶׁ is common in later biblical books, and Ecclesiastes and Song of Songs are both post-exilic biblical compositions.

1:6 Remember that participles may be spelled with or without a ו.

1:7 Like עָמָדֶת in verse 4, לָלָכֶת is a pausal form. The regular infinitive for ה.ל.ך is לֶכֶת.

לֹא־תִשְׂבַּע עַיִן לִרְאוֹת וְלֹא־תִמָּלֵא אֹזֶן מִשְּׁמֹעַ׃
9 מַה־שֶּׁהָיָה הוּא שֶׁיִּהְיֶה וּמַה־שֶּׁנַּעֲשָׂה הוּא שֶׁיֵּעָשֶׂה
וְאֵין כָּל־חָדָשׁ תַּחַת הַשָּׁמֶשׁ׃

לֹא־תִשְׂבַּע עַיִן לִרְאוֹת	The eye is not satisfied with seeing,
וְלֹא־תִמָּלֵא אֹזֶן מִשְּׁמֹעַ	and the ear is not fulfilled from hearing.
9 מַה־שֶּׁהָיָה הוּא שֶׁיִּהְיֶה	What has been, it will be (again).
וּמַה־שֶּׁנַּעֲשָׂה הוּא שֶׁיֵּעָשֶׂה	And what has been done, it will be done (again).
וְאֵין כָּל־חָדָשׁ תַּחַת הַשָּׁמֶשׁ׃	And there is nothing new under the sun."

NEW VOCABULARY

תִּשְׂבַּע satisfied
תִּמָּלֵא fulfilled
חָדָשׁ new

VERB ANALYSIS

VERB	ROOT	PATTERN	MEANING	TENSE	P/G/N	SUFFIX
תִשְׂבַּע	שׂ.ב.ע	פָּעַל	satisfied	imperfect	3fs	
לִרְאוֹת	ר.א.ה	פָּעַל	see	infinitive		
תִמָּלֵא	מ.ל.א	נִפְעַל	be filled	imperfect	3fs	
מִשְּׁמֹעַ	שׁ.מ.ע	פָּעַל	hear	infinitive		
שֶׁהָיָה	ה.י.ה	פָּעַל	be, become	perfect	3ms	
שֶׁיִּהְיֶה	ה.י.ה	פָּעַל	be, become	imperfect	3ms	
שֶׁנַּעֲשָׂה	ע.שׂ.ה	נִפְעַל	make, do	perfect	3ms	
שֶׁיֵּעָשֶׂה	ע.שׂ.ה	נִפְעַל	make, do	imperfect	3ms	

GRAMMATICAL NOTES

In Ecclesiastes 3:1–5, we gave several Hebrew words nonliteral translations. As your skills improve, feel free to do the same; a good translation represents the meaning of the Hebrew in idiomatic English. For now, make sure that you understand how our English translation relates to the basic meaning of the Hebrew. We suggest that you look up these words in a good dictionary and explore the range of meanings within a variety of contexts. See the bibliography for recommended dictionaries.

1:8 Sometimes the regular infinitive functions like an English gerund. **Gerunds** are words that convey verbal information but behave like nouns. English gerunds usually end in -ing. In the clause **I object to his going**, the word **going** is a gerund. For more examples, refer to page 210 in *The First Hebrew Primer.*

3 [1] לַכֹּל זְמָן וְעֵת לְכָל־חֵפֶץ תַּחַת הַשָּׁמָיִם׃
[2] עֵת לָלֶדֶת וְעֵת לָמוּת
עֵת לָטַעַת וְעֵת לַעֲקוֹר נָטוּעַ׃
[3] עֵת לַהֲרוֹג וְעֵת לִרְפּוֹא
עֵת לִפְרוֹץ וְעֵת לִבְנוֹת׃
[4] עֵת לִבְכּוֹת וְעֵת לִשְׂחוֹק

[1] לַכֹּל זְמָן	For everything there is a season,
וְעֵת לְכָל־חֵפֶץ	and there is a time for every affair
תַּחַת הַשָּׁמָיִם׃	under heaven.
[2] עֵת לָלֶדֶת וְעֵת לָמוּת	A time to be born, and a time to die;
עֵת לָטַעַת	a time to plant,
וְעֵת לַעֲקוֹר נָטוּעַ׃	and a time to uproot what is planted;
[3] עֵת לַהֲרוֹג וְעֵת לִרְפּוֹא	a time to kill, and a time to heal;
עֵת לִפְרוֹץ	a time to break down,
וְעֵת לִבְנוֹת׃	and a time to build up;
[4] עֵת לִבְכּוֹת וְעֵת לִשְׂחוֹק	a time to weep, and a time to laugh;

NEW VOCABULARY

זְמָן	a season	לַהֲרוֹג	to kill
חֵפֶץ	affair	לִרְפּוֹא	to heal
לָטַעַת	to plant	לִפְרוֹץ	to break down
לַעֲקוֹר	to uproot	לִבְכּוֹת	to weep
נָטוּעַ	what is planted	לִשְׂחוֹק	to laugh

VERB ANALYSIS

VERB	ROOT	PATTERN	MEANING	TENSE	P/G/N	SUFFIX
לָלֶדֶת	י.ל.ד	פָּעַל	bear, beget	infinitive		
לָמוּת	מ.ו.ת	פָּעַל	die	infinitive		
לָטַעַת	נ.ט.ע	פָּעַל	plant	infinitive		
לַעֲקוֹר	ע.ק.ר	פָּעַל	uproot	infinitive		
נָטוּעַ	נ.ט.ע	פָּעַל	plant	p. participle	ms	
לַהֲרוֹג	ה.ר.ג	פָּעַל	kill	infinitive		
לִרְפּוֹא	ר.פ.א	פָּעַל	heal	infinitive		
לִפְרוֹץ	פ.ר.ץ	פָּעַל	break	infinitive		
לִבְנוֹת	ב.נ.ה	פָּעַל	build	infinitive		
לִבְכּוֹת	ב.כ.ה	פָּעַל	weep	infinitive		
לִשְׂחוֹק	שׂ.ח.ק	פָּעַל	laugh	infinitive		

GRAMMATICAL NOTES

This selection is unusually instructive for the regular infinitive. If you have trouble recognizing the infinitive now, you won't after working through Ecclesiastes 3! For an infinitive review, see pp. 209–214 in *The First Hebrew Primer.*

3:2 שׂ.ח.ק, a near homophone of צ.ח.ק, is the Late Hebrew root for **to laugh**. As you progress, we will point out other features that indicate the late date assigned to Ecclesiastes.

עֵת סְפוֹד וְעֵת רְקוֹד׃
5 עֵת לְהַשְׁלִיךְ אֲבָנִים וְעֵת כְּנוֹס אֲבָנִים
עֵת לַחֲבוֹק וְעֵת לִרְחֹק מֵחַבֵּק׃
6 עֵת לְבַקֵּשׁ וְעֵת לְאַבֵּד
עֵת לִשְׁמוֹר וְעֵת לְהַשְׁלִיךְ׃
7 עֵת לִקְרוֹעַ וְעֵת לִתְפּוֹר

עֵת סְפוֹד וְעֵת רְקוֹד׃	a time to mourn, and a time to frolic;
5 עֵת לְהַשְׁלִיךְ אֲבָנִים	a time to throw stones,
וְעֵת כְּנוֹס אֲבָנִים	and a time to gather stones;
עֵת לַחֲבוֹק	a time to embrace,
וְעֵת לִרְחֹק מֵחַבֵּק׃	and a time to abstain from embracing;
6 עֵת לְבַקֵּשׁ וְעֵת לְאַבֵּד	a time to seek, and a time to lose;
עֵת לִשְׁמוֹר	a time to keep,
וְעֵת לְהַשְׁלִיךְ׃	and a time to throw away;
7 עֵת לִקְרוֹעַ	a time to tear apart,
וְעֵת לִתְפּוֹר	and a time to sew together;

NEW VOCABULARY

לִרְחֹק	to abstain	סְפוֹד	to mourn
מֵחַבֵּק	from embracing	רְקוֹד	to frolic
לְאַבֵּד	to lose	כְּנוֹס	to gather
לִקְרוֹעַ	to tear apart	לַחֲבוֹק	to embrace
לִתְפּוֹר	to sew together		

VERB ANALYSIS

VERB	ROOT	PATTERN	MEANING	TENSE	P/G/N	SUFFIX
סְפוֹד	ס.פ.ד	פָּעַל	mourn	infinitive		
רְקוֹד	ר.ק.ד	פָּעַל	frolic	infinitive		
לְהַשְׁלִיךְ	ש.ל.ך	הִפְעִיל	throw	infinitive		
כְּנוֹס	כ.נ.ס	פָּעַל	gather	infinitive		
לַחֲבוֹק	ח.ב.ק	פָּעַל	embrace	infinitive		
לִרְחֹק	ר.ח.ק	פָּעַל	abstain	infinitive		
מֵחַבֵּק	ח.ב.ק	פִּעֵל	embrace	infinitive		
לְבַקֵּשׁ	ב.ק.ש	פִּעֵל	seek	infinitive		
לְאַבֵּד	א.ב.ד	פִּעֵל	lose, perish	infinitive		
לִשְׁמוֹר	ש.מ.ר	פָּעַל	keep, watch	infinitive		
לְהַשְׁלִיךְ	ש.ל.ך	הִפְעִיל	throw	infinitive		
לִקְרוֹעַ	ק.ר.ע	פָּעַל	tear	infinitive		
לִתְפּוֹר	ת.פ.ר	פָּעַל	sew together	infinitive		

GRAMMATICAL NOTE

3:5 Though they have similar pronunciations and definitions, ש.ל.ך is not the same root as ש.ל.ח from Genesis 22:10 and 22:11. ש.ל.ח means **to send** and occurs in all the major patterns. ש.ל.ך means **to throw** or **to cast** and appears only in the הִפְעִיל.

עֵת לַחֲשׁוֹת וְעֵת לְדַבֵּר׃
8 עֵת לֶאֱהֹב וְעֵת לִשְׂנֹא
עֵת מִלְחָמָה וְעֵת שָׁלוֹם׃
9 מַה־יִּתְרוֹן הָעוֹשֶׂה בַּאֲשֶׁר הוּא עָמֵל׃ 10 רָאִיתִי
אֶת־הָעִנְיָן אֲשֶׁר נָתַן אֱלֹהִים לִבְנֵי הָאָדָם לַעֲנוֹת בּוֹ׃
11 אֶת־הַכֹּל עָשָׂה יָפֶה בְעִתּוֹ

עֵת לַחֲשׁוֹת וְעֵת לְדַבֵּר׃	a time to be silent, and a time to speak;
8 עֵת לֶאֱהֹב וְעֵת לִשְׂנֹא	a time to love, and a time to hate;
עֵת מִלְחָמָה וְעֵת שָׁלוֹם׃	a time for war, and a time for peace.
9 מַה־יִּתְרוֹן הָעוֹשֶׂה	What (then) is the profit of the worker
בַּאֲשֶׁר הוּא עָמֵל׃	in that which he works?
10 רָאִיתִי אֶת־הָעִנְיָן	I have seen the task
אֲשֶׁר נָתַן אֱלֹהִים לִבְנֵי הָאָדָם	that God gave to the sons of men
לַעֲנוֹת בּוֹ׃	to be busy with.
11 אֶת־הַכֹּל עָשָׂה	He has made everything
יָפֶה בְעִתּוֹ	beautiful in its time,

NEW VOCABULARY

רָאִיתִי	I have seen	לַחֲשׁוֹת	to be silent
הָעִנְיָן	the task	לִשְׂנֹא	to hate
לַעֲנוֹת	to be busy	יִתְרוֹן	the profit
יָפֶה	beautiful	עָמֵל	he works

VERB ANALYSIS

VERB	ROOT	PATTERN	MEANING	TENSE	P/G/N	SUFFIX
לַחֲשׁוֹת	ח.שׁ.ה	פָּעַל	be silent	infinitive		
לְדַבֵּר	ד.ב.ר	פִּעֵל	speak	infinitive		
לֶאֱהֹב	א.ה.ב	פָּעַל	love	infinitive		
לִשְׂנֹא	שׂ.נ.א	פָּעַל	hate	infinitive		
הָעוֹשֶׂה	ע.שׂ.ה	פָּעַל	make, do	participle	ms	
רָאִיתִי	ר.א.ה	פָּעַל	see	perfect	1cs	
נָתַן	נ.ת.ן	פָּעַל	give, set	perfect	3ms	
לַעֲנוֹת	ע.נ.ה	פָּעַל	be occupied	infinitive		
עָשָׂה	ע.שׂ.ה	פָּעַל	make, do	perfect	3ms	

GRAMMATICAL NOTES

3:9 The adjective עָמֵל has the force of a verb, and appears only in Ecclesiastes. Translate the word as **toiling** or **working**.

3:10 The verb ע.נ.ה and its derivative עִנְיָן appear only in Ecclesiastes and might be Aramaic loan words. Because עִנְיָן is common in late, nonbiblical texts, it is another clue that Ecclesiastes is a postexilic text.

3:10 The **it** in **with it** (בּוֹ) is redundant; leave it out of your translation.

גַּם אֶת־הָעֹלָם נָתַן בְּלִבָּם מִבְּלִי אֲשֶׁר לֹא־יִמְצָא
הָאָדָם אֶת־הַמַּעֲשֶׂה אֲשֶׁר־עָשָׂה הָאֱלֹהִים מֵרֹאשׁ
וְעַד־סוֹף׃ 12 יָדַעְתִּי כִּי אֵין טוֹב בָּם כִּי אִם־לִשְׂמוֹחַ
וְלַעֲשׂוֹת טוֹב בְּחַיָּיו׃ 13 וְגַם כָּל־הָאָדָם שֶׁיֹּאכַל וְשָׁתָה
וְרָאָה טוֹב בְּכָל־עֲמָלוֹ מַתַּת אֱלֹהִים הִיא׃

גַּם אֶת־הָעֹלָם נָתַן בְּלִבָּם	(and) he has also set eternity in their mind,
מִבְּלִי אֲשֶׁר לֹא־יִמְצָא הָאָדָם	so that man should not find out
אֶת־הַמַּעֲשֶׂה אֲשֶׁר־עָשָׂה הָאֱלֹהִים	what work God has done
מֵרֹאשׁ וְעַד־סוֹף׃	from beginning to end.
12 יָדַעְתִּי כִּי אֵין טוֹב בָּם	I know there is nothing good for them
כִּי אִם־לִשְׂמוֹחַ	except rejoicing
וְלַעֲשׂוֹת טוֹב בְּחַיָּיו׃	and doing good things in their lives.
13 וְגַם כָּל־הָאָדָם שֶׁיֹּאכַל וְשָׁתָה	And also, that every man eats and drinks
וְרָאָה טוֹב בְּכָל־עֲמָלוֹ	and sees good things in all his labor:
מַתַּת אֱלֹהִים הִיא׃	that is God's gift.

NEW VOCABULARY

מִבְּלִי אֲשֶׁר	so that not
סוֹף	end
כִּי אִם	except
לִשְׂמוֹחַ	rejoicing
עֲמָלוֹ	his labor
מַתַּת	gift

VERB ANALYSIS

VERB	ROOT	PATTERN	MEANING	TENSE	P/G/N	SUFFIX
נָתַן	נ.ת.ן	פָּעַל	give, set	perfect	3ms	
יִמְצָא	מ.צ.א	פָּעַל	find	imperfect	3ms	
עָשָׂה	ע.שׂ.ה	פָּעַל	make, do	perfect	3ms	
יָדַעְתִּי	י.ד.ע	פָּעַל	know	perfect	1cs	
לִשְׂמוֹחַ	שׂ.מ.ח	פָּעַל	be happy	infinitive		
וְלַעֲשׂוֹת	ע.שׂ.ה	פָּעַל	make, do	infinitive		
שֶׁיֹּאכַל	א.כ.ל	פָּעַל	eat	imperfect	3ms	
וְשָׁתָה	שׁ.ת.ה	פָּעַל	drink	rv perfect	3ms	
וְרָאָה	ר.א.ה	פָּעַל	see	rv perfect	3ms	

GRAMMATICAL NOTES

3:11 Remember that לֵב means **will**, **mind**, or **heart**.

3:11 The conjunction מִבְּלִי means **so that there is not**. The additional לֹא in this construction is redundant.

3:12 כִּי אִם is an idiom for **except**.

3:13 The basic translation of טוֹב is **good**, **good thing**, or the collective plural **good things**. When applied to work, טוֹב can have the sense of **prosperous** or **prosperity**.

14 יָדַעְתִּי כִּי כָּל־אֲשֶׁר יַעֲשֶׂה הָאֱלֹהִים הוּא יִהְיֶה
לְעוֹלָם עָלָיו אֵין לְהוֹסִיף וּמִמֶּנּוּ אֵין לִגְרֹעַ וְהָאֱלֹהִים
עָשָׂה שֶׁיִּרְאוּ מִלְּפָנָיו׃ 15 מַה־שֶּׁהָיָה כְּבָר הוּא וַאֲשֶׁר
לִהְיוֹת כְּבָר הָיָה וְהָאֱלֹהִים יְבַקֵּשׁ אֶת־נִרְדָּף׃ 16 וְעוֹד
רָאִיתִי תַּחַת הַשָּׁמֶשׁ מְקוֹם הַמִּשְׁפָּט

14 יָדַעְתִּי כִּי	I know that
כָּל־אֲשֶׁר יַעֲשֶׂה הָאֱלֹהִים	everything that God does,
הוּא יִהְיֶה לְעוֹלָם	it endures forever;
עָלָיו אֵין לְהוֹסִיף	there is nothing to add to it,
וּמִמֶּנּוּ אֵין לִגְרֹעַ	and there is nothing to take away from it.
וְהָאֱלֹהִים עָשָׂה	God has made it
שֶׁיִּרְאוּ מִלְּפָנָיו׃	so that they stand in awe before him.
15 מַה־שֶּׁהָיָה כְּבָר הוּא	What is, it has already (been),
וַאֲשֶׁר לִהְיוֹת כְּבָר הָיָה	and what will be, it has already (been),
וְהָאֱלֹהִים יְבַקֵּשׁ אֶת־נִרְדָּף׃	and God seeks the pursued.
16 וְעוֹד רָאִיתִי תַּחַת הַשָּׁמֶשׁ	Moreover, I have seen under the sun
מְקוֹם הַמִּשְׁפָּט	a place of justice,

NEW VOCABULARY

לִגְרֹעַ	to take away
שֶׁיִּרְאוּ מִלְּפָנָיו	so that they stand in awe before him
כְּבָר	already
נִרְדָּף	the pursued

VERB ANALYSIS

VERB	ROOT	PATTERN	MEANING	TENSE	P/G/N	SUFFIX
יָדַעְתִּי	י.ד.ע	פָּעַל	know	perfect	1cs	
יַעֲשֶׂה	ע.שׂ.ה	פָּעַל	make, do	imperfect	3ms	
יִהְיֶה	ה.י.ה	פָּעַל	be, become	imperfect	3ms	
לְהוֹסִיף	י.ס.ף	הִפְעִיל	add to	infinitive		
לִגְרֹעַ	ג.ר.ע	פָּעַל	diminish	infinitive		
עָשָׂה	ע.שׂ.ה	פָּעַל	make, do	perfect	3ms	
שֶׁיִּרְאוּ	י.ר.א	פָּעַל	fear	imperfect	3mp	
שֶׁהָיָה	ה.י.ה	פָּעַל	be, become	perfect	3ms	
לִהְיוֹת	ה.י.ה	פָּעַל	be, become	infinitive		
הָיָה	ה.י.ה	פָּעַל	be, become	perfect	3ms	
יְבַקֵּשׁ	ב.ק.שׁ	פִּעֵל	seek	imperfect	3ms	
נִרְדָּף	ר.ד.ף	נִפְעַל	be pursued	participle	ms	
רָאִיתִי	ר.א.ה	פָּעַל	see	perfect	1cs	

GRAMMATICAL NOTES

3:14 You saw the formula for **to stand in awe of** (י.ר.א. מִן־) in I Kings 3:28, which was discussed on page 103. The Hebrew root י.ר.א. can signify awe, reverence, or fear. Translations of the word must rely on context and interpretation.

3:15 כְּבָר is another Late Hebrew word, the adverb **already**. When it follows ה.י.ה, translate כְּבָר as **has already been**.

שָׁמָּה הָרֶשַׁע וּמְקוֹם הַצֶּדֶק שָׁמָּה הָרָשַׁע׃ 17 אָמַרְתִּי
אֲנִי בְּלִבִּי אֶת־הַצַּדִּיק וְאֶת־הָרָשָׁע יִשְׁפֹּט הָאֱלֹהִים
כִּי־עֵת לְכָל־חֵפֶץ וְעַל כָּל־הַמַּעֲשֶׂה שָׁם׃ 18 אָמַרְתִּי
אֲנִי בְּלִבִּי עַל־דִּבְרַת בְּנֵי הָאָדָם לְבָרָם הָאֱלֹהִים
וְלִרְאוֹת שְׁהֶם־בְּהֵמָה הֵמָּה לָהֶם׃

שָׁמָּה הָרֶשַׁע	there was wickedness;
וּמְקוֹם הַצֶּדֶק	and in the place of righteousness,
שָׁמָּה הָרָשַׁע׃	there was wickedness.
17 אָמַרְתִּי אֲנִי בְּלִבִּי	I thought (lit. said in my mind),
אֶת־הַצַּדִּיק וְאֶת־הָרָשָׁע	the righteous and the evil
יִשְׁפֹּט הָאֱלֹהִים	God judges,
כִּי־עֵת לְכָל־חֵפֶץ	for there is a time for every affair
וְעַל כָּל־הַמַּעֲשֶׂה שָׁם׃	and for every work.
18 אָמַרְתִּי אֲנִי בְּלִבִּי	I thought,
עַל־דִּבְרַת בְּנֵי הָאָדָם	it is for the sake of the sons of men
לְבָרָם הָאֱלֹהִים וְלִרְאוֹת	(that) God is testing them and showing
שְׁהֶם־בְּהֵמָה הֵמָּה לָהֶם׃	(them) that they are like animals.

NEW VOCABULARY

הָרֶשַׁע	wickedness
הַצֶּדֶק	righteousness
שָׁמָּה	there
חֵפֶץ	affair
עַל-דִּבְרַת	for the sake of
לְבָרָם	(he) is testing them

VERB ANALYSIS

VERB	ROOT	PATTERN	MEANING	TENSE	P/G/N	SUFFIX
אָמַרְתִּי	א.מ.ר	פָּעַל	say	perfect	1cs	
יִשְׁפֹּט	שׁ.פ.ט	פָּעַל	judge	imperfect	3ms	
לְבָרָם	ב.ר.ר	פָּעַל	test, prove	infinitive	3mp	
וְלִרְאוֹת	ר.א.ה	פָּעַל	see	infinitive		

GRAMMATICAL NOTE

3:16–17 These verses contain two awkward articles, הַ- (**the**), and one redundant adverb, שָׁם (**there**). Remember that an idiomatic translation will not include every word from the original text.

19 כִּי מִקְרֶה בְנֵי־הָאָדָם וּמִקְרֶה הַבְּהֵמָה וּמִקְרֶה
אֶחָד לָהֶם כְּמוֹת זֶה כֵּן מוֹת זֶה וְרוּחַ אֶחָד לַכֹּל
וּמוֹתַר הָאָדָם מִן־הַבְּהֵמָה אָיִן כִּי הַכֹּל הָבֶל׃ 20 הַכֹּל
הוֹלֵךְ אֶל־מָקוֹם אֶחָד הַכֹּל הָיָה מִן־הֶעָפָר וְהַכֹּל שָׁב
אֶל־הֶעָפָר׃ 21 מִי יוֹדֵעַ רוּחַ בְּנֵי הָאָדָם הָעֹלָה הִיא
לְמָעְלָה

19 כִּי מִקְרֶה בְנֵי־הָאָדָם	For the fate of the sons of men
וּמִקְרֶה הַבְּהֵמָה	and the fate of the animals
וּמִקְרֶה אֶחָד לָהֶם	is one fate for (all of) them.
כְּמוֹת זֶה כֵּן מוֹת זֶה	As the one dies, so the other dies;
וְרוּחַ אֶחָד לַכֹּל	and there is one breath for all.
וּמוֹתַר הָאָדָם מִן־הַבְּהֵמָה אָיִן	And there is no advantage for the man over the animals,
כִּי הַכֹּל הָבֶל׃	for all is vanity
20 הַכֹּל הוֹלֵךְ אֶל־מָקוֹם אֶחָד	all go to one place;
הַכֹּל הָיָה מִן־הֶעָפָר	all come from dust,
וְהַכֹּל שָׁב אֶל־הֶעָפָר׃	and all return to dust.
21 מִי יוֹדֵעַ רוּחַ בְּנֵי הָאָדָם	Who knows the spirit of the sons of men,
הָעֹלָה הִיא לְמָעְלָה	if it ascends upwards,

NEW VOCABULARY

מִקְרֶה	the fate of
וּמוֹתַר	and there is advantage
הָבֶל	vanity
לְמָעְלָה	upwards

VERB ANALYSIS

VERB	ROOT	PATTERN	MEANING	TENSE	P/G/N	SUFFIX
הוֹלֵךְ	ה.ל.ך	פָּעַל	walk, go	participle	ms	
הָיָה	ה.י.ה	פָּעַל	be, become	perfect	3ms	
שָׁב	שׁ.ו.ב	פָּעַל	turn, return	participle	ms	
יוֹדֵעַ	י.ד.ע	פָּעַל	know	participle	ms	
הָעֹלָה	ע.ל.ה	פָּעַל	go up	participle	fs	

GRAMMATICAL NOTE

3:19 בְּנֵי הָאָדָם occurs here and in Ecclesiastes 3:10, 3:18, and 3:20. The word אָדָם refers to **Adam** (the first man), **man** (one human being), or **men** (humanity). Sometimes אָדָם includes women in its meaning, and at other times אָדָם contrasts with a separate word for woman or women. When אָדָם follows בְּנֵי it refers to humans or mortals as a class. You may translate בְּנֵי הָאָדָם as **sons of men**, **humanity**, **human beings**, or **mankind**, depending on your understanding and preference.

וְרוּחַ הַבְּהֵמָה הַיֹּרֶדֶת הִיא לְמַטָּה לָאָרֶץ׃ 22 וְרָאִיתִי
כִּי אֵין טוֹב מֵאֲשֶׁר יִשְׂמַח הָאָדָם בְּמַעֲשָׂיו כִּי־הוּא
חֶלְקוֹ כִּי מִי יְבִיאֶנּוּ לִרְאוֹת בְּמֶה שֶׁיִּהְיֶה אַחֲרָיו׃

וְרוּחַ הַבְּהֵמָה	and the spirit of the animal,
הַיֹּרֶדֶת הִיא לְמַטָּה לָאָרֶץ׃	if it descends downwards to earth?
22 וְרָאִיתִי	And I have seen
כִּי אֵין טוֹב	that there is nothing better
מֵאֲשֶׁר יִשְׂמַח הָאָדָם בְּמַעֲשָׂיו	than that a man should enjoy his work,
כִּי־הוּא חֶלְקוֹ	for that is his lot;
כִּי מִי יְבִיאֶנּוּ לִרְאוֹת	who can bring him to see
בְּמֶה שֶׁיִּהְיֶה אַחֲרָיו׃	what will be after him?

NEW VOCABULARY

לְמַטָּה	downwards
יִשְׂמַח	(he) should enjoy
חֶלְקוֹ	his lot
בְּמֶה	what

VERB ANALYSIS

VERB	ROOT	PATTERN	MEANING	TENSE	P/G/N	SUFFIX
הַיֹּרֶדֶת	י.ר.ד	פָּעַל	go down	participle	fs	
וְרָאִיתִי	ר.א.ה	פָּעַל	see	perfect	1cs	
יִשְׂמַח	שׂ.מ.ח	פָּעַל	be happy	imperfect	3ms	
יְבִיאֶנּוּ	ב.ו.א	הִפְעִיל	bring	imperfect	3ms	3ms
לִרְאוֹת	ר.א.ה	פָּעַל	see	infinitive		
שֶׁיִּהְיֶה	ה.י.ה	פָּעַל	be, become	imperfect	3ms	

GRAMMATICAL NOTE

3:22 לִרְאוֹת is an example of the regular infinitive +לְ expressing purpose. You now know four primary functions of the regular infinitive, summarized below. Verses and page references in parentheses refer to a full discussion of each use.

1. to express purpose (Psalm 67:3, page 137)
2. as the subject or object of a sentence (I Kings 3:7, page 87)
3. in temporal clauses (I Kings 3:18, page 95)
4. as a gerund (Ecclesiastes 1:8, page 159)

GUIDE TO EKS TERMINOLOGY

EKS NAME	TRADITIONAL NAME
Throaty Five Letters	Gutturals, Laryngeals
ו Meaning and	ו Conjunctive, the Conjunction
Hebrew Verb Patterns	Verb Conjugations, Stems
Hebrew Word Pair	Construct Chain
Hebew Word Pair Form	Construct State
ה of Direction	Directive ה, Directional Article
Reversing ו	ו Consecutive, ו Conversive
Clipped Form	Apocopated Form
Command	Imperative
Regular Infinitive	Infinitive Construct
Infinitive of Emphasis	Infinitive Absolute
Question ה	Interrogative ה
פָּעַל	Qal, G

SUGGESTIONS FOR FURTHER READING

Hebrew Editions of the Hebrew Bible

Elliger, K. and W. Rudolph, eds. *Biblia Hebraica Stuttgartensia.* Stuttgart: Deutsche Bibelgesellschaft, 1966/77.

JPS Hebrew-English Tanakh: The Traditional Hebrew Text and the New JPS Translation. 2d ed. Philadelphia: Jewish Publication Society, 1999.

English Translations of the Hebrew Bible

Fox, Everett, trans. *The Five Books of Moses: Genesis, Exodus, Leviticus, Numbers, Deuteronomy.* New York: Schocken Books, 1995.

May, Herbert G. and Bruce M. Metzger, eds. *The Holy Bible: Revised Standard Version Containing the Old and New Testaments.* New York: Oxford University Press, 1973.

Metzger, Bruce M. and Roland E. Murphy, eds. *The New Oxford Annotated Bible with the Apocryphal/Deuterocanonical Books: New Revised Standard Version.* New York: Oxford University Press, 1991.

Tanakh: A New Translation of the Holy Scriptures According to the Traditional Hebrew Text. Philadelphia: Jewish Publication Society, 1985.

Grammars for Biblical Hebrew

Greenberg, Moshe. *Introduction to Hebrew.* Englewood Cliffs, New Jersey: Prentice-Hall, 1965.

Kittel, Bonnie Pedrotti, Vicki Hoffer, and Rebecca Abts Wright. *Biblical Hebrew: A Text and Workbook.* New Haven: Yale University Press, 1989.

Lambdin, Thomas O. *Introduction to Biblical Hebrew.* New York: Charles Scribner's Sons, 1971.

Seow, C. L. *A Grammar for Biblical Hebrew.* rev. ed. Nashville: Abingdon Press, 1995.

Simon, Ethelyn, Irene Resnikoff, and Linda Motzkin. *The First Hebrew Primer: The Adult Beginner's Path to Biblical Hebrew.* 3d ed. Albany, California: EKS Publishing Co., 1992.

Waltke, Bruce K. and M. O'Connor. *An Introduction to Biblical Hebrew Syntax.* Winona Lake, Indiana: Eisenbrauns, 1990.

Weingreen, J. *A Practical Grammar for Classical Hebrew.* 2d ed. Oxford: Clarendon Press, 1959.

Lexicons and Dictionaries

Brown, Francis, S. R. Driver, and Charles A. Briggs. *A Hebrew and English Lexicon of the Old Testament.* Oxford: Clarendon Press, 1951.

Hebrew-English Lexicon of the Bible. New York: Schocken Books, 1975.

Holladay, William L., ed. *A Concise Hebrew and Aramaic Lexicon of the Old Testament.* Grand Rapids, Michigan: William B. Eerdmans Publishing Co., 1988.

Jastrow, Marcus, comp. *A Dictionary of the Targumim, the Talmud Babli and Yerushalmi, and the Midrashic Literature.* New York: Judaica Press, 1975.

Other Translation Aids

Beall, Todd S. and William A. Banks. *Old Testament Parsing Guide: Genesis-Esther.* Chicago: Moody Press, 1986.

Beall, Todd S., William A. Banks, and Colin Smith. *Old Testament Parsing Guide: Job-Malachi.* Chicago: Moody Press, 1990.

Botterweck, G. J., H. Ringgren, and H. J. Fabry, eds. *Theological Dictionary of the Old Testament.* Translated by J. T. Willis, G. W. Bromily, and D. E. Green. Grand Rapids: William B. Eerdmans Publishing Co., 1974.

Einspahr, Bruce, comp. *Index to Brown, Driver, and Briggs Hebrew Lexicon.* Chicago: Moody Press, 1976.

Even-Shoshan, ed. *A New Concordance of the Old Testament Using the Hebrew and Aramaic Text.* 2d ed. Jerusalem: Kiryat Sefer Publishing House, 1993.

Freedman, David Noel, ed. *The Anchor Bible Dictionary.* New York: Doubleday, 1992.

Landes, George M., comp. *A Student's Vocabulary of Biblical Hebrew Listed According to Frequency and Cognate.* New York: Charles Scribner's Sons, 1961.

Williams, Ronald J. *Hebrew Syntax: An Outline.* 2d ed. Toronto: University of Toronto Press, 1986.

HEBREW-ENGLISH GLOSSARY

א ב ג ד ה ו ז ח ט י כ ל מ נ ס ע פ צ ק ר ש ת

* Everyone should know or learn these words. They are included in the *First Hebrew Primer.*
** These words should be added to your working vocabulary. They appear often in the Hebrew Bible.

א

א.ב.ד	פָּעַל lose, perish **
אָב, אָבוֹת, אֲבִי-, אֲבוֹת-	father, ancestor *m* *
אֶבֶן, אֲבָנִים, אֶבֶן-, אַבְנֵי-	stone *f* *
אַבְרָהָם	Abraham *
אַבְרָם	Abram **
אָדוֹן, אֲדוֹנִים	lord, master *m* *
אַדִּיר	majestic, lofty
אָדָם	Adam, person, humanity *m* *
אֲדָמָה, אַדְמַת-	ground, earth *f* *
א.ה.ב	פָּעַל love *
אֹהֶל, אֹהָלִים, אֹהֶל-, אָהֳלֵי	tent *m* *
אֹהֶל מֹעֵד	tent of meeting *m* *
אַהֲרֹן	Aaron *
אוֹ	or *
א.ו.ה	הִתְפַּעֵל crave
אוּלַי	perhaps
אוֹר, אוֹר-	light *m* *
אוֹת	sign *f* **
אָז	then *
אֹזֶן, אָזְנַיִם, אֹזֶן-, אָזְנֵי-	ear *f* *
אָח, אַחִים, אֲחִי-, אֲחֵי-	brother *m* *
אֶחָד, אַחַת, אַחַד-, אַחַת-	one *
א.ח.ז	פָּעַל grasp **
	נִפְעַל be caught
אֲחֻזָּה	property, possession *f* **
אַחַר, אַחֲרֵי	after, behind *
אַחֲרֵי כֵן	afterward(s) *

אַחֵר, אַחֶרֶת, אֲחֵרִים, אֲחֵרוֹת	other, another *
אַחֲרִית	end or latter part (of time) *f* **
אַי	where
א.י.ב	פָּעַל be hostile to **
אַיֵּה	where
אַיִל, אֵילִים, אֵיל-, אֵילֵי-	ram *m* *
אַיָּלָה, אַיָּלוֹת	doe *f* **
אֵין	there is not, there are not *
אִישׁ, אֲנָשִׁים, אִישׁ-, אַנְשֵׁי-	man, person *m* *
אַךְ	but, only *
א.כ.ל	פָּעַל eat, consume *
אַל	do not *
אֵל	God, god, (the god) El *m*
אֵלִים	gods *m*
אֱלוֹהַּ	god *m*
אֱלֹהִים	God, gods *m*
אֶל	to *
אֵלֶּה	these *m & f* *
אֶלֶף, אֲלָפִים, אַלְפֵי-, אַלְפַּיִם	thousand *
אֵם, אֵם-	mother *f* *
אִם	if *
אָמָה, אֲמַת-	maid, handmaid *f* **
אֻמָּה, אֻמִּים, אֻמּוֹת	tribe, people *f*
א.מ.ן	הִפְעִיל believe **
	נִפְעַל made sure
א.מ.ר	פָּעַל say *
	נִפְעַל be said
אֱמֹרִי	Amorite **

אֱמֶת truth *
אֲמִתַּי Amittai
אָנָּה I/we beg you!
אֲנַחְנוּ we *
אֲנִי, אָנֹכִי I *
אֳנִיָּה, אֳנִיּוֹת ship *f*
אֲנָשִׁים people, men *m* *
א.ס.ף פָּעַל gather *
נִפְעַל be gathered
אַף, אַף- anger, nose *m* *
אֶפֶס, אַפְסֵי- ends, extreme limits *m*
אֵצֶל, אֶצֶל- beside **
אַרְבָּעָה, אַרְבַּע, אַרְבַּעַת-, אַרְבַּע- four *
אָרוֹן, אֲרוֹן- ark *m* *
אֶרֶז, אֲרָזִים, אַרְזֵי- cedar *m* **
אֹרַח, אֳרָחוֹת, אָרְחוֹת- way, path *m* **
א.ר.ך הִפְעִיל prolong
אֹרֶךְ length *m* **
אֶרֶץ, אֲרָצוֹת, אֶרֶץ-, אַרְצוֹת- land, country *f* *
אֵשׁ fire *f* **
אִשָּׁה, נָשִׁים, אֵשֶׁת-, נְשֵׁי- woman, wife *f* *
אֲשֶׁר that, who, which, where*
— בַּאֲשֶׁר לְמִי- on account of whom?
— כַּאֲשֶׁר when, as
— יַעַן אֲשֶׁר because
— עֵקֶב אֲשֶׁר because
— בַּאֲשֶׁר לְמִי- on account of whom?
אַתְּ you *f s* *
אֵת, אֵתִים, אִתִּים ploughshare *m*
אֶת-, אֵת direct object marker *
אֶת-, אֵת with *
אַתָּה you *m s* *
אַתֶּם you *m p* *
אַתֶּן you *f p* *

ב

בְּ- in, with *
בְּאֵר שָׁבַע Be'er Sheva
בַּאֲשֶׁר לְמִי- on account of whom?
בֶּגֶד, בְּגָדִים, בֶּגֶד-, בִּגְדֵי- garment, clothing *m* *
בְּהֵמָה, בְּהֵמוֹת, בֶּהֱמַת- animal, cattle *f* *
ב.ו.א פָּעַל come *
הִפְעִיל bring
ב.ו.ש פּוֹלֵל delay
ב.ח.ר פָּעַל choose **
בִּי excuse me! Pray . . .
ב.י.ן הִפְעִיל understand **
נִפְעַל be discerning
הִתְפּוֹלֵל inspect
בֵּין between, among *
בַּיִת, בָּתִּים, בֵּית-, בָּתֵּי- house *m* *
בֵּית לֶחֶם Bethlehem *
ב.כ.ה פָּעַל weep **
בְּכוֹר, בְּכוֹרִים, בְּכֹר- בְּכוֹרֵי- firstborn *m* **
בְּלִי without **
ב.ל.ע פָּעַל swallow
בָּמָה, בָּמוֹת high place *f* **
בֵּן, בָּנִים, בֶּן-, בְּנֵי- son, child *m* *
ב.נ.ה פָּעַל build *
נִפְעַל be built
בְּעִיר cattle, beasts *m*
ב.ק.ע פִּעֵל cut to pieces **
בֹּקֶר morning *m* *
בְּקֶרֶב- in the midst of, within, among *
ב.ק.ש פִּעֵל seek *
ב.ר.ח פָּעַל flee **
בְּרִית, בְּרִית- covenant, agreement, contract *f* *
ב.ר.ך פִּעֵל bless *

ב.ר.ךְ הִתְפַּעֵל bless oneself

ב.ר.ר פָּעַל test, prove

בָּשָׂר, בְּשַׂר־ flesh, meat *m* *

בְּשֶׁלְּמִי on account of whom

בָּשָׁן Bashan

בַּת, בָּנוֹת, בַּת־, בְּנוֹת־ daughter *f* *

בְּתוֹךְ־ in the midst of, within *

ג

גְּבוּל, גְּבוּל־ border *m* *

גִּבְעָה, גִּבְעַת־ hill *f* **

גִּבְעוֹן Gibeon

גָּדוֹל, גְּדוֹלָה, גְּדוֹלִים, גְּדוֹלוֹת big, great *

גּוֹי, גּוֹיִם a people, nation *m* *

ג.ו.ע פָּעַל perish, die

גּוֹרָל, גּוֹרָלוֹת lot *f*

ג.ז.ל פָּעַל seize, rob

ג.ז.ר פָּעַל cut, divide

גֶּזֶר, גְּזָרִים part, portion *m*

גַּיְא, גֵּיא־ valley *m*

גַּם also *

— גַּם כִּי even though

ג.נ.ב פָּעַל steal

גֶּפֶן vine *f* **

גֵּר sojourner, visitor *m* **

ג.ר.ע פָּעַל diminish

ד

ד.ב.ר פִּעֵל speak *

פָּעַל speak

דָּבָר, דְּבָרִים, דְּבַר־, דִּבְרֵי־ word, thing *m* *

דִּבְרָה, דִּבְרַת־ cause, reason *f*

דָּג fish *m*

דָּוִד David *

דּוֹר, דּוֹרוֹת generation *m* *

דַּל weak, poor

דָּם, דָּמִים, דַּם־, דְּמֵי־ blood *m* *

דָּרוֹם south *m*

דֶּרֶךְ, דְּרָכִים, דֶּרֶךְ־, דַּרְכֵי־ road, way *m & f* *

דֶּשֶׁא grass, new grass *m*

ד.שׁ.ן פִּעֵל make fat

ה

הַ־, הָ־, הֶ־ the *

הֶבֶל, הֲבָלִים, הֲבֵל־ vapor, vanity, breath *m***

ה.ד.ר פָּעַל swell, honor

הָדָר, הֲדַר־ ornament, splendor *m*

הֲדָרָה, הַדְרַת־ adornment, glory *f*

הוּא he, it *m* *

הִיא she, it *f* *

ה.י.ה פָּעַל be, become *

הַיּוֹם today *

הֵיכָל temple, palace *m* **

הַכֹּל everything *

הַלַּיְלָה tonight *

ה.ל.ךְ פָּעַל walk, go *

הִפְעִיל lead

הִתְפַּעֵל walk about

ה.ל.ל פָּעַל praise *

הִתְפַּעֵל praise oneself, boast

הֵם, הֵמָּה they *m* *

הָמוֹן multitude **

הֵנָּה they *f* *

הִנֵּה behold! *

ה.ר.ג פָּעַל kill **

ה.ר.ה פָּעַל conceive

הַר, הָרִים, הַר־, הָרֵי־ mountain, hill *m* *

הַשָּׁמַיְמָה toward the heavens, heavenward(s) *

ו

וְ-, וָ-, וֵ-, וֶ-, וַ-, וִ- and *

ז

זֹאת this *f* *

ז.ב.ח פָּעַל sacrifice **

זֶבַח, זֶבַח- sacrifice *m* **

זֶה this *m* *

זָהָב gold *m* *

זוּלָה, זוּלַת except, only *f*

ז.ו.ר פָּעַל be a stranger

זָכָר male *m* **

ז.כ.ר פָּעַל remember *

נִפְעַל be remembered

זְמָן time, appointed time *m* **

ז.נ.ה פָּעַל fornicate **

זַעַף storming, raging *m*

ז.ע.ק פָּעַל cry, cry out **

זָקֵן, זְקֵנָה, זְקֵנִים, זְקֵנוֹת old *

ז.ר.ח פָּעַל rise

זֶרַע, זֶרַע- seed, descendants *m* *

זְרֹעַ, זְרוֹעַ arm *f* **

ח

חֹבֵל sailor *m*

ח.ב.ק פִּעֵל embrace

ח.ב.ש פָּעַל bind

חַג feast, festival, gathering **

חֶדֶר chamber, room *m*

חָדָשׁ new

חֹדֶשׁ, חֳדָשִׁים, חֹדֶשׁ- month *m* *

ח.ו.ה הִשְׁתַּפֵּל worship **

ח.ו.ל הִפְעִיל make tremble

ח.ו.ל פּוֹלֵל bring forth

חוֹל sand *m*

חוּץ, חוּצוֹת outside *m* *

חִזָּיוֹן vision *m*

ח.ז.ק פָּעַל be strong *

פִּעֵל strengthen, harden, support

הִפְעִיל strengthen, grasp

הִתְפַּעֵל strengthen oneself

חָזָק, חֲזָקָה strong **

חֵטְא sin *m*

חַטָּאת, חַטַּאת- sin *f* *

חַי, חַיָּה, חַיִּים, חַיּוֹת alive, living *

ח.י.ה פָּעַל live *

חַיִּים, חַיֵּי- life *m p (no s)* *

חַיִל, חֵיל- strength, power, army *m* *

חָכָם, חֲכָמָה, חֲכָמִים, חֲכָמוֹת wise *

ח.ל.ה פִּעֵל implore **

חֲלוֹם, חֲלֹם- dream *m* **

ח.ל.ל פִּעֵל defile, profane **

חֵלֶק portion, lot *m* **

ח.מ.ד פָּעַל desire

חֲמוֹר donkey *m* **

חֲמִשָּׁה, חָמֵשׁ, חֲמֵשֶׁת-, חֲמֵשׁ- five *

חֵן favor, grace *m* *

חֲנִית spear *f*

ח.נ.ן פָּעַל be gracious **

חֶסֶד, חֲסָדִים goodness, kindness *m* **

ח.ס.ר פָּעַל lack, need

ח.פ.ץ פָּעַל please, delight **

חֵפֶץ delight, pleasure, (late) affair

ח.צ.ב פָּעַל cleave, divide

חֲצִי half *m* **

חֵק, חֵיק bosom, breast *m*

חֹק law, statute *m* **

חֻקָּה, חֻקּוֹת statute *f* **

חֶרֶב, חֶרֶב־ sword *f* *

חֹרֵב Horeb

ח.ר.ד הִפְעִיל terrify

ח.ר.ה פָּעַל burn **

חָרוֹן, חֲרוֹן־ burning (anger) *m*

חֶרֶט engraving tool *m*

חֵרֵשׁ deaf

ח.שׂ.ך פָּעַל withhold

ח.שׂ.ף פָּעַל strip bare

ח.שׁ.ב פָּעַל think, plan **

ח.שׁ.ה פָּעַל be silent

ח.ת.ר פָּעַל dig, row

ט

טוֹב, טוֹבָה, טוֹבִים, טוֹבוֹת good *

ט.ו.ל פִּעֵל cast, hurl

הִפְעִיל cast, hurl

טוֹטָפוֹת bands *f*

י

י.א.ר הִפְעִיל make shine

יְבוּל produce *m*

יַבָּשָׁה dry land, dry ground *f*

יָגֵעַ weary, wearisome

יָד, יָדַיִם, יַד־, יְדֵי־ hand *f* *

י.ד.ה הִפְעִיל praise **

י.ד.ע פָּעַל know *

הִפְעִיל cause to know, announce

נִפְעַל be known

י.ה.ב פָּעַל credit, attribute

יְהוָה Tetragrammaton, the name of Israel's God

יוֹם, יָמִים, יוֹם־, יְמֵי־, יוֹמַיִם day *m* *

יוֹנָה Jonah

יוֹסֵף Joseph *

יוֹשֵׁב, יוֹשְׁבִים, יוֹשֵׁב־, יוֹשְׁבֵי־ resident, inhabitant *

יַחְדָּו together **

יָחִיד only, only one

י.ט.ב פָּעַל be pleasing **

יַיִן, יֵין־ wine *m* *

י.כ.ח הִפְעִיל judge, reprove**

י.כ.ל פָּעַל be able *

י.ל.ד פָּעַל bear, beget *

הִפְעִיל cause to have a child, beget

נִפְעַל be born

יָם, יַמִּים, יַם־ sea *m* *

יָמָּה toward the sea, westward(s) *

י.נ.ק הִפְעִיל nurse

י.ס.ף הִפְעִיל add to *

יַעַן because **

יַעַן אֲשֶׁר — because

יַעֲקֹב Jacob *

יַעַר, יְעָרִים, יְעָרוֹת wood, forest *m* **

יָפֶה fair, beautiful **

יָפוֹ Joppa

י.צ.א פָּעַל go out *

הִפְעִיל bring out

יִצְחָק Isaac *

י.ק.ץ פָּעַל awake

י.ר.א פָּעַל fear *

י.ר.ד פָּעַל go down *

הִפְעִיל cause to go down, lower

י.ר.ה הִפְעִיל teach **

יְרוּשָׁלַםִ Jerusalem *f* *

יָרֵחַ the moon *m* **

יְרִיעָה curtain *f* **

יַרְכָה, יְרֵכָה recesses, extreme parts

י.ר.ש פָּעַל possess *

יִשְׂרָאֵל Israel *m* *

יֵשׁ there is, there are *

י.שׁ.ב פָּעַל sit, dwell *

יְשׁוּעָה, יְשׁוּעוֹת, יְשׁוּעַת- salvation *f* **

יְשָׁרָה, יִשְׁרַת- uprightness *f*

יִתְרוֹן advantage, profit *m*

כ

כְּ- as, when, while *

כַּאֲשֶׁר when, as *

כ.ב.ד פִּעֵל honor **

כָּבֵד heavy, massive

כָּבוֹד, כְּבוֹד- honor *m* *

כְּבָר already

כֹּה thus, so *

כֹּהֵן, כֹּהֲנִים, כֹּהֵן-, כֹּהֲנֵי- priest *m* *

כּוֹכָב, כּוֹכָבִים, כּוֹכַב-, כּוֹכְבֵי- star *m* **

כ.ו.ן הִפְעִיל establish *

נִפְעַל be established

פּוֹלֵל set up

כּוֹס cup *f*

כֹּחַ, כֹּחַ- strength *m* *

כ.ח.ש פִּעֵל deceive

כִּי that, because *

כִּי אִם except **

כֹּל, כָּל- all, every, the whole *

כ.ל.ה פִּעֵל complete **

כְּלִי, כֵּלִים, כְּלִי-, כְּלֵי- vessel, implement, dish *m* *

כְּמוֹ like, as *

כִּמְעַט almost, just, hardly

כ.מ.ר נִפְעַל grow tender

כֵּן thus, so *

כ.נ.ס פָּעַל gather

כְּנַעַן Canaan **

כָּנָף, כְּנָפַיִם, כְּנַף-, כַּנְפֵי- wing *f* *

כִּסֵּא, כִּסֵּא- seat, throne *m* *

כֶּסֶף, כֶּסֶף- silver, money *m* *

כַּף, כַּפּוֹת, כַּף-, כַּפּוֹת- palm (of the hand), sole (of the foot) *f* *

כ.ר.ת פָּעַל cut, make *

הִפְעִיל cut off

נִפְעַל be cut off

כ.ר.ת בְּרִית make a covenant

כ.ת.ב פָּעַל write *

כ.ת.ת פִּעֵל beat, crush

ל

לְ- to, for *

לֹא no, not *

לֵאָה Leah *

לֵב, לֵבָה, לֵב-, לְבַב- heart *m* *

לְבַד alone **

לְבָנוֹן Lebanon

ל.ב.ש פָּעַל put on, wear *

הִפְעִיל cause to wear, clothe, dress

לֶהָבָה, לֶהָבוֹת, לַהֲבוֹת- flame *f*

לוּ if only . . . !

ל.ו.ן פָּעַל pass the night **

ל.ח.ם נִפְעַל fight *

לֶחֶם, לֶחֶם- bread, food *m* *

לַיְלָה, לֵילוֹת night *m* *

לָכֵן therefore **

ל.מ.ד פָּעַל learn **

לָמָּה why? *

לְמַעַן in order that, for the sake of *

לְעוֹלָם forever *

— לְעוֹלָם וָעֶד forever and ever *

לִפְנֵי before, in front of *

ל.ק.ח פָּעַל take *

מ

מְאֹד very *

מְאֹד muchness, force *m* **

מֵאָה, מֵאוֹת, מְאַת-, מָאתַיִם a hundred *f* *

מְאוּמָה something

מֵאַיִן from where

מַאֲכֶלֶת knife *f*

מַבּוּל flood *m*

מִבְּלִי so that not, from want of

מָגוֹר, מְגוּרִים, מְגוּרֵי- sojourning *m*

מִדְבָּר, מִדְבַּר- wilderness, desert *m* *

מַה, מָה, מֶה what, how *

מַהֵר quickly

מוֹאָב Moab *m* *

מ.ו.ל נִפְעַל be circumcised

מוֹעֵד, מוֹעֲדִים, מוֹעֲדֵי appointed time *m* *

מ.ו.ת פָּעַל die *

הִפְעִיל kill

מָוֶת, מוֹת- death *m* *

מוֹתָר advantage, pre-eminence *m*

מִזְבֵּחַ, מִזְבְּחוֹת, מִזְבַּח- altar *m* *

מְזוּזָה, מְזוּזוֹת, מְזוּזַת- doorpost, gatepost *f*

מִזְמוֹר melody, psalm *m* **

מַחֲנֶה, מַחֲנוֹת, מַחֲנֵה-, מַחֲנוֹת- camp *m* *

מָחָר tomorrow *m* **

מַטָּה downward(s)

מַטֶּה, מַטּוֹת, מַטֵּה-, מַטּוֹת- tribe, staff *m* *

מִי who? *

מַיִם, מֵי- water *m p* *

מִישׁוֹר uprightness, fairness *m*

מַכָּה, מַכּוֹת hard blow, hit, plague *f* *

מִכְשׁוֹל stumbling block *m*

מ.ל.א פָּעַל be full, fill **

נִפְעַל be filled

מָלֵא full **

מַלְאָךְ, מַלְאָכִים, מַלְאַךְ-, מַלְאֲכֵי- messenger, angel *m* *

מְלָאכָה, מְלֶאכֶת- occupation, work *f* **

מַלָּח, מַלָּחִים mariner, sailor *m*

מִלְחָמָה, מִלְחָמוֹת war, battle *f* *

מ.ל.ך פָּעַל rule, reign *

הִפְעִיל make reign

מֶלֶךְ, מְלָכִים, מֶלֶךְ-, מַלְכֵי- king *m* *

מִלִּפְנֵי from before **

מַמְלָכָה, מַמְלֶכֶת- kingdom *f* **

מֶמְשָׁלָה, מֶמְשֶׁלֶת- rule, dominion *f*

מִן, מִ-, מֵ- from *

מ.נ.ה פָּעַל appoint

נִפְעַל be numbered

מִנְחָה, מִנְחַת- gift, offering *f* *

מְנֻחָה, מְנוּחָה, מְנוּחוֹת rest, quiet *f*

מַסֵּכָה, מַסֵּכַת- molten metal or image *f*

מִסְפָּר, מִסְפַּר- number, amount *m* *

מַעְגָּל, מַעְגַּל-, מַעְגְּלֵי- path, entrenchment *m*

מֵעֶה, מֵעִים, מְעֵי- belly, womb *m*

מְעַט a few, a little **

מֵעַל upon, beside **

מַעְלָה higher, upward(s)

מַעֲשֶׂה, מַעֲשִׂים, מַעֲשֵׂה-, מַעֲשֵׂי- deed *m* *

מִפְּנֵי from before **

מ.צ.א פָּעַל find *

נִפְעַל be found

— מ.צ.א חֵן בְּעֵינֵי	find favor in the eyes of *
מִצְוָה, מִצְוֹת, מִצְוַת-, מִצְוֹת-	commandment f*
מִצְרַיִם	Egypt f*
מָקוֹם, מְקוֹמוֹת, מְקוֹם-	place m*
מִקֶּרֶב-	from within, from among *
מִקְרֶה	accident, chance, fortune m
מ.ר.ה פָּעַל	be rebellious
מְרִיבָה	Meribah
מֹרִיָּה	Moriah
מִרְיָם	Miriam
מֹשֶׁה	Moses *
מִשְׁכָּב	couch, bed m
מִשְׁעֶנֶת	staff f
מִשְׁפָּחָה, מִשְׁפָּחוֹת, מִשְׁפַּחַת-, מִשְׁפְּחוֹת-	family f*
מִשְׁפָּט, מִשְׁפָּטִים, מִשְׁפַּט-, מִשְׁפְּטֵי-	law, justice m*
מִשְׁתֶּה, מִשְׁתֵּה-	feast, drink m
מִתּוֹךְ-	from the midst of *
מַתַּת	gift f

נ

נָא	please (word of politeness) *
נְאֻם, נְאֻם-	speech, declaration m*
נ.א.ף פָּעַל	commit adultery
נָבִיא, נְבִיאִים, נְבִיאֵי-	prophet m*
נ.ג.ד הִפְעִיל	declare, tell *
נֶגֶד	opposite, in front of *
נָגִיד	leader, ruler, prince m
נְגִינָה, נְגִינוֹת	music f
נֶגַע, נְגָעִים, נִגְעֵי-	stroke, mark m**
נ.ג.שׁ הִפְעִיל	bring **
נ.ד.ר פָּעַל	vow
נֵדֶר, נֶדֶר, נְדָרִים	vow m**
נ.ה.ל פִּעֵל	lead, guide
נ.ה.ר פָּעַל	stream
נָהָר, נְהָרוֹת, נְהַר	river m*
נָוֶה, נְאוֹת, נְוֹת-	pasture, meadow f
נ.ו.ח פָּעַל	rest **
הִפְעִיל	give rest to
נֶזֶם, נְזָמִים, נִזְמֵי-	ring m
נ.ח.ה הִפְעִיל	guide
נ.ח.ל פָּעַל	inherit **
נַחַל	torrent, stream, wadi m**
נַחֲלָה, נַחֲלַת-	property, inheritance f*
נ.ח.ם פִּעֵל	comfort **
נִפְעַל	be sorry
נ.ט.ה פָּעַל	stretch out **
נ.ט.ע פָּעַל	plant **
נ.ט.ר פָּעַל	keep, maintain
נִינְוֵה	Nineveh
נ.כ.ה הִפְעִיל	strike, smite *
נ.ס.ה פִּעֵל	test, try
נָעֳמִי	Naomi *
נ.ע.ר פִּעֵל	shake off
נַעַר, נְעָרִים, נַעַר-, נַעֲרֵי-	young man m*
נַעֲרָה, נְעָרוֹת	young woman f*
נ.פ.ל פָּעַל	fall *
הִפְעִיל	cast
נֶפֶשׁ, נְפָשׁוֹת, נֶפֶשׁ-, נַפְשׁוֹת-	soul, person f*
נ.צ.ח פִּעֵל	direct **
נ.צ.ל הִפְעִיל	save, rescue, snatch away *
נ.ק.ה פִּעֵל	exonerate
נָקִיא	innocent
נ.ק.ם פָּעַל	avenge
נ.שׂ.א פָּעַל	lift, carry *
נִפְעַל	be raised
— נ.שׂ.א עֵינַיִם	lift one's eyes, look up *

נ.ת.ן פָּעַל	give, set *
נִפְעַל	be given
נָתָן	Nathan

ס

ס.ב.ב פָּעַל	go around, turn **
פּוֹלֵל	go about
סָבִיב	around, roundabout *
סָבִיב	circuit
סְבַךְ	thicket *m*
סוֹף	end *m*
סוּף	reeds, rushes *m*
ס.ו.ר פָּעַל	turn aside *
הִפְעִיל	remove
סִיחוֹן	Sihon
סֶלַע	cliff, crag, rock *m* **
ס.ע.ר פָּעַל	storm, rage
סַעַר	storm *m*
ס.פ.ד פָּעַל	mourn
סְפִינָה	vessel, ship *f*
ס.פ.ר פָּעַל	count *
פִּעֵל	recount, tell
נִפְעַל	be counted
סֵפֶר, סְפָרִים, סֵפֶר־	scroll, book *m* *

ע

ע.ב.ד פָּעַל	work, serve, *
הָפְעַל	work, serve
עֶבֶד, עֲבָדִים, עֶבֶד־, עַבְדֵי־	slave, servant *m* *
עֲבוֹדָה, עֲבוֹדַת־	work, service *f* *
ע.ב.ר פָּעַל	pass over *
הִפְעִיל	make pass
עִבְרִי	Hebrew **
עֵגֶל	calf, young bull *m*
עַד	until, as far as *
— עַד עוֹלָם	forever *
עֵד, עֵדָה	witness **
עֵדָה	congregation *f* **
עוֹג	Og
עוֹד	again, still, another, yet, more *
ע.ו.ה הִפְעִיל	sin
עָוֶל	injustice *m*
עַוְלָה	unrighteousness, injustice *f*
עוֹלָם	eternity, forever, universe *m* *
עָוֹן, עֲוֹנוֹת, עֲוֹן־, עֲוֹנוֹת־	sin, transgression *m* *
עוֹף, עוֹף־	bird *m* *
ע.ו.ר הִפְעִיל	stir up
פּוֹלֵל	rouse
עִוֵּר	blind
עֹז, עוֹז	strength *m* **
עַיִן, עֵינַיִם, עֵין־, עֵינֵי־	eye *f* *
עִיר, עָרִים, עִיר־, עָרֵי־	city *f* *
עַל	upon, about, on, over *
— עַל־דִּבְרַת	for the sake of
— עַל יַד	near, next to *
— עַל כֵּן	therefore *
ע.ל.ה פָּעַל	go up *
הִפְעִיל	bring up, offer
עֹלָה, עוֹלוֹת, עֹלֹת	burnt offering *f* **
עַם, עַמִּים, עַם־ עַמֵּי־	a people, nation *m* *
עִם	with *
ע.מ.ד פָּעַל	stand *
הִפְעִיל	cause to stand, erect
עָמִית	associate, fellow *m*
ע.מ.ל פָּעַל	labor
עָמָל	trouble, labor, toil *m & f* **

ע.נ.ה פָּעַל answer, reply *

ע.נ.ה פִּעֵל afflict **

ע.נ.ה פָּעַל be occupied

עִנְיָן occupation, task m

עָפָר, עֲפַר– dust m *

עֵץ, עֵצִים, עֵץ–, עֲצֵי– tree, wood m *

עָצוּם mighty, numerous

עֶצֶם, עֲצָמוֹת, עֶצֶם–, עַצְמוֹת– bone, essence f *

ע.ק.ד פָּעַל bind

ע.ק.ר פָּעַל uproot

עֶרֶב evening m *

ע.ר.ך פָּעַל arrange **

עֹרֶף neck, back of neck m

ע.שׂ.ה פָּעַל make, do *

נִפְעַל be done

עֲשָׂרָה, עֶשֶׂר, עֲשֶׂרֶת–, עֶשֶׂר– ten *

עֶשְׂרִים twenty m & f *

ע.שׁ.ק פָּעַל oppress

עֹשֶׁר riches m

ע.שׁ.ת הִתְפַּעֵל think

עֵת, עֶת– time f *

עַתָּה now *

פ

פֶּה, פִּי– mouth m *

פֹּה here **

פ.ל.א נִפְעַל be wonderful **

פ.ל.ל הִתְפַּעֵל pray *

פֶּן lest *

פָּנִים, פְּנֵי– face, faces m *

פֶּסֶל sculpted image m

פְּעֻלָּה, פְּעֻלַּת wages, recompense f

פַּעַם, פְּעָמִים, פַּעֲמַיִם a time, occurrence f *

פ.ק.ד פָּעַל attend to, visit **

פַּר, פָּרִים, פַּר– bull m *

פ.ר.ה הִפְעִיל make fruitful **

פָּרָה, פָּרוֹת cow f *

פְּרִי, פְּרִי– fruit m *

פַּרְעֹה pharaoh *

פ.ר.ץ פָּעַל break **

פ.ר.ק פִּעֵל remove

הִתְפַּעֵל remove

פ.ת.ח פָּעַל open *

פֶּתַח, פֶּתַח– opening, entrance m *

צ

צֹאן, צֹאן– flock of sheep (or goats) f *

צָבָא, צְבָאוֹת, צְבָא– army, military force m *

צְבִי, צְבִיִּם, צְבָאִים, צְבָאוֹת gazelle m

צַדִּיק, צַדִּיקָה, צַדִּיקִים, צַדִּיקוֹת righteous *

צֶדֶק righteousness m **

צְדָקָה, צִדְקַת– righteousness f *

צ.ו.ה פִּעֵל command *

צ.ו.ר פָּעַל form, fashion

צ.ח.ק פִּעֵל laugh

צִיּוֹן Zion **

צַלְמָוֶת deep darkness m

צִן Zin

צָפוֹן north f **

צַר adversary, foe m **

צ.ר.ר פָּעַל be hostile to

ק

ק.ב.ר נִפְעַל be buried **

קָדוֹשׁ, קְדוֹשִׁים holy *

ק.ד.שׁ פִּעֵל sanctify *

הִפְעִיל treat as sacred

נִפְעַל be sanctified

הִתְפַּעֵל make oneself holy, sanctify oneself *

קָדֵשׁ Kadesh

קֹדֶשׁ, קֳדָשִׁים, קֹדֶשׁ-, קָדְשֵׁי- holy thing *m* *

— קֹדֶשׁ הַקֳּדָשִׁים the holy of holies *

ק.ה.ל הִפְעִיל call assembly

נִפְעַל assemble

קָהָל, קְהַל- assembly *m* **

קֹהֶלֶת Kohelet, preacher

קוֹל, קוֹל- voice, sound *m* *

ק.ו.ם פָּעַל arise *

הִפְעִיל raise up

קָטָן, קְטַנָּה, קְטַנִּים, קְטַנּוֹת little *

ק.ט.ר הִפְעִיל burn incense **

ק.ל.ל פִּעֵל insult, curse **

הִפְעִיל make light

קַנָּא jealous

ק.ר.א פָּעַל call, proclaim *

נִפְעַל be called

ק.ר.ב פָּעַל come near **

קֶרֶב inward part, midst *m* *

קֶרֶן horn *f* **

ק.ר.ע פָּעַל tear **

קָשֶׁה, קָשָׁה, קְשֵׁה-, קְשַׁת- stiff, hard

ק.ש.ר פָּעַל bind, join

ר

ר.א.ה פָּעַל see *

נִפְעַל appear

רְאֵם, רְאֵמִים wild ox *m*

רֹאשׁ, רָאשִׁים, רֹאשׁ-, רָאשֵׁי- head, top, leader *m* *

רִאשׁוֹן, רִאשׁוֹנָה first **

רַב chief *m* **

רַב, רַבָּה, רַבִּים, רַבּוֹת many, much, a lot of *

רֹב, רֹב- multitude, abundance *m* **

ר.ב.ה הִפְעִיל make numerous **

רִבֵּעַ, רִבֵּעִים pertaining to the fourth

ר.ב.ץ הִפְעִיל make lie down

רִבְקָה Rebecca *

ר.ג.ז פָּעַל be perturbed

רֶגֶל, רַגְלַיִם, רֶגֶל- רַגְלֵי- foot, leg *f* *

ר.ד.ם נִפְעַל be fast asleep

ר.ד.ף פָּעַל pursue **

נִפְעַל be pursued

רוּחַ, רוּחוֹת, רוּחַ- wind, spirit, breath *m* *

רְוָיָה saturation, well filled *f*

ר.ו.ם הִפְעִיל raise, lift **

רוּת Ruth *

רְחוֹב, רְחֹבוֹת plaza, square *f*

רָחֵל Rachel *

רַחֲמִים compassion, feeling *m*

רָחֹק, רָחוֹק far, distant **

ר.י.ב פָּעַל quarrel **

רָכִיל slander, tale bearer *m*

רִמּוֹן pomegranate *m*

ר.נ.ן פִּעֵל shout with joy **

רָע.רַע, רָעָה, רָעִים, רָעוֹת evil, misery, distress *

רֵעַ, רֵעִים friend *m* *

רָעָב famine, hunger *m* *

ר.ע.ה פָּעַל shepherd **

ר.ע.ם הִפְעִיל thunder

ר.פ.א פָּעַל heal **

ר.פ.ה הִפְעִיל let go

ר.צ.ח פָּעַל murder

רַק only *

ר.ק.ד פָּעַל frolic

הִפְעִיל make skip

ר.ק.ע פָּעַל beat, spread

רָשָׁע, רְשָׁעִים wicked, evil *

רֶשַׁע wickedness *m*

שׂ

Hebrew	Stem	English
ש.ב.ע	פָּעַל	satisfied **
שָׂדֶה, שָׂדוֹת, שְׂדֵה-, שְׂדֵי-		field *m* *
שֶׂה		lamb
ש.ח.ק	פָּעַל	laugh
ש.י.ם	פָּעַל	put, place *
שָׂכִיר		worker, hired laborer
שָׂכָר		hire, wages *m*
ש.מ.ח	פָּעַל	be happy **
ש.נ.א	פָּעַל	hate **
שָׂפָה, שְׂפָתַיִם, שְׂפַת-, שִׂפְתֵי-		lip, edge, shore *f* *
שַׂר, שָׂרִים, שַׂר-, שָׂרֵי-		commander, chief *m* *
שָׂרָה		Sarah *
שִׂרְיֹן		Sirion

שׁ

Hebrew	Stem	English
-שֶׁ		that, who, which, where **
בְּשֶׁלְּמִי —		on account of whom
שָׁאוּל		Saul
ש.א.ל	פָּעַל	ask **
ש.א.ף	פָּעַל	gasp
שֵׁבֶט, שְׁבָטִים, שִׁבְטֵי-		rod, staff *m* **
ש.ב.ע	הִפְעִיל	make swear **
	נִפְעַל	swear
שִׁבְעָה, שֶׁבַע, שִׁבְעַת-, שְׁבַע-		seven *
שְׁבִיעִי —		seventh **
ש.ב.ר	פָּעַל	break *
	פִּעֵל	break, shatter
	נִפְעַל	be broken
שַׁבָּת, שַׁבָּתוֹת, שַׁבַּת-		Sabbath *f* *
שַׁדַּי		Almighty
שָׁוְא		emptiness, vanity *m* **
ש.ו.ב	פָּעַל	turn, return *
	הִפְעִיל	restore
ש.ו.ב	פּוֹלֵל	restore
שׁוּק, שְׁוָקִים		street *m*
שׁוֹר		ox *m* **
ש.ח.ט	פָּעַל	slaughter **
ש.ח.ת	פִּעֵל	go to ruin
שִׁיר, שִׁירִים		song *m* **
ש.כ.ב.	פָּעַל	lie, lie down *
	הִפְעִיל	lay down
ש.כ.ם	הִפְעִיל	rise early **
ש.כ.ן	פָּעַל	dwell **
שָׁלוֹם, שְׁלוֹם-		peace, completeness *m* *
ש.ל.ח	פָּעַל	send *
	פִּעֵל	send away, set free
שֻׁלְחָן		table *m* **
ש.ל.ך	הִפְעִיל	throw *
שֶׁלֶם, שְׁלָמִים		peace offering *m* **
שְׁלֹמֹה		Solomon
שָׁלִשׁ, שָׁלִשִׁים		pertaining to the third
שְׁלֹשָׁה, שָׁלֹשׁ, שְׁלֹשֶׁת-, שְׁלֹשׁ-		three *
שָׁם		there *
שֵׁם, שֵׁמוֹת, שֵׁם-, שְׁמוֹת-		name *m* *
שָׁמָּה		to there
שָׁמַיִם, שְׁמֵי-		heavens, sky *m* *
שֶׁמֶן		fat, oil *m* **
שְׁמֹנָה, שְׁמוֹנֶה, שְׁמוֹנַת- שְׁמוֹנֶה-		eight *
ש.מ.ע	פָּעַל	hear *
	הִפְעִיל	cause to hear, announce
	נִפְעַל	be heard
ש.מ.ר	פָּעַל	keep, watch *
	נִפְעַל	be guarded, be kept
שֹׁמֵר, שֹׁמְרִים, שׁוֹמֵר-, שׁוֹמְרֵי-		guard *m* *
שֶׁמֶשׁ		sun *m* or *f* *
שָׁנָה, שָׁנִים, שְׁנַת-, שְׁנֵי-, שְׁנָתַיִם		year *f* *

שְׁנַיִם, שְׁתַּיִם, שְׁנֵי־, שְׁתֵּי־	two *
ש.נ.ן	פִּעֵל teach diligently
שַׁעַר, שְׁעָרִים, שַׁעַר־, שַׁעֲרֵי־	gate *m* *
ש.פ.ט	פָּעַל judge *
שֹׁפֵט, שֹׁפְטִים, שֹׁפְטֵי־	judge *m* *
שֵׁפֶל	low estate, condition *m*
ש.ק.ה	הִפְעִיל give drink **
ש.ק.ר	פִּעֵל deal falsely
שֶׁקֶר	deception *m* **
שִׁשָּׁה, שֵׁשׁ, שֵׁשֶׁת־, שֵׁשׁ־	six *
ש.ת.ה	פָּעַל drink *
ש.ת.ק	פָּעַל be quiet

ת

תְּאֵנָה	fig tree *f*
תְּבוּנָה	understanding *f*
תּוֹךְ־	the middle of *
תּוֹרָה, תּוֹרַת־	law, instruction, Torah *f* *
תַּחַת	under, instead of *
תְּמוּנָה	likeness, form *f*
תָּמִיד	continually, regularly *
תָּמִים	blameless **
ת.פ.ר	פָּעַל sew together
תַּרְשִׁישׁ	Tarshish
תִּשְׁעָה, תֵּשַׁע, תִּשְׁעַת־, תְּשַׁע־	nine *
תִּשְׁעִים	ninety **

INDEX OF GRAMMATICAL NOTES

negative command, 57
noun: adjective as, 37; suffixed, 81
numbering, verse, 65
numbers, large, 23, 85
Numbers, title of, 51
paragogic nun, 63, 121
parallel construction, 77, 135
participle: marking vowel, 73; in Psalm 136, 141; spelling of, 157
particle: at beginning of word, 151; at end of word, 31, 109
past event, 95
past tense: and perfect verb, 111; from imperfect verb, 139
pausal form, 157: at end of verse or sentence, 99; for fs participle, 155
perfect tense: as command, 89; for completed action, 91, 111; from imperfect verb, 139
plural, collective, 105, 145
Polel, 25
prohibition: with imperfect tense, 37; as negative command, 57
pronoun: demonstrative, 99; repetition of , 101
Psalm 29, origins of, 131, 135
Psalm 67, interpretation of, 137
Psalm 136, interpretation of, 141, 149
repetition, use of, 101; of verbs, 103
rv perfect verb as command, 89
Sea of Reeds, 145
Shema, 67
shepherd imagery, 129
shin, 31
Sirion range, 133
suffixed noun, 81
superlative, 141
synecdoche, 57
Ten Commandments: accounts of, 61; prohibitions of, 57
Tetragrammaton, 93
verb: feminine verbal endings, evolution of, 153; geminate, 151; impersonal constructions with, 46, 100; infinitive as object of, 87; as jussive, 139, order and tense of, 139; pattern, 97; repetition of, with direct object, 103; rv perfect tense, as command, 89. *See also* hollow verb
verse: numbering of, 65; parallelism in, 135
vowels: history of change of, 55; participles marking, 73
wordplay, 5
adjective as noun, 37
adjuration, formula for, 153
age, Hebrew expression of, 3
Amorites, 147
anthropomorphizing, 107
balance in verses, 135
Bashan, 147
cognate accusative, 103, 115, 155
cohortative, 3, 31, 109, 119
collective plural, 105, 145
command: attachment for, 31, 109; Psalm 136 as, 149; rv perfect as, 89
consonants, history of change of, 55
covenant between Israel and God, 35
Deuteronomy: *Shema* in, 67; verse numbering of, 65
direct speech, introduction of, 5
etiology, 51
feminine: with collective man, 173; verbal endings, evolution of, 153
geminate verb, 151
gerund, 159
God/God Almighty, translation of, 3, 141
Hishtafel, 13
Hofal, 57
Holiness Code, 41
hollow verb, 25; pattern, 151; verb pattern replacing, 97
idioms: for anger, 30, 40; for compassion, 34; for long life, 91; for making a covenant, 53
imperfect tense: as cohortative, 3, 31; as customary action, 85; as jussive, 19, 139; in negative commands, 57; as past or perfect tense, 139; as prohibition, 37
incipit, 41
infinitive: of emphasis, 39; as gerund, 159; as object of verb, 87; as purpose, 175; as purpose of preceding action, 137; in temporal clause, 95; using regular, 161
Jonah, origin of, 117
jussive, 19: atachment for, 109; translation as, 139
Kadesh, 43, 133
Lebanon range, 133
Leviticus, title of, 41
Massah, 51
mater lectionis, 73
Meribah, 51
metonymy, 53
names: etiology of, 51; wordplays on, 5

לְ: of authorship, 127; of specification, 147
לֹא, in prohibitions, 37
לֵאמֹר, 5
לֵב, 67, 89, 167
לָמָּה, 33
מְאֹד, 3, 67
מַטֶּה, 47
מִלִּפְנֵי, 105
מִמַּעַל, 17
מְרִיבָה, 51
-נָא, 109
נְאֻם, 21
נ.פ.ל + פָּנִים, 45
נִפְעַל, meaning of, 33
נֶפֶשׁ, 67
סֶלָה, 137
עֹלָה, derivation of, 15
פּוֹלֵל, 25, 81, 127, 151
קֹהֶלֶת, 155
קְשֵׁה-עֹרֶף, 31
רַב, 109
-שֶׁ, 151, 157
שָׁוְא, 65
שׁוּב, meanings of, 33, 113
שֵׁם, 79
אָה, with commands, 31
א, written next to שׁ, 31
אַבְרָם, 5
אַל, in negative commands, 57
אֵל-שַׁדַּי, 3
אָנָּא\אָנָּה, 115
אֲשֶׁר, with prepositions, 21, 153
בִּי, 95
בַּיִת, 75, 81
בָּמוֹת, 85
בְּנֵי אֵלִים, 131
בְּנֵי הָאָדָם, 173
בְּנֵי יִשְׂרָאֵל, 75
גַּם . . . גַּם, 93
ה of direction, 105
ה.ל.ך with participles, 113
הִנֵּה, suffixed, 11
הָפְעַל, 57
הִשְׁתַּפֵּל, 13, 57
הִתְפּוֹלֵל, 97
ו, in reversing ו constructions, 7
חוֹל, as symbol, 23
יַם-סוּף, 145
י.ר.א מִן-, 103
כְּתִיב קְרֵי, 55

Other Books and Materials from EKS Publishing

LEARN THE ALPHABET

Teach Yourself to Read Hebrew: cassettes and book

Teach Yourself to Read Hebrew: book only

Handy Hebrew Alphabet

Handy Hebrew Writing Guide

LEARN PRAYERBOOK HEBREW

Prayerbook Hebrew the Easy Way

Prayerbook Hebrew the Easy Way: Companion Audio Tape Set

Top 100 Hebrew Flashwords

Og the Terrible: A Comic Book Introduction to Prayerbook Hebrew

Og Returns: Og's Further Adventures in Prayerbook Hebrew

LEARN BIBLICAL HEBREW

The First Hebrew Primer

Primer Answer Book

Primer Flashcards

Handy Hebrew Verb Charts

Handy Hebrew Grammar Charts

The First Biblical Hebrew Speller

Tall Tales Told in Biblical Hebrew